Praise for *Parentspeak*

"Underlying her friendly, enjoyable critique of certain phrases parents use reflexively—the kind that l~~~ ~~ ~~ ~~~~~~ 'How did ~~ mother get in my larynx?'—**Lehr off(** essage **of respect for kids.** The chap :e of the book by itself, but I highl ing."
　　—**Alfie Kohn**, author of *l* and *The Myth of the*

"*Parentspeak* is the antidote to all those words we find ourselves saying to our children automatically, because everyone else says them: 'Good job!' ... 'Say you're sorry.' ... 'Don't cry, you're okay.' ... 'Where's my kiss?'" Lehr holds these and other thoughtless responses up to the light, where we suddenly see through them. **I love Lehr's clarity, her respect for children, and her ability to make it fun for readers as they have their worldview dismantled and renovated.** Important for all parents; I will be recommending it to everyone."
　　—**Dr. Laura Markham**, author of *Peaceful Parent, Happy Kids: How to Stop Yelling and Start Connecting*

"**Smart, audacious, and often hilarious.** Takes everything you thought you knew about parenting and turns it on its ear."
　　—**Jennifer Jason Leigh**, actress, *LBJ*

"**I'm obsessed with this brilliant gem of a book.** I'm sharing it with my spouse, in-laws, extended family, and babysitters as a way to start discussions about when to ask for hugs, whether 'please' and 'thank you' are always necessary, and that awful thing that constantly comes out of my mouth: 'Be careful!' What I love about Jennifer is that she deals out the most incisive, specific, modern advice, but then shares honest, authentic, and even awful true stories about her own mistakes. **It's like getting on the phone with the best expert and your best friend all at once.**"
　　—**Jill Soloway**, creator of *Transparent*

"If the phrase 'Good job, buddy!' has ever made you cringe and you're not sure why (except that you just heard it 6,873 times on the playground, including 146 times coming from your own mouth), this book is for you. Jennifer Lehr's serious, skeptical look at why we sound so patronizing, controlling, and fake nice when we talk to our kids may change not only the way you talk to yours, but even the way you bring them up. **Language is power, and this powerful book blows my mind—a fascinating read.**"

> **—Lenore Skenazy,** founder of the book, blog, and movement *Free-Range Kids*

"Beautifully bold. This book bucks convention so well you'll wonder why you never questioned these platitudes before. Jennifer Lehr deeply understands kids, and her book is a lifesaver. **Get ready to shake up your brain, ditch old habits, and discover what the parent-child relationship can really be.**"

> **—Heather Shumaker,** author of *It's OK Not to Share* and *It's OK to Go Up the Slide*

"Children, even the youngest ones, are not dolls or pets; they are human beings, more intelligent than most adults realize. In this **often witty, always highly engaging book**, Jennifer Lehr helps us think about how to talk to and with these small humans. **I recommend it for all new parents**, and also for aunts, uncles, grandparents, early educators, and anyone else who interacts with young children."

> **—Peter Gray,** research professor at Boston College and author of *Free to Learn: Why Unleashing the Instinct to Play Will Make Our Children Happier, More Self-Reliant, and Better Students for Life*

"**Funny, relatable, and packed with wisdom**, *Parentspeak* encourages parents to proceed with compassion and meet kids where they are: in the thick of childhood. **Lehr has a profound understanding of how language impacts children** and provides practical strategies to help parents do what they often ask of their own kids . . . to choose your words carefully."

> **—Katie Hurley,** LCSW, author of *The Happy Kid Handbook*

"Wow. I had more EUREKA! moments in the first fifteen pages of this book than I have had in most of my 9 years of parenting. This book is now my forever shower gift. Thanks to the painstaking research and consideration of Jennifer Lehr, I now can understand why so many of my well intentioned impulses have not always provided the calm, confident, loving outcomes I dream of. . . . It is never too late to examine or change the way we talk to and with our children. Words fly out so fast as a parent—this book gives us a second to step back and hear what we are actually saying. **Bravo!**"
   —**Kathryn Hahn**, actress, *Bad Moms*

"Jennifer Lehr adds a new twist to the parenting literature. With humor and clear examples from her own and others' experiences, she **unravels messages that parents might not intend to give to their children but unknowingly are.** This book will make them rethink how they interact and the language they use."
   —**Tovah P. Klein**, author of *How Toddlers Thrive* and director of the Barnard College Center for Toddler Development

"Language matters. It shapes our perceptions and influences how our children view themselves and their world. As such, *Parentspeak* is an important book in our time. With humor and grace, Lehr brings to light the issues with our common parental language and offers practical solutions. **Well researched and insightful, *Parentspeak* will challenge you in the best possible way.** Read it and grow."
   —**Rebecca Eanes**, author of *Positive Parenting: An Essential Guide*

"**Finally someone who says what we shouldn't say to our children— and, more importantly, why.** If we want our children to follow their hearts, be resilient, and find their potential, then we must stop trying to lead and manipulate their way. Lehr shows us how we can derail their paths to success—and how to get back on track."
   —**Bonnie Harris**, MSEd, author of *When Your Kids Push Your Buttons and What You Can Do About It*

PARENT SPEAK

What's Wrong
with How We Talk
to Our Children

—and What
to Say Instead

Jennifer Lehr

WORKMAN PUBLISHING · NEW YORK

Library of Congress Cataloging-in-Publication Data is available.

ISBN 978-0-7611-8151-4

Design by Galen Smith
Cover design by John Passineau
Author photo by Diana Koenigsberg

Workman books are available at special discounts when purchased in bulk for premiums and sales promotions as well as for fund-raising or educational use. Special editions or book excerpts also can be created to specification. For details, contact the Special Sales Director at the address below, or send an email to specialmarkets@workman.com.

Workman Publishing Co., Inc.
225 Varick Street
New York, NY 10014-4381
workman.com

WORKMAN is a registered trademark of Workman Publishing Co., Inc.

Printed in the United States of America

First printing December 2016

10 9 8 7 6 5 4 3 2 1

Inspired by Jules and Hudson Lehr

Entirely impossible without the long-enduring
and unwavering support of John Lehr

"Sticks and stones may break bones,
but words can shatter souls.
Words matter. Choose wisely."

—L. R. Knost

CONTENTS

THE PERVASIVENESS OF PARENTSPEAK

"Language exerts hidden power,
like the moon on the tides."
—Rita Mae Brown

P arentspeak. It's the second (or third or fourth) language we never set out to learn yet can't seem to help but speak.

If you have kids or you work with kids—hell, if you've ever talked to a kid!—I imagine you just might speak it, too. And if you're a kid yourself, you know it when you hear it. While dialects vary, Parentspeak sounds something like this: "Ohhh! You're sooo cute!" . . . "Shhh, don't cry. You're okay!" . . . "That's not nice!" . . . "Who's a big boy?" . . . "Say 'Sorry'!" . . . "Share!" . . . "Be careful!" . . . "Good job!" . . . "Do you want a time out?" . . . "What's the magic word?" . . . "I'm gonna tickle you!" . . . "Where's my hug?" . . . Sound familiar?

I'd never really noticed it until I became a mom myself back in 2006—to one Jules Walker Lehr. But then, slowly but surely, with every visit with family, friends, and fellow parents, and with each trip to the pediatrician's office, park, library, grocery store, or birthday party, I noticed more and more that adults do indeed talk to kids *differently.* It got to the point where I could predict what people would say to kids in a variety of situations with a fair amount of accuracy. I started calling it Parentspeak, as in *Here comes the Parentspeak!* (Though it certainly isn't only parents who speak it.) And sometimes it could really trigger me: My jaw would clench, my chest would become jittery, and I'd be awash in feelings I couldn't quite tease out. I assumed my intense reaction was the result of some childhood baggage. Which is not to say I wouldn't catch myself speaking it. I would!

While I figured we were all speaking Parentspeak with nothing but a genuine desire to do right by our kids—to help them feel loved, encouraged, and secure, while also aiming to instill the self-control and manners they need to navigate the world—I doubt any of us ever consciously chose to start using it. After all, there are an infinite number of ways to say something, and yet the language of Parentspeak is decidedly limited. More likely we default to it because our parents did and/or because everyone else does. It's in the ether. It creeps up on us innocuously enough with a "Shhh, don't cry!" lovingly whispered to our newborns, and soon we're excitedly applauding "Good job!" for every roll over, new step, and bite of broccoli. We start off warning our curious toddlers to "Be careful!" and before we know it, enough's enough and we're threatening, "If you don't . . ." with a wagging finger. And boom, we've become our parents. Or our teachers. Now we are the authority figures speaking with "authority." The tables have officially turned. I began to wonder if Parentspeak was having undue influence not only on how I responded to Jules and soon to her younger brother, Hudson, but also on how I perceived their behavior in the first place. Was I responding to them, and the unique situations in front of me, or was Parentspeak—i.e., our upbringing and culture—holding me hostage, dictating not only what I said but how I felt about what my kids were doing?

Considering the undeniable power of language and its ability to shape the way kids think about themselves, their relationships, the ways of the world, and their place in it, I had to question if our best intentions were translating. Does "You're okay!" really *feel* comforting? Is "Good job!" actually encouraging? Does "Say 'Sorry'!" cultivate remorse? Is "Do you want a time-out?" the best way to enlist "cooperation"? (And what do I mean by "best," anyway? Easiest? Quickest?)

Speaking to the profound influence language has on impressionable young brains, the late psychologist Thomas Gordon—a pioneer in teaching communication skills and three-time Nobel Peace Prize nominee—explained, "Every time you talk to a child you are adding a brick to define the relationship that is being built between the two of you. And each message says something to the child about what you think of him. He gradually builds up a picture of how you perceive him as a person. Talk can be constructive to the child and to the relationship or it can be destructive."

Echoing Gordon, author L. R. Knost cautioned, "Sticks and stones may break bones, but words can shatter souls. Choose wisely." Indeed, the way we talk to kids becomes their inner voice—the sound track they'll involuntarily play back to themselves throughout their lives that tells them if they are worthy of respect and compassion, if they're capable and competent, and if their ideas, perceptions, interests, feelings, and voices matter. What messages, I wondered, were Jules's and Hudson's developing brains recording? Were they helpful, or something they'd want to later try to record over or erase?

As curious as I was concerned, I started deconstructing a bunch of phrases that I considered Parentspeak classics to see if

> The way we talk to kids becomes their inner voice—the sound track they'll involuntarily play back to themselves throughout their lives.

they were, as Gordon said, constructive or destructive, helpful or harmful. Were my best intentions translating? If not, why not? What would be wiser? Soon, with too many thoughts and questions swirling around to keep track of, I took on the project more formally and started researching this book. What I've come to realize is that Parentspeak is a language of control, too often further marred by condescension. In various ways—some obvious, some not so—we use Parentspeak to tell our children how *we* want them to feel ("You're okay!"); what *we* want them to say ("Can you say 'Thank you'?"); how *we* want them to act ("Be nice!"); what *we* want them to do ("Share!"); when *we* want them to do it ("I'm gonna count to three . . ."); how proud *we*'ll be if they do it ("Good job!"); and what will happen to them if they don't ("Do you want a time-out?"). And therein lies the Achilles' heel of Parentspeak. No one, of any age, at any time, responds well to being controlled—or patronized. Control triggers one of two responses: rebellion or submission, accompanied by various less than healthy coping mechanisms. It might "work" in the short run, but it's bound to backfire over time.

> No one, of any age, at any time, responds well to being controlled— or patronized.

Alas, Parentspeak distances us from our children instead of connecting us to the real them. And feeling connected to those you love—feeling seen, heard, felt, understood, considered, truly cared for, celebrated, enjoyed, and ultimately accepted—well, isn't that *everything*? Isn't it what we all long for? Isn't that what we want for our children, for them to feel like they are a part of a family that knows and loves them and their totally unique personality and interests—mistakes, bad moods, human frailties, and all? Ultimately, this feeling of being *accepted* and *connected* is what makes our kids genuinely want to be with us. And it's what makes us want to be with them. It's what allows us to get to know them. It's what builds trust and makes them want to work with us to solve problems. And it's what will make our kids—some fifteen, twenty, or thirty years from now—look forward to getting together with us during the holidays instead of dreading it. Bottom line: How our children *feel* when they are with us determines the degree to which they will flourish. And control—the current running through Parentspeak—is a flourish-inhibitor if ever there was one. And the condescension? Well, it just adds insult to injury.

I've chosen fourteen Parentspeak classics to explore in depth here, each one illustrative of a different way in which our best intentions get bungled. Taking a good hard look at these habitually overused phrases has helped me pinpoint the disconnect between the messages we hope we're sending and the messages our kids are likely receiving. And because we often use Parentspeak to address issues fundamental to raising children, I've found that teasing these phrases apart has helped me clarify how ideally I'd like to relate and respond to Jules and Hudson—and all children. All people! Because kids are people and deserve to be spoken to and treated as such. As the psychotherapist John Peterson so perfectly put it, "Children are our equals, not in skill or knowledge, but in human dignity."

My goal hasn't so much been to come up with some new language to use with my children as it has been to let go of Parentspeak and the control and condescension inherent in it. My goal is to be conscious, present, and calm enough to respond with compassion, respect, and authenticity while maintaining my boundaries— a tall order, for sure!—especially when life is at its most haywire, which, when you have young kids, can feel like most of the time. That said, I have found some alternative language and different ways of responding that I can count on when I feel like I'm drowning. They bring me back to a more centered place where I can be a part of the solution instead of just creating a bigger problem— which, I'd noticed, was all too often the case. My hope is that these approaches will help you, too.

CHAPTER ONE

"GOOD JOB!"

"I was trained to make my mother
happy. . . . [I am] addicted to attention,
acclaim, validation."
—Howard Stern

"Hate to break it to you . . ." So read the subject line of a
mass email from my friend Ana. (This is *way* back in
2007, before everyone and their mother turned to social
media to spread the good—or bad—word.) "Read and weep!"
she wrote and attached an article from *Parents* magazine called
"Hooked on Praise," by Alfie Kohn, a ruckus-making scholar in
the worlds of education, parenting, and beyond. Even though I
only had a precious few minutes left to get stuff done before Jules
awoke from her nap, I was curious to see what news was so bad that
Ana hated to break it to me—and all the other new-parent friends
she'd cc'd.

I quickly skimmed the article, hoping I'd land on just the right sentences that would tell me whatever I needed to know— it seems nothing makes a person more ADD than having a baby. Scanning, I gathered that, contrary to popular belief, our national habit of saying "Good job!" to kids is not only *not* helpful, but it can be manipulative and can actually turn them into "praise junkies." *Praise junkies?* I thought skeptically. *Really? Isn't that overstating things a bit?* I didn't quite think "Whatever!" but I certainly wasn't reading and weeping. Then Jules woke up, so I quickly replied to Ana with a perfunctory "Interesting! Thx for sending" and ran off to get my angel. I figured that was that.

But she wrote back.

"I know! The article really hit home for me and Greg. We both grew up desperately wanting to please our parents. I was always trying to be the person my parents wanted me to be, grasping for the answers I thought my parents wanted to hear, molding myself into whatever person would elicit a 'Good job!' Believe me, it's no surprise Greg and I met at Yale! It was our parents' wet dream. Twenty years and tons of therapy later, I realized that I'd never really asked myself *What do I think? How do I feel? What do I want?* Oh, the wasted years! We're definitely going to try to be really mindful about praising Tessie. Two people-pleasers in the house is two too many."

Whoa! I should have actually read the whole article, I thought, hitting reply.

"Amazing how parents mean well but cause damage in ways they never could have imagined—to put it mildly. Wonder what I'm doing to screw up Jules. Isn't it inevitable? Guess we should start a therapy fund now! :) I appreciate the heads-up. I'll definitely be laying off 'good job.' See you soon? xo"

Then I hit Google. "What creates a people-pleaser?" I asked the great and powerful wizard.

"Parents do!" the wizard replied, just like Alfie Kohn said they do.

I clicked on a *Psychology Today* article forebodingly entitled "From Parent-Pleasing to People-Pleasing: How Craving Others' Approval Can Sabotage Healthy Self-Development," by Dr. Leon Seltzer, who explained that "Children learn to say and do what their parents approve of either for fear of not getting the approval or worse, either a withholding of love or some kind of punishment." Among his long list of characteristics that defined people-pleasers, Seltzer included:

> Very organized; easily liked . . . friendly and gregarious; helpful and supportive; courteous and considerate; always smiling; interested in others' welfare . . .

Ana to a T! I thought. She's about as lovely, warm, and welcoming as a person can be. I could imagine if someone had read only those positive attributes, she might wonder *How can I raise that child? Praise? Done!* But unfortunately, those are only the traits people-pleasers display to their parents and later to the world. On the inside, life isn't so rosy:

> [People-pleasers are] fearful of losing approval; fearful of failure and rejection . . . ignoring personal needs and rights; feeling lonely and isolated . . . feeling undeserving, and "not good enough"; excessively concerned about satisfying others' demands; insecure about personal abilities, skills, or knowledge; fearful of letting friends and family down; fearful of being "found out" as not being as good as they seem . . . [they suffer from] exhaustion from always trying so hard to be perfect . . . feeling unappreciated and taken for granted . . .

Whoa! I thought, feeling for Ana. *That's a lot to try to recover from.* Constantly trying to be the person you think other people want you to be. Never feeling you are enough. To some degree, I could definitely relate. Like many, I suppose, as a kid I acted differently with my grandparents than I did with my teachers than I did with my friends than I did with my parents than I did with boys I had crushes on. Certainly different people bring out different parts of one's personality, but I was more calculating than that. I acted in ways I figured would make them like me more, only sharing certain stories or spinning them in ways I thought would make them think I was a "good girl" or cool or funny or sophisticated or tough or whatever. But isn't that normal? Is it really possible to just truly be "yourself"—whoever that is—with everyone?

I found some insight into my experience in psychologist Robin Grille's book, *Parenting for a Peaceful World*. Explaining how rewards and praise can harm parent's relationships with their children, Grille writes, "As a result of early manipulation, we grow up trying hard to please, or we learn to use our wiles to impress, in order to get the goodies—at the expense of being our natural selves. We develop a phony or false self that distorts our relationships with others." *Hmmm.* I could see how constructing a version of oneself to be more liked could leave a kid (me!) feeling insecure and wondering if she would be as lovable or deserving if people knew the real her (me). As Jules wasn't yet a year old, I assumed she was still blissfully unaware of needing to please. *Isn't she?* I didn't want her to feel she had to act a certain way to be loved, I just wanted her to know she was. As is. Always. Could praise really lead to such deep-rooted insecurity?

Praise Addicts: In Their Own Words

Apparently so.

I did a little digging and discovered that other thinkers, in particular Carl Rogers, one of the most influential

> It was heartbreaking to think of a kid trapped in a continuous state of calculation, always on the prowl for a "Good job!" to assure herself that she is "good" or smart or clever or caring enough.

psychologists of the twentieth century, and Hungarian pediatrician Dr. Emmi Pikler agree that praise can breed insecurity. I also got a sense of what being a praise addict can feel like, according to a few of them in their own words. Christie Pettit, a blogger who identifies herself as a "recovering praise addict"; Howard Stern, the self-proclaimed king of all media; and a recent Harvard graduate who laments that she realized she hadn't "formed an identity beyond making people proud of me" all have spoken directly about how their lives have been adversely affected by praise.

Explaining her addiction, Pettit writes that praise addicts are "not just after pleasing others, but hearing encouragement and affirmation from others. The praise—positive words that will stroke the junkie's fragile ego—is the coveted prize. Motivation to do even the most considerate things for other people ultimately comes from the praise that will be received in return. Most praise junkies are probably not aware that this is what drives them, but as I stop to really look at my heart, this is the sad truth." It was heartbreaking to think of a kid trapped in a continuous state of calculation, always on the prowl for a "Good job!" to assure herself that she is "good" or smart or clever or caring enough. I got it. That's what Alfie Kohn meant when he said kids can become "extrinsically motivated." They don't do things because they're genuinely interested or curious but because they feel compelled to please their parents upon whom the quality of their life literally depends.

In Neil Strauss's revealing *Rolling Stone* interview "Howard Stern: Deeply Neurotic, Desperate for Approval and Happier than Ever," Stern directly traces his crippling dependence on praise to his early relationship with his mom, divulging, "I was trained to make my mother happy." Some fifty years later, the affects of that early training continue to plague him. "I just can't walk out of here and say, 'I did a good show today and I'm very satisfied,'" Stern explains. "No, I gotta know, do you think I did a good show and are you satisfied? And that's the neurosis and that's the source of all problems for me. . . . The pressure I put on myself is horrible. It's excruciating. . . . It's desperate. . . . One person not laughing can make me insane." And this is despite his stratospheric success, millions of devoted fans, a seemingly happy marriage, being the proud father of three children, more than a decade of psychotherapy, and a consistent transcendental meditation practice. So I wasn't surprised when I later came across this sobering admission from an unnamed recent Harvard graduate featured in the wildly popular photography blog Humans of New York:

> I'd always been an overachiever. I graduated at the top of my class in high school. . . . But when I got to Harvard, everyone around me was just as smart or smarter. My grades fell, and suddenly I was no longer exceeding expectations. All that external validation that I'd become accustomed to suddenly stopped. And I crumbled. I felt lost. I learned that I hadn't formed an identity beyond making people proud of me. I'm still not exactly sure who I am. But I'm working on it.

While these stories were enough to make me never want to say "Good job!" again, I was still confused because for so long I'd thought of parents praising their kids as nothing short of part of the job description. *We're our kids' support system. Their champions. If not us, who?* I figured Ana, Pettit, and Stern were extreme cases. *Surely,* I thought, *you can be encouraging and supportive without creating an insecure praise addict. Can't you?* Everything in moderation, right?

Not All "Good Job!"s Are Created Equal

Until I could get a handle on what was okay to praise or how to do it without making a mess of Jules, I decided I'd just lay off "Good job!" for a while. Better safe than sorry. What I didn't realize however, was that this new focus on praise had apparently planted some kind of homing-device inside of me, because it seemed that wherever I went, if someone said "Good job!" I heard it. Which means I heard it *everywhere* and *often*. Alas, not all "Good job!"s are created equal. Sometimes it was said as if a child had literally cured cancer and a Nobel Peace Prize nomination was imminent, even though all he'd done was taken his shoes off before getting into the sandbox.

"Good job, buddy! Thatta boy!"

Or jumped off the swing.

"Good job! Way to go!" Applause, applause, applause.

Or finished a meal.

"Good job! What a good eater you are!"

At the other end of the spectrum, however, some "Good job!"s sounded so lifeless—probably because the good jobber was mid-text or maybe because saying it had become so rote.

In between, however, were some low-key, yet supportive "Good job!"s that seemed to be saying, *I care and think you're great. Keep on rocking it.* Like when a six-year-old boy said, "Hey, Dad, check this out!" and then he swung across the monkey bars. Inevitably, his dad called out, "Good job, buddy!" He didn't overdo it. He didn't under do it. I mean, what else was he supposed to say? *That's not manipulative, is it?* I wondered. *What could possibly be wrong with that?*

Other times, however, I swear if I was blind I would've thought people were training their dogs instead of "complimenting" their kids. "Stay seated. . . . Good job!" or "Wait your turn! . . . Good job!" and "Good standing in line!" Some folks would even clap.

Why, I wondered, are we all good-jobbing everything all the time? Our incessant, albeit well-meaning, praise started to seem so intrusive. It felt kind of *Big Brother*-ish—no action, no matter how seemingly inconsequential, was immune from our judgment. I wondered if kids who have become so used to receiving a constant stream of praise are more likely to seek it out when their efforts aren't automatically acknowledged with fanfare:

> **Wherever I went, if someone said "Good job!" I heard it.**

"Watch this, Mom!"

"Good job!"

"Now watch this!"

"That's great, honey!"

"What about this?"

"Awesome!!"

"And this!"

Because if it isn't praised, does it count? Is it satisfying?

However, on the other hand, I imagine some continually praised kids might feel relieved to be "off the clock." *Phew, they're gone. Finally I can just play without having to do a good job of it all the time.*

Praise at Your Own Risk

While praising kids has been steadily gaining momentum over the last several decades, "Good job!" is now *the* signature phrase of the twenty-first-century American parent, teacher, coach, doctor, nanny, babysitter—i.e., any person who comes in contact with a child. Along the way, though, there have been many detractors waving their arms and yelling, "CAUTION: Danger Ahead!" One early alarm sounder was the Hungarian pediatrician Dr. Emmi Pikler, who, back in the 1930s, conducted extensive research on the natural gross motor development of infants. In her audaciously titled book *What Can Your Baby Do Already?*—a pointed comment on parents' unhealthy obsession with their children's rate of development—Dr. Pikler cautioned, "We hinder the child when we acknowledge certain accomplishments in an exaggerated way. . . . The effect is incalculable. As a result, the child will not . . . try out what gives him pleasure, but that which he assumes will please adults."

> **Thus our "encouragement" can actually make children more insecure—literally and figuratively.**

Celebrating an accomplishment *with* a child, Dr. Pikler believed, is quite different from trying to push a baby toward mastering a new milestone like standing or walking using praise as a reward—"You can do it! Come on! . . . Good job!" Because when we do try to encourage our children's development by applauding their efforts to reach certain milestones, we send the message that where they are—say, as a crawler—isn't good enough for us. There's also a risk that children may actually end up weaker and less coordinated because they are trying to rush their progress to please us instead of listening to the wisdom of their bodies. Thus our "encouragement" can actually make children more insecure—literally and figuratively. *Mom and Dad want me to walk. That will make them happy with me! Oh gosh, why does my body still want to crawl sometimes? Got. To. Stand. Up.*

For Dr. Pikler, honoring a child's initiative and unique rate and way of developing was essential to healthy growth—both physically and psychologically. In an effort to reassure anxious parents, she explained, "An infant's own movements and the development of these movements and every detail of this development are a constant source of joy to him. If one does not interfere, an infant will learn to turn, roll, creep on the belly, go on all fours, stand, sit, and walk with no trouble." It is our meddling—which often comes in the form of well-meaning encouragement and praise—that's not only not helpful to their development but teaches that we value product over process.

Looking at the world through Pikler-colored glasses, I began noticing things I'd never thought to pay attention to before and was surprised by just how subtle and easy-to-miss the seeds of creating a people-pleaser could be. For instance, I was over at my friends Nick and Tanya's trying to help them decide on a paint color for their living room when, all of a sudden, they literally went "Good job!" crazy over their nine-month-old daughter, Lola.

"Good job, Lola!" applauded Tanya, beaming. "Good job!"

"Good job!" Nick concurred. "That's my girl!"

Lola looked up from gumming a red rubber ball and smiled a big smile.

What just happened? I couldn't help but wonder. One minute Lola was happily playing while we debated whether Moonlight Gray would be too dark, and now she was ten feet away in the dining room playing with a ball. Obviously I'd missed something pretty spectacular. My face must've betrayed my confusion because Tanya explained, "That was *only* Lola's second time crawling up a step! Wasn't it, Lola? Good job, baby girl!"

"Oh, wow! Great," I said as I thought *Hmmmm.*

Of course, I could relate to their excitement. It is amazing to watch your child go from a weak and helpless newborn to a coordinated kid on the go (who climbs stairs!) in such a short time. Nature *is* truly astonishing. But considering that as a normally growing and developing Homo sapiens, Lola literally couldn't *not* learn to crawl up the step, I wondered how she might process getting praised for something inevitable? Certainly no lioness is applauding when her cubs start to walk. It's just as it is. Praising your child for crawling up a stair is just a few steps away from praising a child for breathing. *That's my girl! Inhale in and exhale out! Good job!* I could see how a child might become reticent to try something she isn't naturally good at for fear of not getting the praise she's come to expect for things that come naturally. The irony! Or perhaps, as Dr. Pikler suggested, a child will continue to do whatever won the accolades and attention in the first place, hoping for more. Sadly, of course, she'll eventually learn that the "accomplishment" has become old news and is no longer praiseworthy, and that she'll need to up her game if she wants more attention. *Maybe Mom and Dad will like this? No? Hmmm, let me try this. . . .*

> Praising your child for crawling up a stair is just a few steps away from praising a child for breathing.

The Power of Observation

None of this is to say that children aren't proud of their accomplishments—they may well be. And we can enjoy and support their feeling of pride. But they also may not be, and instead just absorb their new abilities as part of the natural flow of life. After all, babies are in a near constant state of learning and acquiring skills—it's just that some of those skills are more dramatic and visible than others. Dr. Pikler believed the key to being a supportive parent is *observation*. Too often, before children even have a chance to register how they feel about *their* big moment, we're telling them how we feel about it or how we think they should feel about it. Maybe Lola was excited that her newfound ability had allowed her to explore the next room or enabled her to get that ball she'd been eyeing! In that case, instead of a rote "good job," parents can reflect their child's excitement:

"I see! You can climb steps now!"

Or "You got your ball!"

Silence Is Golden

O r, if Lola seems unfazed by her new ability and was just engrossed in her play, then there's really no need to say anything at all. If she isn't excited about it, then her parents' praise can seem random, which may send the message that they're perpetually on the lookout for things she does that are praiseworthy. Of course, if we're excited (and watching our children master new things is exciting—even mind-blowing!), we can always share our feelings with friends and partners: "Can you believe it? She's already climbing steps. It happened so fast!"

Happily, I've found Dr. Pikler's appeal to parents to allow their children to develop without pressure or fanfare is alive and well in the widely read parenting blog of Janet Lansbury, a RIE (Resources for Infant Educarers) expert. Lansbury was a student of Dr. Pikler's protégé, the late Magda Gerber, founding director of RIE. She shared on Facebook a story from a mom who managed to swallow her impulse to "Good job!" her daughter, thus allowing her to bask in her own moment of glory.

> Tonight it was time for bed and I was carrying my baby while my 2yo followed along. We got to the baby gate and I asked my toddler if she would like me to pick her up or if she would like

to try to get over the gate on her own. (Something she's been working on but hasn't quite been able to do.) She said, "Yes, Emmy try it herself." And then she got over and was so excited! She threw her arms up and said "Emmy tried and tried and didn't do it, but now Emmy did it by herself!" I responded, "You did it! And you seem to be very proud of yourself!" I love how the excitement came from HER accomplishment. SHE had worked on something and mastered it on her own, and that was enough for her. She didn't need MY praise.

Precisely.

"Sweetheart! You *have* done it. How exciting. I'm so happy for you." That's celebrating *with*.

Prizing Instead of Praising

Another alarm-sounder was Carl Rogers, who, as I mentioned, was one of the twentieth century's most influential psychologists, and someone I've come to think of as the granddaddy of the notion that praise can derail a life. A founder of the humanistic approach to psychology in the 1950s, Rogers developed the paradigm-shifting theory of "unconditional positive regard," which holds that essential to a child's healthy development is feeling that she's unconditionally loved by her parents. That is to say, in order for a child to be on the path to reaching her innate potential, she needs parents who do not withdraw their love just because she acts in ways they don't approve of or makes a mistake. I like David G. Myers's description of unconditional positive regard from the textbook *Psychology:*

This is an attitude of grace, an attitude that values us even knowing our failings. It is a profound relief to drop our pretenses, confess our worst feelings, and discover that we are still accepted. In a good marriage, a close family, or an intimate friendship, we are free to be spontaneous without fearing the loss of others' esteem.

Rogers called this attitude of valuing our children for who they are "prizing" them, which is so different from praising them for what they do. A child who feels prized will develop the confidence and freedom to go out on a limb and experiment, unafraid that she is in any way diminished by challenges, mistakes, or setbacks. On the other hand, if the love and affirmation a child receives is conditional, then she starts to feel good about herself only when she performs or acts in ways that make her parents happy or proud, rather than when she does something that brings her personal joy.

> **A child who feels prized will develop the confidence and freedom to go out on a limb and experiment.**

Indeed, before my very eyes, I witnessed a four year old girl doing something just to make her mother happy one drizzly afternoon when I was picking Jules up from preschool—a veritable hotbed of "Good jobs!" Paula, a fellow mom who must've been in a hurry, tried to get her daughter, Georgia, to put on her raincoat.

"Here you go, honey," Paula said holding up her jacket.

Georgia frowned and shook her head.

"Come on, sweetheart, we've *got* to go!" Paula pleaded.

Georgia shook her head again and firmly said, "No!"

Some parents call this being "obstinate." Others call it being "uncooperative," or even "misbehaving." At this point, I'd come to see it as a child who knows what she wants and how she feels and is simply trying to communicate it.

What Is RIE?

Resources for Infant Educarers, more commonly known as RIE (pronounced "rye"), is a philosophy and methodology of raising children with respect. The organization was founded in the 1970s by the late Magda Gerber, largely based on the work of her mentor, the Hungarian pediatrician Dr. Emmi Pikler. Gerber coined the term "educarer" to emphasize the idea that the way we care for our children is an essential part of their education. My husband, John, and I started taking a weekly parent-infant class with Jules when she was just three months old and continued for two years. In each class, for the first half hour the children play and the parents observe. Then we talk about our observations and address any questions we may have. Here are some of the tenets from the RIE philosophy that really helped me:

1. Tell your child what you are going to do before you do it—"I'm going to pick you up now. Are you ready?" This allows babies to relax because they know you're not going to just move their bodies without fair warning.

2. Use caregiving times—e.g., dressing, changing, feeding, and bathing—to slow down and really connect, inviting your child to participate in the process.

3. From the earliest age, give your baby plenty of uninterrupted time to explore and play in their own way.

4. While car seats are necessary and strollers are helpful to a point, putting a baby into play centers, exersaucers, walkers, swings, and bouncy seats restricts their freedom to move and develop naturally.

5. Passive toys (i.e., no bells and whistles) make active babies. Simple toys that can be used in a variety of ways encourage a child's imagination, creativity, attention span, and competence.

6. Don't try to rush your child's development (i.e., don't try to help your child roll over, sit up, or walk). They will do it on their own when they have gained the necessary strength and coordination.

7. If your child's days are consistent and predictable, she'll start to anticipate what will come next, which creates a great sense of security.

8. Reflecting or acknowledging achievements is more helpful than praising.

9. Don't talk about your child in the third person in front of them.

10. Don't ask your child to perform ("Show Grandma how you can clap your hands!") or label them (shy or rude, or what have you), because it only gives them, as Gerber once said, a script to live up to.

So Paula switched tactics.

"I know you can do it, sweetheart. First this arm . . ." she said, touching Georgia's right arm and flashing a big smile.

And in Georgia's right arm went.

"Good job!" her mom exclaimed, happy finally to be moving in the right direction.

Georgia smiled back.

"Now your other one!" she instructed with equal enthusiasm and warmth.

In her left arm went.

"Good job, honey! And now let's zip you up! Good job! Okay! We're ready to go!" Paula said, tapping Georgia's nose.

Three "Good job!"s over the course of the single act of putting on a coat. *Wow!* I thought.

The Gift of Why

O nly months earlier, this interaction wouldn't have even registered, but now it made me gulp. Georgia clearly hadn't wanted to put on her coat, and instead of asking her *why* she didn't want to, Paula good-jobbed her into it, not giving Georgia's reluctance any credence. After all, it's not like Paula was complimenting Georgia on her ability to put her arm through a sleeve—she'd likely mastered that a couple of years earlier. Rather, she was essentially praising Georgia for being "cooperative" (a kissing cousin to "obedient") her maternal warmth and approval given upon the condition that her request was fulfilled.

Now, I don't doubt that Paula had sound reasons for wanting Georgia to wear the raincoat. Maybe she thought it was about to start pouring. Maybe they were going to the supermarket, where she knew Georgia would be freezing if she were damp. We've all had our valid reasons for wanting our kids to comply with our requests. But what gave me pause was that Paula didn't take that extra few seconds to *explain* to her daughter *why* it was important that she put the coat on. Nor did she ask Georgia *why* she didn't want to put it on in the first place. Instead, likely in the interest of time, she sweet-talked Georgia into doing something she clearly hadn't wanted to do—thus leveraging her coveted parental approval.

I can imagine for Georgia's part that she, too, had a valid reason for not wanting to wear the raincoat. Maybe she didn't want to put it on because she was hot from running around so much at school. Maybe she knew from experience how restricting the stiff raincoat would feel when she was strapped into her car seat. Or, perhaps Georgia didn't want to wear the coat because she thought the rain was magical and loved how it felt when it lightly hit her skin. I don't know. But neither did Paula. The problem is that Georgia acquiesced not because she understood why it was important that she wear the coat, but seemingly to please her mom. Even if Georgia felt hot and bulky in it, she probably figured—subconsciously, of course—that it was a small price to pay for Mom being happy with her.

This may seem like a ridiculously minor situation of little consequence. I imagine many would admire Paula's warmth and patience. After all, she didn't lose her cool or resort to threats—and her need to get to the next thing in her day matters, too. While I don't want to make mountains out of molehills, the truth is that many molehills a mountain make. That's the way brain wiring works. A child's experience, when coupled again and again with like experiences, impacts her understanding of herself and her place in the world. And so it follows that depending on how we respond to our children,

> **We've all had our valid reasons for wanting our kids to comply with our requests.**

they will come to either value their own point of view or they won't. North Dakota State professor and family science specialist Sean Brotherson explains how this works in his article "Understanding Brain Development in Young Children":

> As the synapses in a child's brain are strengthened through repeated experiences, connections and pathways are formed that structure the way a child learns. If a pathway is not used, it's eliminated based on the 'use it or lose it' principle.

Alas, seeing that it took my super smart friend Ana years of therapy just to be able to ask herself *What do I think? What do I feel?* it seems reasonable to deduce that the belief that her feelings were important literally didn't get wired into her brain when she was a child. And my guess is that it's because her parents never really thought about considering her perspective, but instead were intent on teaching her what they felt was important. Getting Ana to go along with their program—i.e., to be a good girl—was vital. And so their beliefs became hers. We're all born with a perspective, but if it's not valued, we can lose it. (We can find it again—often with the help of a therapist—but it's a search that requires a lot of fortitude.)

And so it stands that the more we value our children's perspective—that is, the more we ask them why they do or don't want to do something, and give their response genuine consideration—the stronger their belief will be that their thoughts, feelings, and experiences are important. However, if, on the other hand, we want children who follow our directions regardless of their personal circumstances, then giving conditional positive regard will help us achieve that goal. What we can't have, however, is our cake and to eat it too—unquestioning, compliant children who become self-assured adults. This reality was perfectly captured in an unattributed cartoon I came across of a mother saying to her daughter, "Honey, when you grow up, I want you to be assertive, independent, and strong-willed. But while you're a kid, I want you to be passive, pliable, and obedient." It just doesn't work that way. Challenging our parents is practice for the future. And it's up to us to meet our children's challenge to our "authority" with curiosity as to where they're coming from. Essentially what happened with Paula's sweet-talking Georgia into putting on the coat she didn't want to wear was that Paula—who is actually one of the biggest feminists I know—not only denied her daughter her voice but sent the message

> The more we value our children's perspective, the stronger their belief will be that their thoughts, feelings, and experiences are important.

that at best her experience wasn't important and at worst it was wrong or bad. Not a big deal if it's only one instance, but I could see how over time this is how a child becomes a people-pleaser. *It's fine! I can live with the discomfort as long as everyone else is happy. Mother knows best.* It's incumbent upon us as parents to value our children's point of view. To *prize* them. Because it is only then, when their feelings and needs are on the table, that parents and kids can work together to find solutions that work for everyone.

For instance, if Paula understood that the raincoat felt too stiff, I can imagine them deciding that Georgia would wear the coat to the car but then could take it off before getting in. Or maybe once Paula understood how much Georgia loved the feeling of the rain on her skin (which is common for kids here in drought-ravaged southern California), she might realize it's only a little water and that the coat isn't as important as she thought.

Believe me, I get that it's often inconvenient to pause and try to figure out why our children are resisting us. We have things to do! Places to go! But when we do take the time, we're telling our children that how they feel and think is *important*—which is especially critical when it's a matter related to their own bodies. We want them to trust their instincts. But alas, like many of us, Paula used praise to reward Georgia for "cooperating," and as a result Georgia became more oriented to her mom's approval than to an experience of enjoying the magic of the rain or avoiding the discomfort of the jacket. It's exactly as the psychologist and author Jay Earley describes: "Often, parents will simply tell kids what to do and never encourage them to assert themselves. When the kids obey, the parents give them conditional love. Once established, such behaviors become self-reinforcing, which makes them difficult to uproot. They get rewarded by bosses, co-workers, and friends just as they do by parents, prompting pleasers to assume doormat postures over and over again in hopes of receiving more kudos." If Ana, Christie Pettit, or Howard Stern are any indication, "difficult to uproot" is a serious understatement.

I totally got how it can happen that a child who wants to be a filmmaker might grow up to be the doctor of his parents' dreams—burying his or her own innate interest, talents, and passions for the unmatched reassurance of his parents' approval. It's a phenomenon with which Julie Lythcott-Haims, former dean of freshmen at Stanford University, is all too familiar. The author of *How to Raise an Adult: Break Free of the Overparenting Trap and Prepare Your Kids for Success*, Lythcott-Haims discloses, "I heard plenty of stories from college students who believed they *had* to study science (or medicine, or engineering), just as they'd *had* to play piano, *and* do community service for Africa, *and, and, and.* I talked with kids completely uninterested in the items on their own résumés. Some shrugged off any right to be bothered by their own lack of interest in what they were working on, saying, 'My parents know what's best for me.'"

This is precisely what I want to avoid, because I know there is simply no way for me to know what the best path is for Jules and Hudson. I'm not them, and crystal balls aren't real. Certainly I can share my concerns and thoughts, and they theirs. And then we can weigh them together.

If Not "Good Job!" Then What?

The good news is that not all praise is manipulative. Sometimes we "Good job!" our kids to let them know we're rooting for them, we think they nailed it, or that we're impressed or proud. But the more I thought about it, the more crazy—or maybe just lazy— it seemed that we use the same two, über-generic, all-purpose words to send such a variety of messages. So, if not "Good job!" then what? As a mother of two young children, I've had many, many occasions to contemplate this question and experiment with how I respond when my kids say, "Watch this!" One such occasion proved particularly pivotal to my thinking.

Describe What You See

Jules's brother Hudson was three when he went through a love affair with tape—Scotch tape, packing tape, colored tapes—and he essentially hyperventilated at the sight of caution tape. And just in case he was overcome with the desire to tape things together—furniture, blocks, action figures, cars, what have you—he often kept a pair of children's scissors tucked into his Pull-Ups.

"Maw-om!" he called out one day.

"Yes, Hudson?"

"Come!" he said meaning, *I'm on a roll here, and you're gonna love it. Check this out!*

Now upon seeing his complex creation of various colored tapes zigzagging across the house, I could certainly have said, "Wow, Hudson! This is amazing! Good job, honey. Good job!" And likely he would have smiled with pride and then returned to his work. I genuinely did find it amazing, and clearly he had been working really hard. He had indeed done a good job in creating whatever it was he'd created. But I stopped myself. This time, instead of telling him how great it was, I slowed down and *described* what I was looking at.

"Hudson! This is so elaborate. I see you've wound the caution tape all the way from the legs of the dresser in your bedroom, in and out through the banister along the staircase . . . down into the living room, under the sofa, around the coffee table and taped it onto the bookshelf! This is your longest construction ever! What a lot of work."

> **Describing what I was looking at, I found I actually became more aware of what I was seeing.**

Describing what I was looking at, I found I actually became more aware of what I was seeing. Instead of just doing a perfunctory, drive-by "Good job!" I was more present. (And as an extra bonus, I was using words like "elaborate" and "banister" and "attached" that could certainly help develop his vocabulary a lot more than "good job" ever would.) I also found myself genuinely intrigued by his "setup" (as he called it), so I asked about it.

Can You Tell Me About It?

"I'm interested in all of these little strips of orange tape that you cut and attached to the black tape. Can you tell me about them?"

It's a question that has turned out to be a gift that keeps on giving.

"Wait!" Hudson said. "First I've got to hide this guy in this bucket." Then he turned a plastic pail over an action figure and started drumming on it as he explained, "There are a lot of rabbits. Rabbits are here. And here. And here. And they all climb across the caution tape, to the black tape, hanging by their hands and they climb and climb to this rope and then they all climb down into the hole. There's only one hole for all the rabbits. And it's small."

"It must be crowded down there. What are all the rabbits doing in the hole?"

"They're trying to work it out," he explained.

"I see. So many rabbits in one place—I bet that's challenging. How is it going for them?"

"Good. They're working it out."

"And what about this area? With these blocks and magnet tiles?"

"Those aren't blocks, Maw-om!" he said, unable to hide his contempt, as his drumming came to an abrupt halt. "Those are *buildings*. And they're all taped together because this is all water and they'll float away if they're not together. There's a *flood*."

Wow, I thought. *Wow.*

Hudson's explanations of his creation were infinitely more interesting and illuminating than my telling him how "good" I thought what he had made was. This time I gave him what he really craved: a mom who genuinely was interested in his work. As Carl Rogers explained, "If you value someone, you listen. You pay attention. You aim to understand. You give time." Had I thrown out a pat "Good job!" I would have reduced all of his intricate work to two words that did little more than cast my judgment of his creation. If we take the time to learn about them, kids' creations can be a fascinating window into their thoughts and feelings. In this case, Hudson seemed to be working through problems with lots of other rabbits (who I suspected were stand-ins for kids at preschool) and finding solutions to challenges. "Good job" wouldn't have begun to address the complexity of what he created, and most sadly, it would have ended a really interesting conversation before it began.

Is Praise Encouraging?

Thinking about Hudson's work, I answered one of my initial questions: Do my children need my praise to encourage them to keep on creating, exploring, and advancing their skills? Apparently not. They're naturally curious and involved in what they're doing, be it building, pretending, dancing, jumping, drawing, reading, cartwheeling, or dressing up. Of their own volition, driven by their innate curiosity and need to express themselves, they continue to acquire skills and make each project more complex in some way. As the late educator John Holt explained in his 1967 book *How Children Learn*, "Children are born passionately eager to make as much sense as they can of things around them. If we attempt to control, manipulate, or divert this process . . . the independent scientist in the child disappears . . . We can best help children learn, not by deciding what we think they should learn [but by] paying serious attention to what they do." Or as Neil deGrasse Tyson, the renowned astrophysicist and cosmologist, said, "Children are born curious. Period. I only have one piece of advice: Get out of their way."

When a young child is given the space to follow his interests, he is intensely engaged, motivated, and learning on a deep level. A "Good job!" from a parent is really beside the point—the thrill of discovery and the satisfaction of creating are the child's reward. That said, certainly children like to share their efforts and accomplishments with their friends, parents, and teachers, not because they want it evaluated, but rather because they're proud and want to connect. They want to share more of who they are with those they love. As Alfie Kohn wrote in his book *Unconditional Parenting: Moving from Rewards and Punishments to Love and Reason*, "When unconditional love and genuine enthusiasm are always present, 'Good job!' isn't necessary; when they're absent, 'Good job!' won't help."

Appreciating Instead of Evaluating

A seemingly innocuous exchange with my husband made me realize just how patronizing being praised can feel. At least to me. I figured, seeing that kids are human, too, that it just may feel similarly to them. This dawned on me one evening when John essentially praised me for stopping at Target to buy a pump to blow up our air mattresses for an upcoming camping trip.

When he came home and saw the pump box on the front table, he yelled up, "I'm proud of you for getting the pump! Good job, babe!"

I thought to myself, *Good job? What the hell? He's proud of me for picking up a pump? I'm forty-three years old. I've been perfectly capable of driving over to a store and purchasing something for twenty-seven years now. What exactly is he proud of?*

It was a backhanded compliment, a dig disguised as praise. The subtext was something like, "You usually forget to pick up things we need. Good job remembering this time! You're really growing into a responsible adult." It's true, I'm a bit of a scatterbrain, but I was becoming more organized and didn't appreciate the subtle reminder of my shortcomings when I was supposedly receiving a compliment.

When I called him on it, John agreed.

"Sorry, babe! You're right. Thank you. I've had such a busy week, I appreciate you handling that."

Ahhh, knowing I was helping my husband out felt so much better than being evaluated by him, even if the evaluation was full of adulation. It was as psychologist Marshall Rosenberg observed: "[praise] destroys the beauty of sincere gratitude." To explain what he meant, Rosenberg, founder of the Center for Nonviolent Communication, told this story about a conversation he had with a woman who came up to him after a talk to tell him how brilliant he'd been.

> I said, "That is no help. I have been called a lot of names in my life, some positive and some far from positive, and I could never recall learning anything of value from someone telling me what I am . . ."
>
> She said, "What do you want to hear?"
>
> "What did I say in the workshop that made life more wonderful for you?"
>
> She thought for a moment and . . . said, "I have this 18-year-old son, and when we fight, it is horrible. It can go on for days. I have been needing some concrete direction, and these two things have made such a difference for me."

She was grateful because Rosenberg gave her both real hope and a path to follow about something vitally important to her. I got it. Essentially, the difference between praise and gratitude is: "I think you did a good job" vs. "Thank you for enriching my life." It made so much sense.

In fact, it was on the very school camping trip for which I bought the mattress pump that my friend Allison essentially expressed the same sentiment as Rosenberg. God bless her, Allison had taken on the enormous job of orchestrating the Sunday breakfast that ended the camping trip, which meant figuring out how to get more than 400 mouths fed at 7 a.m. in the middle of nowhere. After said breakfast went off rather seamlessly (thanks to months of preparation and a well-organized small army of volunteers), I happened to be sitting on a bench with Allison as a bunch of folks walked by calling out things like, "Hey! Good job on the breakfast!" or "That was awesome!" She smiled and thanked them all.

But then, after about the sixth person essentially said the same thing, instead of replying with her usual gracious "Thank you!" she finally said, "I'm glad everyone liked it so much, but *what* made it so good?" The truth is that while Allison had indeed done one hell of a good job, it's not what she wanted to hear. What she craved were details! How had her efforts made their life more wonderful?

"Well, for one thing," Julia replied, "the food was *hot* this year when I got it. Somehow the lines moved faster...."

"And," Eric added, "there was enough coffee. Bless you! It was so annoying last year when I finally got to the front of the line and it was all gone! I even had two cups."

"Nice!" Allison said. "That was actually one of my priorities." Clearly, knowing that all of the time she had spent mulling the kinks from the year before and searching for creative solutions had made a positive difference was more gratifying than the string of generic "Good Job!"s she'd been getting.

I try to express my gratitude and to be as specific as possible about what I appreciate because I know it's likely to be more satisfying.

Now I try to express my gratitude and to be as specific as possible about what I appreciate because I know it's likely to be more satisfying. So, for instance, when Jules and Hudson cleaned up after making a huge mess in the living room, instead of complimenting them on a job well done, I said something like, "Thank you for putting everything back where it goes. I love it when things are right where they should be. The house looks so inviting—just in time for our guests."

After a performance of Jules and Hudson's Black Band, their brother-sister duo known for sporting black clothes and playing music, I applauded like any good audience member would and then told them specifically what I enjoyed so much.

"Jules, you sing with so much emotion and abandon. It's so exciting to watch. And Hudson, I love how you support your sister's singing with your rhythmic guitar playing—you add a real sense of cool to the show. What a fun way to end the evening. I'm a big fan!"

Or instead of "Good job carrying in the groceries!" I'll simply say, "Thanks for helping me carry in the groceries. I know you wanted to go play. Now I can get dinner started faster."

Life Beyond Praise

Today, many years after my initial attempt to retire "Good job!" from my vocabulary, I find I literally can't even bring myself to say it. Admittedly, it's an extreme reaction to two innocent, congenial little words. But I don't miss them. Not only does their predictability still drive me a little insane, but I know that trapped inside them is so much substance, connection, and gratitude waiting to get out. Because it's so important to me that my kids know and value their own thoughts, feelings, and interests, I err on the side of caution.

CHAPTER TWO

"WHO'S MY BIG BOY?"

"The child, the boy, the man should know no other endeavor, but to be at every stage of development, what that stage calls for."
—**Freidrich Froebel**

Look! Big girl underwear!" "Your very own big boy bed!" "No more training wheels! You're ready for a big girl bike!" "Big boys don't need a blankie anymore!" "Aren't you excited? You're gonna be a big sister!"

These are the sales pitches of anxious parents eager to get their kids to do something that, for whatever reason, they don't want to do or aren't yet ready to do—i.e., ditch their diapers, blankie, or pacifier; leave their crib; stop co-sleeping; quit sucking their thumb; lose their training wheels; go to preschool or kindergarten; feel excited about becoming an older sibling, the list goes on. In essence, what's being sold here isn't so much the actual use of a big boy toilet or sleeping in the big girl bed—though these steps are certainly what parents are hoping for—but what we're selling is the *idea* that bigger (i.e., sooner or older) is indeed better. By default, we're telling our kids that the way they are—smaller, younger, or slower—isn't as good as what we're offering. *You wouldn't want to be like a baby now, would you?* It's classic marketing. Ironically, however, before we know it, we'll be trying to put on the brakes, not wanting our children to grow up too fast. "No, you're too young for that outfit, that movie . . . staying up so late . . . dating. . . ." Accepting and appreciating people for where they're at, what they *can* do, and who they are at any given moment instead of lamenting what they can't yet do or can no longer do isn't our culture's strong suit.

> What we're selling is the *idea* that bigger (i.e., sooner or older) is indeed better. By default, we're telling our kids that the way they are—smaller, younger, or slower— isn't as good as what we're offering.

Nevertheless, from personal experience I can tell you this bigger-is-better pitch can be quite compelling. I successfully used it to get Jules to use the toilet *Like a big girl!* But soon after it "worked," it backfired. In fact, it backfiring (both figuratively and literally) was what initially led me to see all of our big girl and big boy pitches for what they really are—attempts to flatter our impressionable, trusting young children into doing what we want, when we want them to.

Big Girl Potty

I t was an ordinary afternoon. Jules, who was two-and-a-half-ish at the time, was playing, while her younger brother Hudson napped. I was in the kitchen putting away groceries, wondering if now was a good time to get the potty-training show on the road. Figuring there's no time like the present, I took a here-goes-nothing breath and called out, "Jules, sweetheart! I have a surprise for you!"

In she ran.

"What?" Jules asked, excited.

"You're getting to be a big girl now," I said.

Quizzical silence.

"Did you know big girls use a big girl potty and wear big girl underwear?!"

Her eyes widened. A smile enveloped her face.

"And that's *just* what I bought for you!" I continued. And then I handed her a fresh six-pack of colorful underwear and presented two mini potties. "I'm going to put these in the bathrooms just for you! Your very own big girl potties."

Well, Jules swooned even harder than I thought she would. So hard that she was almost instantly done with diapers. She was all about her big girl underwear. Within minutes she was running around the house modeling pair after pair after pair; then she went into the bathroom, sat on her potty, and peed. Music to my ears. *My big girl! All grown up!* I didn't think it could have gone any better. And then literally a day or two later, she had the hang of it. For the first week or so, virtually every time she'd pee in her potty I'd exclaim, "That's my big girl!" all jacked up with glee. I was so proud and relieved to have potty-training behind me. *Whew. Done. That was easy!* I thought patting myself on the back. I may have even ever-so-casually bragged about her success to a friend or two, as if

Jules's quickly taking to her big girl potty was evidence of my superior parenting.

What I didn't realize was that while Jules had no problem peeing in the toilet, she didn't like pooping in it, and soon had an accident in her underwear. This felt a lot messier than when it happened in her diaper, and as a result, I think she started trying to hold in her poop. Unfortunately, when that happens, a child gets constipated, which means their stool hardens and it becomes very painful to poop, which makes a child hold it even more.

Occasionally, I found Jules hiding under a table, but I didn't really give it much thought. I didn't notice that her belly was swollen or that she was wearing her waistband much lower than usual. Once in a while she'd complain of a stomachache, but it would pass fairly quickly. Unfortunately, it took us *months* to realize that Jules was seriously constipated, and then only thanks to a visit from my sister who recognized her symptoms (stomachaches and a distended abdomen) because her son had similarly struggled. I immediately made a doctor's appointment for Jules, only to be told (after an examination) that she was fine and not to worry. Still worried, I sought a second opinion. Fortunately, her new doctor was more thorough, and in addition to examining Jules, she asked a series of in-depth questions and even ordered an x-ray that soon confirmed my sister's suspicion.

Constipation, I learned, is not something that should be taken lightly. I think because Jules had been pooping some, her original doctor wasn't concerned. But apparently that was only the poop that managed to make its way around the big hard brick stuck in her overstretched colon. Her new doctor gave us a plan to unclog our angel, and it wasn't going to be fun—or pretty. As instructed, I set the bathroom up with a bunch of towels and then I put my laptop on the floor with a kids' video ready to go. Jules, who up to that point had barely ever seen a video, happily lay down to watch. And then, after giving her a brief description of what was going to happen, which she could barely concentrate on thanks to her video trance, I just did it. I gave her an enema. Remarkably, she barely flinched. I put her in a diaper and we waited. She continued to watch. And then her stomach began to rumble. And rumble. She didn't feel so good.

"Mama, Mama!" she cried. "Ohhhh, Mama!"

Oh, God, I thought. *This is awful. My poor baby.* But I tried to keep my composure. "I know, honey. You're going to go poop soon. Then you'll feel better. I'm right here with you."

And then, just as her doctor had predicted, Jules soon passed an incredibly large, dark mass. *How could* that *come out of someone so small?* I marveled with relief. Jules felt better. Much, much better. Thank goodness! While perhaps not the happiest moment of my life, it's up there. We then kept Jules on a regimen of a cupful of Miralax a day for two months straight, and the crisis was behind us. I thought I'd wanted a "big girl" in "big girl panties!" who used a "big girl potty," but what I'd actually wanted was a comfortable two-year-old with normally functioning plumbing who felt no pressure to do something she wasn't yet ready to do. What was my hurry?

A National Rush to Potty-Train

My honest answer is that I'd just jumped onto the potty-training bandwagon that other parents at Jules's preschool were already on. While I know I was simply doing what I thought I was "supposed to" be doing, in retrospect, I find my "decision" to just start potty-training Jules one random day a curious one, considering I understood—at least theoretically—that all children develop at their own pace (within identifiable parameters, which are often larger than we assume). With my very own eyes, I'd seen my friend's daughter Tatiana start walking before she was ten months old, while our neighbor Bates was still working on it at seventeen months. (Of course, today both walk and run and couldn't care less how old they were when they started.) I remember being amazed to learn that my friend Stephanie's daughter Camille started reading on her own at just three years old (!) while reading didn't take off for her brother Sam until he was almost nine. (Today, both are voracious readers. And although I'd love to be able to say that they couldn't care less when they started, I'm sorry to report that Sam felt ashamed he was in the "lowest reading group," the "one for babies." As it turns out, when a brain is ready to start reading is not related to one's intelligence.) I even remember being surprised when our dentist told me that there's a particularly large developmental span for when human teeth come in. "Did you know," he asked, "that one child might not get a first tooth until he's two years old and another child can actually be born with a tooth showing?" No, I did not. So while I was totally cognizant of the fact that every child develops according to his or her unique timetable, I wasn't considering that fact in relation to a child's readiness to use the toilet. It didn't even dawn on me. I simply accepted the equation that two years old equals potty-trainable, and so *I* chose one day when *I* felt ready to start the process and set out to entice Jules with the excitement of being "big." Unfortunately, at Jules's considerable expense, I learned that an aesthetic attraction to undergarments isn't a sound barometer for assessing a child's readiness to use the toilet. And by "readiness," I mean just how infant specialist Magda Gerber defined it: "Readiness is when they do it."

I know I'm not alone in rushing my child to give up diapers. Not only is it easy to cave to the pressure to do what everyone else seems to be doing, but disposables (which were our politically

> It is easy to cave to the pressure to do what everyone else seems to be doing.

incorrect diaper of choice) are expensive and horrible for the environment, and changing them is time-consuming, messy, and hard on one's olfactory system. What's more, diapers can also be a source of many a power struggle between changer and changee. Why wouldn't a parent want their child out of them as soon as possible? On top of all that, many preschools—whose entire raison d'être is ostensibly to nurture the healthy development of young children—have policies that require children be potty-trained to attend. The obvious conclusion is that pulling the plug on diapers by three years of age must be developmentally appropriate, right?

You may be as disappointed as I was to learn that these no-diaper preschool policies are largely financially driven. Preschools that do allow children in diapers must meet specific licensing requirements that include adequate diaper stations, a certain number of sinks, and a higher staff-to-child ratio. Simply put, these no-diaper policies were not created in the best interest of the children, but instead because it's cheaper for schools to require kids to be out of diapers, even though it means more accidents for the teachers to deal with and more incidents of discomfort, pressure, shame, and confusion for the children who had their diapers taken away prematurely. Preschool isn't and never was meant to be a place for big boys and big girls—it's supposed to be a nurturing and safe haven for the very young, where a deep understanding of early-childhood development guides policy and best practices. And some of these young children just may still need to be in diapers. The fact that many two- and three-year-olds are ready to use a toilet doesn't mean every child that age is ready to do so. The following Facebook post from a stressed-out mom looking for advice on how to get her son out of diapers in time for the first day of preschool hints at the desperation many parents feel facing a similarly looming deadline.

Sam is supposed to go to preschool on September 2nd, and to go there he has to be toilet trained or they won't accept him!! He is almost three. We've tried for more than a week to stop putting him in diapers, and to put on underwear instead but he won't do anything on any toilet device. He refuses it. When I ask him if he wants to pee, he says no and then pees on the floor a minute later.

I certainly felt for Sam's mom, who was charged with a task that was developmentally inappropriate for her son. I also felt deeply for Sam who, all of a sudden, had a goal imposed on him that he had no interest in achieving and apparently wasn't ready for. It's like saying to a baby, "Come on! I need you to be able to walk by next Monday! Let's practice! You can do it." And yet Sam's not yet being ready to use a toilet had *precisely nothing* to do with his readiness to go to preschool. To sing songs, dig in the sand, dress up, and make friends. It seems unjust to deny him the experience because he's literally *not yet capable* of using the toilet. And it seems callous to stress out him and his parents, who feel forced to put him through the paces of toilet training. When I read about some of the lengths to which parents go to try to meet manufactured deadlines— using a whole slew of rewards and punishments—it's even more heartbreaking. In short, these train-by-a-certain-date policies discriminate against children who literally aren't yet able to use the toilet, effectively denying them access to education based on an ability beyond their control.

What's worse, efforts to get toddlers to conform to manufactured deadlines can have a serious adverse affect on their physical health. It's not just about embarrassing or inconvenient accidents or some bloating. Holding one's feces can actually lead to the type of medical problems that pediatric urologist Dr. Steve Hodges sees daily in his clinic at Wake Forest University Medical Center. Dr. Hodges, who has made toileting issues the heart of his research

and medical practice, is committed to helping families struggling with this issue. In both his book for parents, *It's No Accident:
Breakthrough Solutions to Your Child's Wetting, Constipation,
UTIs, and Other Potty Problems*, and his
children's book *Bedwetting and Accidents
Aren't Your Fault: Why Potty Accidents
Happen and How to Make Them Stop*, Dr.
Hodges explains that it is a research-proven
fact that virtually all childhood potty problems are caused by holding poop, pee,
or both. Based on research reported by
the National Institute of Diabetes and
Digestive and Kidney Diseases, half a mil-
lion kids visit the doctor annually for these
issues. Many toddlers "simply don't understand the importance of eliminating when

These train-by-a-certain-date policies discriminate against children who literally aren't yet able to use the toilet.

nature calls," explains Dr. Hodges. "Knowing how to poop on the
potty is not the same as responding to your body's urges in a judi
cious manner. . . . Kids in diapers don't hold; many toilet-trained
children do." And when children hold poop, it collects and then
hardens in their colons, which, in turn, makes them even more
reticent to use the toilet because it is simply too painful to try to
pass such a large hard mass. It becomes a catch-22. To add insult to
injury, the mass can put pressure on a child's bladder, sometimes
causing him to wet the bed at night. What's more, many children
are blamed for not wanting to go to the bathroom and/or for their
accidents. "Sometimes," says Dr. Hodges, "Mom or Dad flashes that
'Again—are you kidding me?' look when the child comes in at 2:00
a.m. for help changing the sheets. Other times, the blame is more
direct, like when a parent says (or yells), 'You're seven! You're old
enough to know better!'" It's not surprising, then, that the first thing
Dr. Hodges tells his young patients is that their accidents aren't
their fault. And, he reports, "They brighten up immediately."

Learning from My Mistake

So *that's* why with my second child, I wasn't just going to randomly select a day for Hudson to become a big boy! I wasn't going to sell him on anything or shame him into anything. I was going to follow the advice RIE expert Janet Lansbury, author of *Elevating Child Care: A Guide to Respectful Parenting*, gives in her blog post "Three Reasons Kids Don't Need Toilet Training (and What to Do Instead)." Surprising many, Lansbury recommends a decidedly laid-back, follow-your-child's-lead approach as she asks, "why would we add toilet training to our already overloaded job description when doing less works just as well, if not better? Why risk the headaches, power struggles and resistance, frustrations, and failures? Why be a taskmaster when we can relax, enjoy, and take pride in supporting our child's self-directed achievement?" She had me at "why?" In brief, Lansbury recommends:

1. Let your kids see you using the toilet.

2. Make sure a potty is available, but don't force (or even coax) children to use it.

3. Observe your kids and learn their signals. If your child shows a need to eliminate (by pressing their thighs together, touching their diaper, etc.), calmly ask if they would like to use the potty. If the answer is no, accept that.

4. Offer a genuine choice of underwear or diapers.

5. Trust they will transition when they're ready.

So I set out to trust Hudson to lead the way. While I was looking forward to "taking pride in his self-directed achievement," I wasn't holding my breath. I knew waiting for him to show interest in using the toilet would likely be more expensive and less green, but it's not his fault we'd chosen disposables over cloth diapers. Nor is it his fault that scientists have managed to invent a material that is so incredibly absorbent that children aren't uncomfortable enough in a soaked diaper to do anything about it. Meanwhile, I was surprised to learn that Hudson's best friend, Jordan, started using the toilet before he was two, on his own, without a drop of pressure from his parents. Apparently Jordan wanted to try to do what he saw his older sister doing. So one day, without telling anyone, he climbed up on the seat, did his business, and never went back—during the day, that is. At night, Jordan would continue to wear Pull-Ups for many years to come. Interestingly, Hudson's path out of diapers would be almost the inverse of Jordan's.

When Hudson was three, he too decided to stop wearing Pull-Ups on his own accord—but *only* at night. One evening, he announced he wanted to sleep without a diaper. While I couldn't imagine it going well—*I mean, who stops wearing diapers for the first time at night?*—Hudson insisted. To my surprise, there would be no 3:00 a.m. scramble for clean sheets. In fact, Hudson continued to sleep without a diaper on, never once having an accident. When he'd wake up in the morning, he'd pee in the toilet (without being told to) and then he'd put on a Pull-Up, like there was no question about it.

Meanwhile, Hudson and Jordan started having sleepovers. Watching them get ready for bed one night, I realized just how profoundly manufactured, messed-up, and full of judgment our "Who's a big boy?" bigger-is-better culture is.

"Here's a Pull-Up, Jordan," Hudson said, handing Jordan one of his as they got ready for bed.

> "Why add toilet training to our job description when doing less works just as well, if not better?"
> —Janet Lansbury

"No, I need my nighttime kind because they're more thick," Jordan replied as he went over to his sleepover bag and grabbed an ultra-absorbent nighttime Pull-Up.

As he put it on, Hudson took his off for the night. Once in their pajamas, the boys climbed in bed next to each other ready for a book—"potty-trained" Jordan in a Pull-Up and Pull-Ups-wearing Hudson going commando under his PJs. The next morning, Jordan took off his *super-full* Pull-Up (I could see what he'd meant!) just as Hudson sat on the toilet, peed, and then pulled on a fresh Pull-Up. The boys didn't compare themselves: One wasn't a big boy, the other a baby! Or a baby at night and a big boy during the day, or vice versa. There was no applause, no disappointment. They were just *different*, each on his own unique journey with his individual needs at that moment in time. Needs, mind you, that they seemed to enjoy helping each other meet. Ahhhh, the ignorance-is-bliss of no agenda and unconditional acceptance.

Trusting your child when he's by far the last of his friends to do whatever everyone else is already doing can be challenging. But I continued to tell myself that Hudson wouldn't want to wear Pull-Ups forever. And then, finally, one day, Hudson stopped wearing them. He was done. He made no announcement, so I couldn't clap or blow a trumpet or otherwise exclaim how happy I was that my big boy had arrived. He didn't need—nor did he want—any acknowledgment. In Hudson's mind, he wasn't a "baby boy" one day and a "big boy" the next. Pull-Ups didn't define him.

Bigger Isn't Better

My experiences with "potty-training" (a phrase I now think could more helpfully be replaced with the admittedly unwieldy "supporting toilet readiness" or "supporting a child's transition from diapers to using a toilet") helped me see how inherently judgmental and used-car-salesman-like our "big girl!" and "big boy!" lines must feel to many kids, no matter what we're trying to get them to do. *Come on! You can do it! Don't you want to be big? Everyone wants to—you should too! You'll see! It's gonna be great! You'll love it! And Mommy and Daddy will be proud, proud, proud!* I imagine our "encouragement" may feel to a young child how "Chug! Chug! Chug!" might to an undergrad at a keg party desperate to fit in. In a way, isn't this "big girl" approach of trying to get our kids to do something they aren't yet interested in doing teaching our children to cave to peer pressure? To conform? Or to be ashamed if they're "behind" in any way? Isn't the message we're sending something like *everyone should be developing at the exact same pace*?

> Too many of us seem to be in a race to nowhere.

If we've used this bigger-is-better pitch, how can we, with any credibility, tell our children not to compare themselves to others? Because aren't we the ones who've been doing the comparing? Even if it's to the "bigger boy" they aren't yet but that we clearly want them to be? I'm sure, like me, you've heard many a child say to a friend "I'm older!" or "I can do that faster!" or "I'm bigger." "I can swim, he can't!" "I can ride my bike, she can't." And so many of us rush in with "Everyone is different and we all learn at our own pace." And yet we ourselves so often send the message that bigger and sooner and faster is indeed better. The truth is, a child is not bigger or better based on how early she starts using a toilet, or how early she rolls over or sits up or walks, or can identify letters and colors or rides a bike or . . . Indeed, too many of us seem to be in a race to nowhere—as the eponymous title of the award-winning documentary on our education system so perfectly captures. After all, Albert Einstein didn't speak until he was four years old, and he did just fine.

Be Honest with Yourself

Now when I feel the urge to convince my kids that something is going to be great—anything from moving into their own "big boy bed" or going to kindergarten "like a big girl"— I'll ask myself: Why do I feel the need to sell it? What's the real reason?

- Am I worried my child is scared?
- Am I worried my child is developmentally behind?
- Am I worried what others will think?
- Am I trying to get them to conform to a school rule?
- Would the change make life more convenient for me?
- Is the change I seek truly the only viable option due to financial or geographic constraints?

Once I'm honest with myself, how to proceed becomes clearer. For instance, if I'm able to admit that I want my kid to stop carrying his blanket around because I'm worried about what others will either think of him or me as a parent, then I can be an adult and remind myself that caring what others think isn't an acceptable reason to push my child forward. Similarly, wanting my child to stop wearing diapers because I assume it'll make my life easier also isn't an acceptable reason to rush their development. However, if I'm genuinely concerned about a potential developmental delay, then I can educate myself and consult a professional. And if I'm worried about my child's ability to conform to a school rule (like wearing socks or shoes or not bringing a blanket to school), I can talk to the teacher to see if

> If I'm genuinely concerned about a potential developmental delay, then I can educate myself and consult a professional.

there's wiggle room and to my child about finding ways to adhere to the rule that works for her. (Personally, I've been fortunate to find faculty and administration more than willing to work with me and my children. Many folks are surprised by concessions made. My feeling is, "Why not ask? It's school, not the army.") When I'm honest with myself, it seems the answer to my anxiety, more often than not, is to chill out. Patience and trust can be hard to come by in our frenetic, competitive, fear-driven world, but they are, without a doubt, priceless gifts to our kids.

A Beloved Blankie

Ever since I've known him, my husband, John, has had the unusual habit of pinching together a small bit of fabric at the bottom of his T-shirts, which he then gently twists, rubs, and taps—usually while talking to someone or watching TV. One day I asked him about it

"Oh, yeah. I don't even realize I'm doing it," he said. "I think it started when my mom took away my blankie when I was five or six."

"Why'd she take it away?" I asked.

"I don't know really. I guess she thought I was too old for it. Or maybe she thought it was ragged and gross. I never asked her. But man, I loved that thing." (As John's parents are no longer with us, that's all the information I could get.)

I've since learned that having a beloved blanket abruptly taken away one random day is not an uncommon experience for many young children. Some parents will take it away because they believe their child has simply gotten too old for it—*Enough is enough. You're not a baby anymore.* Others worry that their child's attachment to a blanket is a sign of insecurity or that it's being used as an unnecessary crutch. Maybe if they take it away, they reason, their kids will realize how well they can cope without it. *See? You're fine!* Other times, however, as it was with my friend Nancy, it's the child herself who makes the swift break.

One day when Nancy was seven—a day she'll never forget—she overheard her older brother and sister talking to some of the neighborhood kids about Special, her much-loved pillowcase that she carried Linus-style.

"Can you believe Nancy still drags that thing around?" one of them said.

"I know! What a baby!"

Beyond mortified, Nancy immediately ran to get Special and threw it away—tears streaming down her face. Unfortunately, at the time, Nancy's parents were consumed with a difficult divorce and were totally unavailable to her. So at precisely the moment in her life when she was most in need of comfort, she forced herself to give up her greatest source of solace because she couldn't think of anything worse than being considered a baby. When she first told me the story, I didn't quite understand the degree of comfort Special must have given her because I didn't have a special blanket or stuffed animal when I was a kid. But when I read this passage from Dorothy Canfield's 1924 novel *The Home-Maker* that describes the unrivaled bliss such an object can give a child, I really understood how hard it must've been to discard the thing she loved most and how difficult it was to endure the painful period without the comfort Special gave her.

> **Transitional objects soothe the shift from day to bedtime, or from a parent's arms to a sitter's.**

He *loved* Teddy! He loved his Teddy! He was lost in unfathomable peace to have found him again. All the associations of tranquility, the only tranquility in Stephen's life, which had accumulated about Teddy, rose in impalpable clouds about the child. What the smell of incense and the murmur of prayers are to the believer, what the first whiffs of his pipe to the dog-tired woodsman, what a green-shaded lamp over a quiet study table to the scholar, all that and more was Teddy to Stephen. His energetic, pugnacious little face grew dreamy, his eyes wide and gentle.

How truly remarkable, and yet also curious, that an inanimate object can give a child such solace.

Almost thirty years after Canfield so beautifully captured the incomparable relationship between child and lovie, the renowned British pediatrician and psychologist D. W. Winnicott brought serious academic attention to the subject in his 1953 landmark paper "Transitional Objects and Transitional Phenomena." Identifying transitional objects as usually being something soft (like a stuffed animal or blanket), Winnicott explained that their role is to take the place of a parent's loving embrace and reassuring presence, thus easing a child's transition into the world. In other words, transitional objects soothe the shift from day to bedtime, or from a parent's arms to a sitter's. They can comfort when a knee is bleeding or a dream is scary, or when feelings are hurt and life feels overwhelming. Winnicott pinpointed five defining attributes of transitional objects:

- The child has total rights over it.
- It may be cuddled, loved, and mutilated.
- It can only be altered by the child.
- It has some tangible "vitality of its own," like a texture or the ability to give warmth.
- Over time, it gradually loses meaning and becomes relegated to a kind of limbo where it is neither forgotten nor mourned.

I was most struck by the first and last characteristics. The first—that the child has total rights over their object—makes sense because it's the child who literally gives the object life by selecting it from among other available blankets, sheets, and stuffed animals and imbues it with profound comfort-giving capabilities. Because the object truly *belongs* to the child, to my mind, it follows that no one else has the right to limit a child's access to it or take it away. I hope it is the last characteristic—that the child will slowly but surely come to depend on it less and less—that can reassure parents uncomfortable with their child's lingering attachment. Not only is there no need to rush this process along, we can't. We can only interrupt it, thus inadvertently and unnecessarily causing feelings of loss and shame. (And perhaps a lifetime habit of twisting and rubbing one's T-shirt.)

Seeking Comfort Is Nothing to Be Ashamed of

In the meantime, we can help fortify our children should they ever find themselves faced with less-than-kind words about their beloved blanket or stuffed animal. I'm inspired by my friend Eliza, whose daughter Beth has worn heavy bifocals since she was two. In the hope of preempting any teasing, together, at the beginning of each new school year, Eliza and Beth make a short presentation to her class about her eye condition and how glasses help her. Questions, anybody?

While I'm not suggesting the exact same approach in regards to a blanket, I do think we can help our children by 1) being accepting of the blanket ourselves, 2) appreciating the comfort it gives our child, and 3) explaining to our kids and their friends the role transitional objects can play—how they help during challenging times or when a kid needs to recharge during a long day, and how we all need these things in our own way. It also helps to know that research tells us that 60 percent of children attach to a love object— so more people actually have formed relationships with them than not. It's been helpful for Jules and Hudson (both of whom have special transitional objects) to know John had one as a child, too. *Well, if Dad had one, they've gotta be cool.* In fact, because they know that it was taken away before he was ready to say good-bye, they feel for him.

None of which is to say they haven't ever been concerned about what others may think. When Jules was nine and going off to sleep-away camp for the first time, she worried she'd be the only one in her cabin bringing a stuffed animal (her beloved Panda) and security blankets (Beebee 1 and Beebee 2). While, unlike her brother, she never carried them during the day, they are her trusted touch-stones, and she looks forward to cuddling up to sleep with them every night. (If we ever forget them for a sleepover, we have to turn around. No question.) While I assured Jules that others would bring theirs, I also reiterated how needing comfort is nothing to be ashamed of. She was going to be *three thousand* miles away from home and away from us for the longest time she'd ever been away. I was glad to know she would have Panda and Beebees to comfort her. I also shared that my childhood friend Linsey went off to college with her two favorite stuffed animals and that even after she finished graduate school, she brought them to New York City and proudly laid them on her bed. While Linsey no longer depended on them as she had as a child, she thought of them as buddies who had been with her for her whole life, and they made

> Research tells us that 60 percent of children attach to a love object—so more people actually have formed relationships with them than not.

It's Never Too Late to Talk About What Happened

If you are a parent who did take your child's special transitional object away—meaning no harm, of course!—and are now rethinking your decision, it's never too late to talk to him about what happened. It's possible that your child is carrying around feelings that would be healthy to discuss. Perhaps get the conversation started with something like, "Honey, we took away your special blanket when you were [whatever-the-age] years old. Do you remember? We did what we thought was best, but have since learned we may have made a mistake. We'd like to talk about it."

Certainly, it would be important for a child to then have the space and time to share any and all feelings they may have had about it. At this point, a parent's job is to listen and empathize. And apologize if it's warranted.

"Sounds like you really miss your blankie and are still mad we took it away."

"Yeah!"

"You loved it so much, and we took it away without your permission. That was so painful for you. We want you to know how sorry we are. We never would knowingly hurt you. We didn't have all the information we needed. We're sorry."

Acknowledging what happened and apologizing can bring closure.

And of course if your child doesn't remember or seems to have totally gotten over the loss, then you'll be glad to know that.

her smile inside. Much to Jules's relief, when we arrived at her cabin, she found that many kids had stuffed animals on their beds, and so she quickly opened her duffle bag and brought out her triad. A week later, she sent me a letter telling me that some of the girls who had been too embarrassed to bring their stuffed animals had written to ask their parents to send them.

Big Brother! Big Sister!

As mentioned, another occasion when the bigger-is-better pitch is commonly used on a child is when they're on the threshold of becoming a sibling for the first time. Understandably, we want our kids to be as happy about a new child coming into the family as we are. Nonetheless, while it would be nice, it's unrealistic. Children on the verge of being dethroned can feel especially vulnerable and anxious—particularly younger kids. They wonder, if only subconsciously, how their life will change and worry *Will my parents still love me? Will they have enough time for me?* And their concerns are well-founded. The truth is life will be different—as in *very* different. A baby who needs around-the-clock attention is about to enter the house. Weary parents who have been up all night will not only have less time for the older child but often less patience. As a result, an older child may act out and/or regress. Which is quite normal. Dr. Zeenat Malik, a developmental pediatrician at the Children's Hospital of New Jersey, explains that toddlers "think in very concrete terms. They see someone who is wearing diapers and using a bottle getting all this attention, so they want to be like that baby. They think, 'If I wear diapers and drink from a bottle, Mom will give me the same attention.'" A new older sibling may be a ball of contradictions, at once hating the baby for robbing them of their parents, while also being excited by his tiny fingers and the thrill of new life. When you think about it, some "big" brothers and "big" sisters are little more than a year or two old themselves, hardly qualifying as "big" under any other circumstances.

What's more, because toddlers lack the verbal and cognitive skills to express their jealousy, frustration, and anger, they often act out in an attempt to communicate their needs and feelings. And that may involve hurting the new sibling, which may, in turn, cause the child to be reprimanded or worse by the parent. The child isn't understood or supported, but instead punished, which only makes things worse. Rather than chastising a child, we can empathize and reassure them that we're here for them, all the while making it a priority to keep the baby safe. This means not expecting the older child to have more self-control than they are capable of.

Keep Everyone Safe

We may think our children should know better or note that in the past they've demonstrated a certain level of self-control, but that doesn't mean they are capable of reining themselves in under these new, more intense circumstances. If your older child is taking out her feelings of fear, sadness, jealousy, or anger on the baby, it is *essential* to set up the environment so the child can't hurt the baby. This may mean not leaving them in the same room alone or even turning your back for a moment. Using baby gates or a crib to separate the children when they aren't being watched can be a big help. Of course, we'd love not to have to do this, but by not doing it we set up the potential for both children to suffer—the baby by being hurt, and the older child by doing something "bad" that might get him "in trouble" when he may already be hurting enough.

Talking to the older child can be a big relief for him.

Reflect

"Your new brother has really changed our life, huh? It's true, he needs to be fed and held often, just like you did, when you were a baby. Sometimes you feel angry that your brother gets so much attention, is that right?"

Reassure and Problem-Solve

"We have big hearts and enough love for everyone. We want to have our special time with you every day. And if you ever need more love and attention, we want to give it to you. Just tell us. We will make sure you get all the love you need."

While of course we want everyone to love everyone, accepting and empathizing with our older child's very real experience is what will ultimately support him the most. I found the following post on Facebook to be very hopeful. It's from a mom whose older child was devastated by the birth of her sister. As hard as it was, the mother continued to accept her older child's negative feelings toward the baby, without trying to sell her on how great it really is to be a big sister. While it took time, she was happy to report that her daughter came around:

> My toddler had a terrible time with the new baby, literally sobbing for hours on end. Through it all I showed empathy and never pushed her to accept or show love toward the baby, but I secretly regretted having a second and saw no light at the end of the tunnel. Baby just turned 6mos, and this [photo of siblings holding hands] happened today! I just want you to know that there's hope. Keep going.

I have to hand it to her, because I imagine it was a trying and frustrating process during an already stressful time. And yet, they prevailed. Having realistic expectations can make all the difference.

Preparing for the Transition to a Bigger Family

All too often, right when children are feeling particularly vulnerable, well-meaning friends and relatives will ask them, "Aren't you excited about being a big sister?" If the child isn't, she may worry *I should be happy, something must be wrong with me.* We can help our older children when we invite friends and family to be sensitive to their feelings and situation. I was really moved when I received this very thoughtful email chock-full of sage advice from my neighbors on the eve of the birth of their second child.

Dear Friends and Family,

As we plan for the birth next week, we've been doing a lot of reading and talking to friends regarding advice for transitioning to a family of four. We thought we'd pass on some of the best advice we got, which has helped our friends and their children during what can often be a challenging time for the first child. As we're sure you know, the first child can often greet the arrival of a new baby with a whole host of complicated emotions, including feelings of loss and anger. We'd like to help Jacob through this transition, and ask for your help as well. Here are some ideas:

—Try to avoid telling Jacob he is so "big" or a "big boy" or a "big brother." (Remember, he is only 2! Saying he is a brother or a boy is fine because those are descriptive facts.) He may feel big, but he may also want to feel like a baby, and that is OK, too. Many first children experience some form of regression with a new baby (e.g., wanting to use bottles, sleep in a crib, crawl, speak "baby talk," etc.). Most experts explain that the regression is less about jealousy (although that can be a part of it) and more about trying to understand the new baby's world (i.e., what it means to be a baby).

These periods of regression pass, but everyone agrees it is best to just go with them.

—Try to avoid asking Jacob if he loves the baby or if he is happy about the baby. Love is a complicated emotion for a two-year-old, and he may be happy, but also angry, sad, or confused. All of this is OK. Let him take the lead on discussing his feelings about the baby. All of the literature on the topic is in agreement that it is healthy for a child to express negative feelings toward a new baby. Rather than ignore or deny these feelings, the best approach is to acknowledge them. For example, if Jacob were to say, "I don't like the baby," we would want to respond, "I understand that it is hard to get used to having a new person around." We would not want to say, "You don't mean that; you love the baby" or "That is not nice."

—Try to pay special attention to Jacob when you are around the baby. I know we are all excited to hold new babies, but the baby really won't know and/or care, and Jacob does. Examples of this are greeting him first, talking to him, and then maybe asking him to show you the baby if he feels like it. You may also want to talk to Jacob about when he was a baby. Another good technique is saying to the baby, when Jacob can hear, "You wait here. Now I'm going to spend some special time with Jacob." Also, when Jacob is in earshot, you can say to the baby, "You are lucky to have such a nice brother as Jacob."

—There is no need to bring anything for the baby. But if you do, please bring something for Jacob, even something small, so he doesn't feel left out.

—Finally, it is a good idea to use the baby's name rather than the word "baby." It helps the older sibling to see the baby as a person rather than an object.

We really appreciate your help during this transition.

Lots of love,
Alexandra & Jordan

And so when I went to visit, I had a gift for Jacob, and he was thrilled. I never would have thought of it. It was such a small gesture, but it gave him that extra attention he so clearly appreciated during a time that was decidedly not about him. When I thanked his parents for their thoughtful email, they told me that people said they found it helpful. I was so impressed by it that, with their permission, I posted it on my blog and Facebook page. To this day, several years later, it remains my most shared post. Even now, I continue to receive requests for "that amazing letter—you know, the one about not saying he's a big brother." (Feel free to borrow from it yourself.)

Time Passes Quickly Enough

The saying is true: "The days are long, but the years are short." Our kids will be big for most of their lives, but little for only a tiny window of time. So we have to change diapers for six more months or even for another year? So our kid brings his blanket to kindergarten and keeps it in his cubby, just in case? So she uses training wheels until she's ready not to? So he loves his crib? So what? Before you know it, you'll be nostalgic for these early days when the most pressing issue was just diapers.

> Our kids will be big for most of their lives, but little for only a tiny window of time.

I remember when Hudson was six, I was carrying him through a parking lot when a security guard said to him, "Hey, big guy! Aren't you too old for your mom to be carrying you?" His question wasn't a genuine question, of course. It was shaming. And the answer was no. Hudson was not too old for his mom to be carrying him. Why? Because I could still comfortably pick him up, and he wanted the comfort of being picked up. And not that it was any of the man's business, but Hudson had the flu and we were on our way to the doctor's office. Even so, sometimes I still pick him up *because he wants me to*. And yes, at seven he's bigger and heavier than he was at five or four or one, but he's still a little boy who enjoys being in his mom's arms. He has a whole life ahead of him of being too big to be picked up by his mom, and every day he's getting closer and closer to that time. Savor. Respect. And trust.

CHAPTER THREE

"YOU'RE SO CUTE!"

"Beauty is the only gift
that does not keep
on giving."
—Paulina Porizkova

"**M**arta's fat!" Jules announced with glee to everyone in the living room when her favorite babysitter walked in the door.

God bless Marta. She smiled her warm, beautiful smile and gently replied, "It is true, Jules. I am fat."

Beyond mortified, I quickly jumped in. "It's so great to see you, Marta! How are you?"

Another day soon thereafter, my parents came over, and Jules greeted my mom by asking about the drooping skin under her chin—the part famously known as a "wattle," thanks to the popular '90s show *Ally McBeal*.

"Gramma, your skin hangs down here. Why? And you have so many stripes on your face! They're here and here and here and here!" she said, running her little finger along the grooves in my mother's skin.

"I do, Jules. This is what happens to skin when you get older," my mom explained.

These were the observations of a curious three-year-old, without a drop of judgment. Some of us are fat. Some of us have "stripes" and loose skin. It's true of course, but still! This couldn't go on. While I knew that explaining the concept of tact would be lost on someone so young, I felt I at least needed to explain to Jules that while people do love to hear her detailed observations about trees and flowers and the like, it's best to keep her thoughts about how others look to herself. *How to do that,* I wondered, *without giving her the impression that there's anything wrong with being rounder or having wrinkles?*

This question percolating in the back of my mind, Jules and I later headed to the market, where I quickly realized what I was up against. Anything I'd say to Jules—e.g., "It's not polite to comment on people's appearance"—was bound to be undermined by all the people who greeted her by telling her just what they thought of the way *she* looked: cute. Like virtually all big-eyed, button-nosed, plump-faced young children, Jules was cute. And people just love themselves some cute.

The first comment came in produce.

"Hello, sweetheart! Aren't you just darling?" a woman gushed.

Not surprisingly, Jules looked at her blank-eyed, so I returned a polite, knowing smile and nodded my head, as I wondered if Jules had any idea what "darling" even means.

Then in the dairy section, another woman cooed, "Hi there, cutie!"

Again, Jules just stared at her, so I said, "Hello."

"She's *just* adorable!" she confided. "Absolutely precious."

"Thank you," I said, then wondered what exactly I'd thanked her for. I mean, if someone compliments me on my handbag, they're essentially saying "I like your aesthetic sensibility," so "Thank you!" makes sense. But when they say my kid is cute, what does my "thank you" mean? "Thank you for letting me know my daughter's looks give you pleasure"? Or, "I'm so glad you like the way my genes mixed with my husband's. She lucked out, didn't she?" It's kind of weird.

> It's as if people think children are a different species.

The coup de grâce came at checkout. Jules was sitting in the cart while I was swiping my credit card when a tall, überfit man who was animatedly talking on his cell phone started briskly walking toward the exit. As he approached our checkout lane, his eyes widened and he gasped "Oh, my God!" Then, as if he was a relay racer slowing down just long enough to pass the baton, he dove down right in front of Jules's face and shrieked in a stage whisper, "You're sooooo cute!" and then he bounded off.

Whoa. What did Jules make of that? I wondered. She looked like she'd been sideswiped.

"That man was loud, wasn't he?" I said.

She nodded.

"I don't know why he did that. Did he scare you?"

She nodded again.

"I'm sorry that happened, honey. He's gone now. I think he was trying to be nice," I vaguely explained, even though it was hard for me to imagine how he could possibly think it qualifies as nice to aggressively get up in such a little girl's personal space—without even saying hello—and tell her how great he thought she looked before running off. It's as if people think children are a different species. What if I'd done that to him? He would've thought I was crazy.

But that wasn't the end of it. On the way home we stopped at the pet store to pick up our dog, Billie, who was being groomed. I was holding Jules on my hip when the groomer came out to give me an update.

"Hi. It should be no more than—WOW!" she exclaimed, catching sight of Jules. "Your eyes! They're so beautiful. You're *really* cute!"

As usual, Jules didn't say anything, and this time neither did I. "Thank you!" no longer felt quite right.

"Ummm . . . It should be just another five minutes," the groomer finally said, breaking the awkward silence.

"Thank you so much!" I said in my (likely transparent) attempt to compensate for having been rude.

Marta was fat. My mom had stripes and sagging skin. And Jules was darling, cute, and had beautiful eyes. Hmmm. Now what should I say to Jules about commenting on people's appearance? I wondered.

The next morning at the park the usual ogling took a turn for the unexpected.

"Oh! My! God! She's *soooo* cute!" a woman squealed.

Jules and I both looked up to discover that this time it wasn't Jules who was being squealed at, even though she was right there in the sandbox just feet from the astonished woman. Instead, the object of her pleasure was a very petite girl with golden hair who was just walking up to the playground.

What was Jules? Chopped liver? One minute I hated people objectifying her, the next I bristled at her being overlooked, presumably because she wasn't cute enough.

"Can you say thank you?" the little girl's beaming mom prodded. Silence.

"Sofiaaaa?" her mom asked again, this time more slowly and in a tone that was a tad more high-pitched and pointed. "Can you say thank you to the nice lady?"

"Tank ooo," the little girl finally said sheepishly to the sand.

"Good job, honey!" her mom exclaimed, fluffing her hair. Sofia was now free to run off and play.

Although I knew that Sofia's mom was trying to teach her daughter to be polite, I couldn't help but wonder how it felt to Sofia to not only be greeted by a stranger with a shriek, but then to also have to thank her for it. (On some level, kids must think we adults and our bizarre rituals are crazy.) I also worried that Jules noticed she wasn't the one singled out for her looks this time. Was she realizing there's a pecking order to this cute thing? And how must it feel to these girls to have their looks be the most exciting thing about them? Or to be overlooked because they're not exciting enough? I mean, what else could they possibly do to elicit such over-the-top shrieks of delight from adults? Maybe break out into a double backflip or hit the high note in "The Star Spangled Banner"? We know that children quickly pick up on the cues of those around them—whether expressed explicitly or not—so while obviously at two and three years old, these girls weren't consciously pondering these things the way I was, nonetheless, their rapidly growing, highly impressionable brains were processing our messages.

> How must it feel to these girls to have their looks be the most exciting thing about them?

Today, thanks to advances in neuroscience, we know that similar to the way vitamins and minerals help a body grow, interactions with people affect the way a child's brain develops. But decades before neuroscience confirmed it, the late infant specialist Magda Gerber taught that the way we treat and care for children *is* their most fundamental education. In fact, Gerber coined a term for the process: *educaring*. "What parents teach," Gerber explained "is themselves . . . by their moods, their facial expressions and actions. These are the real things parents need to be aware of and how they affect their children."

For more than fifty years, Gerber's mission was to help adults see children—from the *moment* they're born—as fully sentient, unique human beings with their own interests, experiences, thoughts, and feelings. As such, they are deserving of the same level of respect and consideration as anyone else. What may seem like a simple or even obvious concept is actually an enormous challenge for so many of us because the idea that babies are unformed beings is deeply embedded in our culture. We think of them as mere cuties to be adored, entertained, and comforted, not necessarily people, who from day one begin developing their own unique points of view and need to be taken seriously and treated with respect. But if we *can* make a shift in our thinking, then it becomes possible to understand how it might feel to a young child to be greeted by gasps, oohs and ahhs, and other expressions of over-the-top adoration. Just imagine how you would feel if you were working on your computer or cooking or were otherwise engaged and someone got up in your face and started cooing, "Oh, look at you! What a cutie! Can you give me a smile?" It would likely feel invasive and annoying. And yet kids quickly adapt. And therein lies the problem.

Derailed by Cute

Children can get used to exaggerated bursts of attention and soon come to expect them. *Here come the giants to tell me how adorable I am. Ahh, well, if they must. Yes, yes, am I not fabulous?* The over-the-top attention can add hits of excitement to their lives. Eventually, of course, children will grow older and for most, their cheeks will deflate, their noses will take on distinct shapes and sizes, and—unless they've won the genetic lottery—their cuteness will give way to normal. Often, as a result, the adoration will stop coming just as quickly as it began, and it can feel like an unfair fall from grace. *I thought everyone loved me! Oh, they never really loved me? They just liked me for the way my looks made them feel? And now I don't look so good anymore?* As a result, some children will try to do whatever they can to generate the attention they once so effortlessly enjoyed. That is to say a child can go from carefree to calculating. From confident and genuine to insecure and inauthentic. From naturally "cute" to cultivating their cute wiles. Unfortunately, their anxiety-fueled attempts to win back the adulation can backfire, as adults may find their new behavior annoying or cloying. This sad (and avoidable) cycle of deterioration was observed in young children time and again back in the 1930s by the pediatrician Dr. Emmi Pikler. The following passage from her book *What Can Your Baby Do Already?* illustrates her frustration with adult objectification of children and their obliviousness to the harm it can cause:

> Usually the child is seen as a toy or as a "doll," rather than a human being. . . . There is always a fuss being made over her. . . . "How sweet!"—"How cute!" . . . Talk, talk talk, right in front of a child. Talking past the child, not to her. . . . The attention paid her is exaggerated. . . . At first she just tolerates the overwhelming impressions, then gets used to them and begins to enjoy being in this state. She feels at home in this atmosphere. Later she cannot live without all this . . . the child loses naturalness, the unconscious gracefulness which was her most attractive quality . . . They, of course, are not aware that they themselves are responsible for the child's having become like this.

Thirty-plus years later the educator John Holt echoed Dr. Pikler's troubling observations in the chapter "How Children Exploit Cuteness" from his 1974 book *Escape from Childhood*:

Such a cute child soon learns to do almost everything he does, at least around adults, to get an effect . . . He sells his behavior, his personality and himself for rewards . . . I often see such simpering, mincing, cutesy-smiling, fake-laughing children with adults in public places. . . .

Then, recalling one of the most acute examples he'd ever had the misfortune to witness, Holt shares the story of a once-cute girl whose life went into serious decline after she lost her looks.

She knew no way of dealing with other people except for seduction, and when that failed, tears and rage. Now that she was no longer cute but had become a sugar addict, fat, lazy, and inactive, seduction failed more and more. Seduction was all she knew.

While, for obvious reasons, we rarely hear about how this loss of attention feels from the perspective of such young children, we can glean some insight into what they may be internalizing when we consider the experience of others who have grown accustomed to continuous streams of exaggerated praise for their looks, only to have them fade away. Specifically: former child stars and super-models. In her article "7 Reasons Child Stars Go Crazy," Mara Wilson, who played starring roles in movies such as *Matilda* and *Mrs. Doubtfire*, shares her experience:

[After] years of adulation . . . things quickly become normal, and then, just as they get used to it all, they hit puberty— which is a serious job hazard when your job is being cute. . . . A child actor who is no longer cute is no longer monetarily viable and is discarded. He or she is then replaced by some- one younger and cuter, and fan bases accordingly forget that the previous object of affection ever existed.

Wilson goes on to liken the feeling of losing the attention cuteness brings to the withdrawal symptoms of an addict, noting that "... a lot of kids feel very rejected ... useless and ugly." And apparently former supermodel Paulina Porizkova can relate. In her refreshingly honest article "Aging," she writes, "Would I ever have dreamed that I would miss the time I couldn't walk past a construction site unmolested?" So accustomed had she become to the attention her appearance garnered, now in her mid-forties, she found herself profoundly insecure, wishing she had "true confidence ... the kind I tell myself I would have developed already had I relied on wit rather than looks." In other words, the kind of confidence that comes when one's interests and thoughts are given real consideration.

The exaggerated superficial attention kids routinely receive for their looks, similar to the attention child stars and supermodels get for theirs, is the psychological equivalent of empty calories. The attention may feel good in the moment, but it contains no nutrients to help grow one's mind, relationships, and confidence in meaningful ways that can sustain one throughout the various stages of life. Indeed, we have become a society of sexist construction workers whistling at kids' cuteness. It's just that salivating over their adorableness is infinitely more acceptable and welcome—but shouldn't be.

There Are Worse Things—Right?

Out one evening with a bunch of mom friends, I was grumbling about how people were always objectifying Jules and other little kids—more often girls, but certainly not only—when my friend Chrissie rolled her eyes in a "you should count your blessings, there are worse things in the world than being called cute, give me a break" way.

"You know what?" she interrupted, barely able to contain her contempt. "Jules is *lucky* she's cute. Woe is her, poor thing has to deal with people thinking she's so amazing looking! That must be so hard for her to have so much attention. People have real problems in the world, Jennifer. Your daughter being so effing cute is *not* among them!"

I gulped. *Was I really making something out of nothing? Should I really just be grateful people find Jules so cute?* While I realized that children being excessively gawked at was a first-world problem, I still felt strongly that objectifying little kids wasn't the harmless act so many considered it to be.

"My point," I started ever so gingerly, "is that Jules is no cuter than your average kid. I mean, certainly there are cuter kids and less-cute kids, but the truth is, most little kids are cute, and because they are—through no fault of their own—they're being reduced to their appearance all day long, and it's gotta be affecting them. People aren't talking to them, they are squealing *at* them. It's so . . . disrespectful!"

"I don't know." Chrissie started, this time much less sure of herself. "I guess it's just that . . . honestly I'd *love* for someone to spontaneously tell Bella that she's cute. Now that she's ten and, you know, on the heavier side—which I'm sure she'll grow out of with her next growth spurt—*no one* tells her she's cute anymore, except me and Donny! We're always saying it to compensate, because we don't want her to think she isn't. And she is! She's beautiful. Inside and out! It's really breaking my heart. And, of course, everyone is always saying it to Jack. 'Jack is so adorable!' 'Oh, my God! What a little cutie!' And I just see it hurts Bella so much. She's like, *What about me?*"

Then Amy chimed in. "Ohhhh! I feel for Bella!" she sighed. "That was my childhood! When I was around Bella's age, I got braces and my hair went all frizzy on me, and I wasn't so cute anymore—to put it mildly. And of course there was Damon, my super cute little brother who everyone fawned all over. And it *killed* me. It seemed so obvious to me that they were being nice to him *just* because he was cute—but he drank it right up. I distinctly remember trying to be cute so people would like me, too. I'd talk in this high-pitched voice, and I tried to be cutesy. But it didn't matter, because all anyone ever said to me was, 'Oh, my! You're so big now.' And I was like, *Uh, duh. That's because I'm a kid growing up.* He was *soooooo* cute, and I was big. It sucked. And I took it out on Damon. I hated him for basically just being alive. For stealing my show."

"Just my point!" I said. "I mean, don't you think that if people just laid off going crazy over how cute Jack was all the time, it would be better for Bella? How hard is it to bite your tongue and just talk to the kids about . . . I don't know . . . *anything*!? Anything other than how cute we think they are—which they don't give a shit about or have any control over!"

"Our whole culture is looks-obsessed, Jennifer!" Chrissie said. "Of course she'd still care that people don't call her cute! She's a preteen! We can't just shield them from the reality of the world!"

Is there really nothing we can do? I wondered.

Cute for a Reason

The truth is, I don't fault anyone for *finding* little kids cute. How can I? I'm not blind. Young children are cute! And for good reason—at least according to the many evolutionary biologists who believe that it's this very combination of vulnerable, adorable, and needy that has helped ensure the propagation of our species. Let's say a baby has been abandoned for whatever reason. She must be so irresistibly cute that a stranger will *want* to pick her up and raise her despite the enormous burden and lack of a biological tie.

Research shows that when we see a photo of a cute baby, there is increased activity in a portion of the brain called the premotor cortex, which is the part that lights up when we're about to act, so it's not surprising that we feel *compelled* to reach out and pat cute heads and coochie-coochie-coo babies under their chins. But just because we want to, or feel driven to, that doesn't give us license. What's called for is some self-control. I mean, youthful beauty signals fertility, but that doesn't mean it's okay to walk up to every attractive young woman or man we see and regale them with our thoughts about their appearance and then start groping them. No one expects women to thank whistling construction workers for objectifying them. What's the difference, really?

> Many evolutionary biologists believe that it's this very combination of vulnerable, adorable, and needy that has helped ensure the propagation of our species.

Humanize Kids as Quickly as Possible

P art of the problem is, as Holt noted, "when we think of children as cute we abstract and idealize them." We don't see them as dimensional people, just objects to be adored. So then it follows that perhaps part of the solution is to help folks see our cute children as real people with interests, thoughts, and feelings as soon as possible. One way to do this came to me one afternoon with Jules, then four. Out of the blue, she said, "Everyone calls me princess. Why?" (Because if she isn't cute, she's royalty.)

"Do you like it?"

"No."

"Okay . . ." I said, trying to think of how to respond. "Well, if it happens again . . . what about . . . telling them your name?"

Her face lit up.

"You wanna practice?" I said.

She nodded.

"Hi, princess," I said.

> Once you engage with a child and they become a dimensional person, then the importance of how they look recedes.

"I'm Jules Walker Lehr!" she said grinning so much that she started laughing. "Let's do it again!"

It was a start. When objectified, introduce yourself. Once you actually have to engage with a child and they become a dimensional person, then genuine connections are possible and the importance of how they look recedes.

Certainly expecting little kids to remember to introduce themselves under pressure is unrealistic, but we parents can step in and help guide the course of an interaction. Perhaps something like this:

"You're so cute!"

"Hi, there, I'm Jennifer," I can jump in and say. "This is my daughter, Jules. We were just talking about this hole we're trying to dig. For some reason we can't go very deep."

Or:

"She's too precious!"

"Hello, I'm Jennifer. And this is Jules. We love this park. . . . Do you come often?"

Anything to steer the conversation away from how enjoyable a child is to look at.

Be Cool. Get Little

I think one of the reasons that we adults "compliment" kids on everything from their looks to their clothes ("What a cute dress!") when we first meet or see them is to ingratiate ourselves. We want to show them (and/or their parents) how friendly and nice we are. But because young children genuinely couldn't give a rat's ass about what we think of how they look and instead thrive on genuine connection, we're better off playing it cool. Real cool. Getting to know someone—particularly young children who aren't yet adept at the social conventions that help support interactions—is a dance. And it can help to remember that our size alone can be intimidating. I always try to keep in mind the signs Jules's kindergarten teacher, Christine Lonergan, hung around the classroom that read "Get Little." It was a gentle reminder to put our grown-up chitchat away and get down to their level and take in life at a lower altitude. I always found the more I quietly observed the kids, the more respect I had for what they were up to. In that mind-set, a big gush over their looks seems so woefully out of place—disruptive and disrespectful.

> The more I quietly observed the kids, the more respect I had for what they were up to.

If I genuinely want to connect with a little kid, I'll often just start playing alongside her. I'll dig a hole in the sandbox, or start building with blocks. Then I let things unfold, perhaps saying things like:

"Hi. Can I use the shovel?"

"Do you want to dig this hole with me?"

"Your building is so tall. I'm building a cave."

If not coerced, little kids speak when they feel comfortable.

Clothes Matter

One day I realized I was to blame for the over-the-top, unwelcome attention Jules received at a family Passover celebration. For the holiday, I'd bought Jules a pair of green patent-leather shoes with emeralds on them to be worn with a gorgeous navy dress and matching sweater with a sparkling Peter Pan collar. Jules in jewels! I had her all dolled up, as it were. Well, as soon as we walked into my cousin's house, Jules was literally bombarded with compliments. It was like she was a celebrity and my relatives the paparazzi.

"Oh, Jules, you look so beautiful. Sparkling from head to toe!"

"Jules! You look like a doll! A living doll!"

"Come on over here! Those shoes! They're gorgeous! You look like a gem!"

"Can you turn around for me?"

"Absolutely adorable! My goodness!"

It was a full-on Jewish gaspfest. Of the twenty-five adults, not a single one could think of anything to say to Jules beyond how cute she looked. She was overwhelmed, and I was pissed at everyone, even though *I* was the one who had set her and them up for it. If I had dressed Jules more simply, she wouldn't have been so inundated and overwhelmed with everyone's impressions of her, and maybe all the boys (she was the only girl among eight cousins) wouldn't have excluded her from their play, which had never happened before. She didn't care that she had a dress on—she wanted to slide down the pole and dig in the sand, too. It was no wonder she made "ugly" faces every time someone tried to take her picture. *Enough with how I look!* In retrospect, I'm actually relieved that she felt invaded by the attention instead of basking in it. But I could also see that what might seem like nothing more than fun—dressing up young children in darling or cool or chic outfits—isn't harmless.

How we dress our young children before they are old enough to pick out their own clothes can contribute to the degree to which they're objectified. Apparently it's not enough that little kids are cute by nature—we want to make them even cuter. And it starts almost immediately. Think about those headbands parents put on their baby girls to reveal gender and inspire oohs and aahhs. I assure you, no baby *wants* to wear a headband; it is as uncomfortable and unnecessary as the attention it brings.

> She didn't care that she had a dress on—she wanted to slide down the pole and dig in the sand, too.

I admire the approach that my friend Jordana takes to dressing her daughter. She explained to me, "I dress Una in gender-neutral colors. I am really trying to put her in clothes that are utilitarian and cute at the same time but without a lot of bows or frills. I am dressing her for her to be herself! And I want her to be comfortable." Prioritizing comfort over cuteness can help deflect unnecessary, intrusive comments from well-meaning grown-ups.

Cute: A Demeaning Catchall

Unfortunately, the problem with "cute" goes beyond our incessant objectification of children based on their appearance. We don't just use "cute" to describe how children look, we use it to describe virtually everything children say, make, or do. Are any of these sound bites familiar?

"She told us all about her trip. So cute!"

"He asked for it so politely. It was adorable."

"Look how cute they are playing together."

"What a pout—it's the cutest!"

We even find it cute when kids get *angry*. "I can't help it. They just look too cute when they're fighting," I've overheard more than one adult say.

We also use "cute" to describe things adults do with kids.

For instance, I once asked a mom about a Hebrew school program I was interested in for Jules.

"Oh, it's really cute," she responded.

How can a program that's ostensibly about the history, culture, language, and philosophy of a more-than-three-thousand-year-old religion be cute? I wondered. I imagine she meant that the program wasn't highly academic or perhaps that the kids found it fun. Or maybe that it had a lot of art projects. If any of this was the case, it still seems odd that these things would be described as cute. So often we devalue engagement of any kind when children are involved. Their drawings are cute. Their performances are cute. Their stories are cute. Their fights are cute. Their thoughts are cute. Cute. Cute. Cute. The thing is, they don't feel cute when they are drawing or telling a story or fighting or thinking. So, when we call it cute, we essentially erase their whole experience. It's demeaning.

> We may think kids don't notice the condescension and disrespect, but many, if not most, do.

We may think kids don't notice the condescension and disrespect, but many, if not most, do. Hunter is one such kid. At only six years old, he was already so exasperated by adults dismissing his thoughts as cute that he essentially stopped talking about anything of importance with them altogether. His mother shared his experience with me in an email:

Hunter is in love with everything green—renewable energy, composting, anything that addresses global warming. However, whenever he is talking with an adult, sharing his passion for saving the earth, he either gets dismissed with a laugh (you know, one of those condescending "you are so cute but I am older and know better than you" type of laughs) or the adult changes the subject, most often to something very trivial in comparison, like asking if he has watched any new episodes of his favorite cartoon or if he has any new toys. Hunter used to attempt to continue on his subject, but recently I am noticing he has stopped doing so.

Hunter is our future. We need people like him taking the environment seriously. That he cares about climate change, wants to learn more, and be a part of the solution isn't cute, it's inspiring. It's important. His eagerness to connect with others about an issue he's passionate about is moving. Here we have a motivated leader who has already written off a large part of his audience and potential collaborators because he is so discouraged by their lack of respect. Why is it so hard for us to take young children seriously? Are we really unable to look past their full cheeks and button noses?

Author Jonathan Allen captured this frustration that too many children feel in his children's book aptly titled *I'm Not Cute!* In the story, our protagonist Baby Owl bravely sets out to explore the ominous woods only to find that every single animal he encounters just wants to hug and cuddle him. "I'm not cute!" he confides to his mom, at once dejected and weary. He sees himself as a "huge and scary hunting machine with great big soft and silent wings" and yet his bubble is continually burst by the older animals he encounters. Like many children, I imagine, Baby Owl sees his adorable appearance as an unwelcome distraction that keeps others from getting to know him for who he really is.

Look with Your Eyes, Not Your Hands

When I asked Jules and Hudson, then seven and four, how they felt when someone called them cute, Jules said it was "embarrassing" and Hudson said he found it "annoying." Then, thinking about it further, Hudson added, "It's like what Thomas says." Thomas is our neighbor, a father of two.

"What does Thomas say?" I asked.

"You know, he tells people, 'Look with your eyes, not your hands.'"

"Oh, yeah, that's right," I said, remembering that he'd tell strangers that when they'd peer into the baby buggy and sigh. "But I don't get it."

"It's the same," Hudson continued. "Look with your eyes, not with your mouth."

Essentially he was saying, *Okay, so you like how I look. I'm happy for you. But just keep it to yourself. I'm busy leading my life. Let me know if you want to talk to me about something of interest.*

While I imagine many might find his comment cute, hopefully some can see it for the practical solution it is. Kids are full of astute observations and wisdom; we just let "cute" cloud our vision of seeing them for the complex people they are.

CHAPTER FOUR

"GIVE GRANDMA A KISS!"

"If children have been accustomed from the start to having their world respected, they will have no trouble later in life recognizing disrespect . . . and will rebel against it on their own."
—Alice Miller

Your doorbell rings, and it's your parents. You welcome them in and the first thing they do is crouch down with wide-open arms.

"Where's our little angel?" they coo. "Come give Nana and Poppy a little love!"

Now, let's say your child, maybe she's three or six or eight, shakes her head. Maybe she hasn't seen them in a while and feels shy. Or perhaps she doesn't like their wet, mushy kisses. Or maybe she doesn't like being smothered in Grandma's chest and finds her perfume noxious. Perhaps Grandpa has horrible breath. Or. Or. Or. It's not that your daughter doesn't love her grandparents, it's just that she doesn't *want* to kiss and hug them or to be hugged and kissed by them—at that moment.

> **Your daughter is rude and you're permissive. Great.**

And you, you feel for your parents who are a scramble of disappointed, embarrassed, and hurt. *Shit!* Your heart beats faster. Not only do you want your parents to know that your daughter loves them—because she does!—but you want them to approve of the way you're raising her. That is to say, respectful and with manners. Now what? You walk over to your daughter, lean down, and gently whisper, "Sweetheart, why don't you go give Nana and Poppy a little hug? They're *so* happy to see you!"

Let's say your nudge works.

Phew.

Then Grandma and Grandpa hug her tight and tell her how much they adore her. Perhaps you look at your daughter with a glance that says *That wasn't so hard, was it? Look how happy you've made them! Good girl!*

But, let's say she *doesn't* hug them. Maybe she shakes her head again or even runs off.

Aaargh!

Then what?

Then you're mortified. Your child isn't listening to you. In front of your parents, who think, or maybe even say out loud, "I wouldn't have dreamed of treating my grandmother like that!" Perhaps you feel they're really blaming you for your lax parenting. Your daughter is rude and you're permissive. Great. Maybe they even say in an extra loud voice so a certain someone in another room can hear, "Well, clearly someone isn't very happy to see us."

And you, well, you're anxious and rattled. You wish your daughter had just hugged them! *(How hard could it be?)* You wish your parents hadn't made such a big deal out of it. *(Cut her some slack! She's just a little girl.)* You wish you were childless in Hawaii, sipping something cool and full of alcohol. *(If only.)*

"Sorry!" you tell your parents with a shrug that says *Kids! Whatta ya gonna do?* Maybe you add, "I don't know what's gotten into her! She's actually *really* excited to see you."

Then you sigh to yourself and go do what you must. You find your daughter and say as calmly as possible (which isn't quite as calmly as you would like), "Honey, you know that really hurt Nana and Poppy's feelings! Here they are, so excited to see you. When you just run away . . . how do you think that makes them feel? You know better than that!" Maybe you insist she go apologize—not caring if her remorse is genuine, just desperate for the bumps to be smoothed over.

Essential Socialization or Coercion?

Does this scenario sound familiar? I know I've witnessed scenes like it. And I've also seen variations on the theme. I've heard moms tell their kids to go welcome Daddy with a big hug because he's had a long, hard day at work. I've heard parents tell their toddler to give their friend a little snuggle good-bye and then sigh "Ahhhh!" because they look so cute doing it. I've heard parents ask, "Where's my kiss good-bye?" That is to say, I've seen many a child told whom to give affection to, what kind to give, and when to give it—as if it's their duty. And, from what I can gather, it seems many parents view this practice as essential to the socialization process. It's how one goes about raising considerate, well-mannered, loving children. In fact, several years ago I wrote a short piece on the topic for the online parenting magazine *Babble*, and many of the responses I got confirmed this:

"At times I make her hug or speak to people because I don't want her to think she can be rude whenever she chooses to."

"Kids should be made to hug their relatives if they haven't seen them in a while. Not acknowledging relatives is rude, and they shouldn't be allowed to slight them like that. Kids have to be taught manners and how to behave and be friendly."

"If I have to hug my mother-in-law, they have to hug her, too. . . . I won't let my children think their feelings are more important than someone else's."

"I make my kids hug their grandparents. They don't see them often, and I want my parents to not feel worse than they already do by allowing the kids to snub them. . . . It's just a 2-second gesture that means so much to the grandparents."

"Showing affection does not come naturally to everyone, but failing to do so is usually socially crippling. So some children need to be taught how to appropriately show affection to those they love."

> "I don't want her to think she can be rude whenever she chooses."

I get it. I mean, who wants kids to snub their doting grandparents? Not me! And I don't know about you, but I'm easily triggered at family get-togethers and try desperately to steer clear of potential landmines, so getting a visit off to a smooth start can feel extra important. And I have to admit I do love to see people's faces when they melt into utter bliss as they get some love from my children.

> "I remember feeling sick to my stomach when asked to give hugs or kisses to adults I didn't like."

However! We have a problem. Here are some comments to the same *Babble* piece from people young enough to remember how it felt to be told to give affection they didn't genuinely feel:

"I remember feeling sick to my stomach when asked to give hugs or kisses to adults I didn't like, and feeling like I was a horrible person for not liking the same people my mum did."

"I always hated it when a parent asked me to go kiss a random auntie that I didn't even know . . . To me, she had a scary clown mask and kept painfully pinching my cheeks. If I refused, I'd seem like a spoiled brat, impolite, and I'd get disapproval from my parents."

"When I was in high school, my mother always said that I needed to hug her and my father more ('you know, like when you were little') . . . Eventually, they nagged me about it so much that they turned to guilt-tripping me. 'Daddy doesn't feel like you love him, so go hug/snuggle him.' On numerous occasions, I was forced into it, and it felt just as it sounds—like I was being used, like I was a dog that was only meant to follow commands."

"The fact is a lot of parents are hurting their children without even knowing it . . . they think they are these cute, lovable animals. In reality they are human beings like us, waiting to be considered and listened to."

Whoa. Right?

Unconscious Messages

I f your response to these memories is along the lines of *Oh, my goodness! I had no idea* and you want to make sure that your child doesn't feel similarly objectified, coerced, or disrespected, you'll be happy to know this problem is solvable. Children can feel respected while guests feel welcome and parents proud of their well-mannered children. I'll get to how this is possible shortly. However, if your response is closer to *Come on! I don't want my kids to think that the world revolves around them. They can suck it up for two seconds for God's sake,* then I think it's worth taking a closer look at the messages we're unconsciously sending our kids when we insist they perform acts of affection regardless of how they feel about it. Even just for two seconds. We may think we're teaching our children: Consider others. Being affectionate with family and friends is polite. Social conventions will help you navigate the world. We probably don't realize the messages they're internalizing are likely something closer to:

- My body is not entirely my own. It can be directed by authority figures to please others.
- My feelings are inconvenient and disruptive. Listening to my body will only get me in trouble.
- Grown-ups' feelings are more important than mine.
- Affection need not be genuine. (Mom and Dad said so!)
- Feigning love, joy, and excitement is not only expected but mandatory.
- I must always reciprocate when someone wants to be affectionate with me. Otherwise, I'm rude and selfish.
- I'm only "good" when I do what others expect—regardless of how I feel about it.

Harsh? Absolutely.

Far-fetched? Not according to Irene van der Zande, executive director of Kidpower International, an organization whose mission is "To teach people of all ages and abilities how to use their power to stay safe, act wisely, and believe in themselves." Explains van der Zande, "When we force children to submit to unwanted affection in order not to offend a relative or hurt a friend's feelings, we teach them that their bodies do not really belong to them because they have to push aside their own feelings about what feels right to them." And because, as neuroscientists often explain it, "neurons that fire together wire together," if a child is repeatedly sent these messages, they *will* make hard-to-reverse impressions on their developing brains. The messages will influence, if not dictate, the way our children respond to similar situations later in life. Developmental biologist Bruce Lipton explains the impact of one's early experience on future experiences like this:

> "Once a reaction pattern is triggered ... it's very difficult to change the course of one's thoughts and behaviors."
> —*Ellen Domm*

> In humans . . . the fundamental behaviors, beliefs, and attitudes we observe in our parents become "hard-wired" as synaptic pathways in our subconscious minds. Once programmed into the subconscious mind, they control our biology for the rest of our lives . . . unless we can figure out a way to reprogram them.

Put yet another way by the psychologist Ellen Domm, "Once a reaction pattern is triggered . . . it's very difficult to change the course of one's thoughts and behaviors." (Fortunately, however, not impossible!) I was struck by how Emily, a mother who follows my blog, has been affected by her experiences as a child who was "encouraged" to return affection she didn't genuinely feel. Talking about what life might be like for children who've had similar experiences, she wrote, "It may be [for them] as it already is for many of us adults. We feel obliged to consent to activities, behaviors, touching, use of our body, etc., that feels very wrong. We stay in relationships that harm us and our children because we feel guilty for not wanting those behaviors and relationships. We will blame ourselves, and pass those feelings on to our children. But of course there IS a choice. It's a hard cycle to break, but we CAN." And we must.

> We don't want our children going about their lives outfitted with brains that tell them *Ignore my instincts.*

Certainly we don't want our children going about their lives outfitted with brains that tell them *Ignore my instincts. Suppress my feelings. Please others.* When our kids reach middle and high school, we want them to know how to respond if a date wants to take things further than they feel comfortable taking them. And to know what to do if a seemingly trustworthy adult—be it a coach, priest, or some perfectly angelic, great-with-kids uncle with a creepy hidden agenda—acts at all inappropriately. I don't mean to be alarmist, but predators are masters at sniffing out polite children because they are potential prey. The more courteous, considerate, and people-pleasing the child, the better.

According to child abuse expert Pattie Fitzgerald, "a child who's been taught to be polite no matter what the circumstances . . . here's a child who probably won't know how to resist an inappropriate touch or have the ability to tell anyone about it. At the next family gathering, [the predator] decides he may be able to go a little further with his behavior because you've basically laid the groundwork out for him already." In fact, it can all begin with what appears to be very "normal," "fun," and "loving" behavior. Explains Sandra J. Dixon, a nurse who specializes in childhood trauma and is the author of *Invisible Girl*, "Nearly all molesters engage children in tickling, roughhousing, picking the child up, massaging, cuddling, holding, patting, rocking, kissing, and touching. The predator touches the child in front of the parents, at first appropriately, and soon inappropriately. That's how bold they are. If the parents don't stop it, the child thinks that they approve." And given that the statistics show that somewhere between 9 and 28 percent of women have experienced some type of sexual abuse in childhood and 14 to 18 percent of men have, and that most of these assaults were by acquaintances and relatives, it behooves us to take Fitzgerald's, van der Zande's, and Dixon's warnings seriously.

Our Bodies' Wisdom

Part of the problem lies in how we judge our children when they refuse a hug or refuse to hug. As a result of feeling embarrassed or frustrated or rejected, we may jump to interpreting their conduct as rude. Selfish! Inconsiderate! Wrong. But when we stop and think about it, do we truly think our kids are out to snub our guests? To give the impression that they are somehow better than everyone else? To embarrass their parents? Why would they? Particularly if they know it will get them in trouble?

The truth is, our children's bodies—via their emotions and feelings—are trying to tell them something. Something important! Indeed, that's their purpose. The psychiatrist Fredric Neuman explains that

> Our children's bodies—via their emotions and feelings—are trying to tell them something.

feelings are "instructions to behave in certain ways." And in this case, the instruction just may be: "Caution!" Therefore, instead of criticizing and punishing our children's behavior, it's important to try to understand it, to be curious about what may have set off their internal alarm system. I'm not saying it's necessarily because a child has sensed a "tricky" person—perhaps it is her body simply saying, "Alert. Not genuine. I don't really feel affectionate toward this person."

We all have a need for authenticity (because it's the foundation of trust, and it's what makes life truly meaningful), and children, who are less jaded than we adults are, tend to be more in touch with this fundamental need. A child's body may simply be trying to keep things real. Or, as I mentioned, a child's refusal could be the result of an assault on their olfactory system—perhaps bad breath or overpowering perfume—or the discomfort of being squeezed and smothered by a much bigger body. Or a child may simply need time to (re)warm up to a person she hasn't connected with in a while. Whatever the reason (or reasons), it's important to be curious, as understanding their reactions will give us and our kids the valuable information we need to come up with solutions to this dilemma—without any compromise or sacrifice on anyone's part.

So, let's get to it.

Meeting Everyone's Needs

My guide to resolving these types of situations is the late clinical psychologist Thomas Gordon, renowned master of resolving conflicts peacefully and to everyone's mutual satisfaction (hence his three Nobel Peace Prize nominations). In his internationally bestselling book *Parent Effectiveness Training*, Gordon shares an invaluable relationship tool he calls the No-Lose

Conflict Resolution Method. This process is in six parts: 1) describe each person's feelings and needs; 2) brainstorm solutions; 3) evaluate solutions; 4) choose a solution; 5) enact it; and 6) reevaluate. The prerequisite for this win-win approach is that all parties *let go* of what they think the outcome should look like—which in this case would be a child initiating or reciprocating a hug or kiss. Certainly, there's more than one way to be warm, considerate, and welcoming.

Step 1: Family Meeting

The first step is to find a time to discuss the issue when there is *no* heat on it.

"Hey, honey, I noticed yesterday that you looked unhappy when Aunt Martha was hugging you. It seems like sometimes you may be overwhelmed when guests come to the house and they want affection. Is that right? . . . Well, I'd love to find a way for you to be comfortable when guests come over while also making sure they feel welcome. I think if we brainstorm about this a bit, we can come up with some good ideas. I thought we could talk about it before dinner tonight—does that sound okay?"

A family meeting is a perfect opportunity to explain to your children that their bodies are unequivocally their own and that their comfort level and safety is more important than any inconvenience, embarrassment, or hurt feelings. It's a chance to reiterate that you do not expect them to do anything they feel uncomfortable doing or to feign feelings they don't have. Remind them that you, their parents, are their safe haven—always available for support, sans judgment. Then you can explain that you understand there is often an expectation when people greet each other

> There's more than one way to be warm, considerate, and welcoming.

that kisses and hugs will be returned, and that while you don't want your children to feel coerced into doing something they're not comfortable doing, at the same time it is an important family value that guests feel welcome when they visit. You believe that there is more than one way for that to happen, and you'd like to figure out what those ways might be *with* them.

This conversation may trigger some thoughts or feelings in your children. Give them a chance to share how they may have felt in the past when greeting people. They might reveal feelings they previously felt uncomfortable sharing, like:

"Sometimes I feel shy."

"Grandpa's wet kisses are gross."

"It hurts when she pinches my cheeks. . . ."

Our job is to listen and empathize—i.e., to try to put ourselves in their young shoes. This process in and of itself will likely bring families closer and build trust. Do your best to avoid justifying or clarifying someone else's behavior.

If the moment feels right, you can move toward the next step of identifying everyone's needs during these ritual interactions. Try to get beyond the actions to the feelings you're looking for. For example, "hugging Aunt Sonia" is *not* a need, but Aunt Sonia feeling welcome in your home *is* a need. A hug is only one way to achieve that.

To get things started, it will likely help if parents begin by sharing their needs for when guests come to the home. For the sake of clarity, write these down. Here's what that might look like:

Parents' Needs When Guests Arrive

- Kids only give affection that feels genuine (a need for authenticity)
- Guests feel welcome (a need for consideration)

Then, ask the children what they need and write down their responses. Here's what I imagine some of them might be:

Children's Needs

- Only give affection they're comfortable giving (a need for autonomy, a need for safety)
- Adults respect their bodies (a need for respect)
- Confidence in their ability to be courteous without compromising themselves (a need for competence)

Step 2: Brainstorm

If it appears impossible to simultaneously meet such seemingly conflicting needs, the good news is that it's not! The next step is to go crazy brainstorming solutions. At this point in the process, *nothing's too implausible* to mention, because you never know where even a far-fetched idea will lead you. Just write down *every* idea that you and your kids have—without commentary or judgment (or even any slight twitch, frown, or eyebrow raise of disapproval) Parents may need to get the ball rolling. Here are some ideas you may want to throw into your mix.

Ideas for What Parents Can Do to Help Kids When a Guest Arrives

- Give kids the 411 on the guests before they arrive to remind them exactly who they are, the last time they saw them, and perhaps what you did together.
- If the children are young, say between ages one and eight, support them by saying to your guests, "Aiden needs a little time to warm up. I'd love to give you a hug! Welcome! So great to have you!"
- Call Grandma and Grandpa before the visit and explain that your child is working on listening to the cues their body gives

them and why it's so important. Then they're forewarned and may want to be a part of the solution.

(For example: "There's my granddaughter! How shall we say hello? A high five? A hug? Kiss? Hip bump?")

Ideas About How Kids Can Greet Guests

- Wave hello and offer guests a glass of water and/or a chocolate kiss.
- Offer to take guests' coats and ask if they'd like a beverage.
- Say:
  "How about a high five or a fist bump?"
  "I'd prefer to hold hands."
  "I made a drawing for you!"
  "I've picked out a book. Would you like to read it to me?"

Step 3: Role Play!

Once you and your children have generated a list of possible solutions, it's time to go through them and evaluate each idea. If there's something about an idea that doesn't work for someone, cross it off the list. If everything is crossed off, go back to brainstorming. I imagine, however, everyone will find at least a couple of ideas worth trying. Once you've all agreed on one or two, it can be helpful to role-play—both in your real roles and others.' Kids can pretend to be the grandparents. Parents can be the kids. Adopting the perspective of another can't help but sensitize you to that person's feelings. When you're done role-playing, ask yourself the following questions:

- As a guest, did you feel welcome when someone asked for your coat and shook your hand?
- As a host, did you feel proud of how the kids welcomed the guests?

- As a kid, did you feel comfortable when the guest asked if you wanted a high five or a hug?

Then, next time, before your guests arrive, go over the plan and perhaps role-play one more time.

Step 4: Assess

After the visit, check in with your kids and see how they feel. How did the guests seem to respond? Did things go smoothly? Did the preparation help? Any tweaking need to be done? Any other ideas?

Step 5: Practice

Doing this just once likely won't be enough. Kids are young. They need practice. So before guests arrive, go over the plan and role-play if it might help. Try to keep it fun.

Affection with My Kids

Having now thought about this subject more deeply, I've become more sensitive to the cues my kids give *me* regarding the affection I give them or want to give them, whether we are lying in bed together reading a book or when I come home from work. Sometimes they're dying for some hugging and kissing and rolling around. Other times, they're not. Sometimes they really want a kiss and hug good-bye. Other times just a hug, as in, "Your breath smells bad, Mommy." Or they'll just wave because they're busy building or coloring or playing ball. Sometimes they fall all over themselves when my husband, John, comes home to see who can get into his arms first. Other times they're watching a video and

R ecently on Facebook, I've loved seeing a bunch of posts from dads with teenage daughters proudly wearing T-shirts that read:

RULES FOR DATING MY DAUGHTER

1. I don't make the rules

2. You don't make the rules

3. She makes the rules

4. Her body, her rules

We don't have to, nor should we, wait until our kids are teenagers to tell them and those in their lives that it's their bodies and their right to decide. (It's a chant I've taught the kids, "My body, my life, my right to decide," hoping it will stick with them.) If we start then, it's really too late. Affection should be welcomed—a source of joy, warmth, and connection—not stomached to please others.

just call out a "Hi!" Sometimes they want to snuggle super close when we read books, other times they want more space. It's nothing personal. While I really would love the affection, I realize it's not my children's responsibility to satiate my need. And really, who wants to be the recipient of coerced affection?

In fact, when Hudson was three or four, we worked out a code to let me know when he wants affection. When he says "Jinx!" that means *Kiss me! Hug me! Squeeze me!* And then when he roars like a lion—"Rooooaaar!"—that means *Enough! Stop!* Which I do—instantly—in a fun way. I freeze in my hugging position and then he wiggles out. Giving my kids practice having their wishes honored is just the kind of brain wiring I'm going for. Which is not to say I don't ever just spontaneously give my kids affection. I do. But I am very sensitive to their body language and if I sense they want me to back off, I do.

My friend Megan shared that every night at bedtime she asks her son, "Can I kiss you good night? Where? Your head? Elbow? Knee?" She makes it playful and fun. He's four, and so far he's yet to ask for a kiss on the cheek . . . which tells me a lot about our expectations of what a kiss good night *should* be.

How to Be a Guest Who Respects Kids

When I'm a guest, while I may be excited to see children I know well (my kids' close friends and nephews and nieces) and want to offer them affection, I don't want them to feel pressure to return it. Essentially, I want to give them control of the greeting—which is actually really easy.

Usually I'll say something like, "Hey! I'm so happy to see you! Do you want a high five? A hug? Nothing? Something else?"

Responses have run the spectrum from "All three!" and "High five!" to "No, thanks," to which I'll reply, "Well, all right then!" to let them know their response works for me. Sometimes if they are hiding or shy, I'll say, "You know, I'll be here for a while, so maybe we can catch up after I've had a chance to talk with your parents." If it seems helpful, I might say, "I totally get it! I need time to warm up to people, too!" Often I find that later on, if we, say, end up reading a book together, children naturally warm up and may climb into my lap or lay their head on my shoulder. There's a genuineness and a level of comfort that tells me they really do want to be close. Of course if a child is running up to me with open arms, I'm more than happy to hug them back!

What If a Parent Tells Their Kid to Hug *You?*

Once you're sensitive to this issue, it can be hard to be the recipient of a coerced hug or kiss—e.g., "Aren't you going to give Aunt Sandy a hug good-bye?" If you're Aunt Sandy, it can feel like a predicament. On the one hand, you don't want to reject an obedient child coming toward you with affection. At the same time, you don't have to play along, either. (That parent isn't in charge of you and your body!) Perhaps try something like this:

MOM: Go give Aunt Sandy her hug good-bye!

AUNT SANDY: (kneeling down to the child's level) It's time for me to go now. I've enjoyed visiting with you. How would *you* like to say good-bye? Shall we high five? Shake hands? You tell me!

I was impressed with how a nanny I met online handles similar situations with employers and their children:

I've had so many parents try to force their kids to hug and/or kiss me good-bye. . . . Even when I'm leaving the interview! They haven't even officially hired me yet and they're forcing their child to give me kisses?!? I always just kneel down and try to make eye contact. (Quite often, they're hiding, so it's not always possible.) I say, "You don't feel like hugging/kissing someone you don't know, do you? That's okay. I don't hug/kiss strangers, either." The looks on the parents' faces are priceless. Whether or not I get the job, I always feel like I've imparted a bit of wisdom. With people I'm closer to, I explain that I want the kids to grow up knowing and understanding that "No means no," and I believe the best way to teach that is to respect their "no" when it comes to their bodies from an early age. If a child is taught as a toddler that "no" or "stop" just means someone will force you into their arms or keep tickling you or kiss you anyway, what do we expect from them as teens and adults? Not everyone gets it, but most see my point.

I'd hire her in a heartbeat.

Respect Is a Lifelong Gift

Respecting our children's bodies is a gift that will last them a lifetime. As the distinguished psychoanalyst Alice Miller wrote in her 1984 bestselling book *Thou Shall Not Be Aware: Society's Betrayal of the Child*, "If children have been accustomed from the start to having their world respected, they will have no trouble later in life recognizing disrespect directed against them in any form and will rebel against it on their own." Isn't that what we all want—for our children to feel confident speaking up when something doesn't feel right? To be able to set a boundary and expect to have it respected?

CHAPTER FIVE

"BE CAREFUL!"

"Adventure without risk is Disneyland."
—Douglas Coupland

'm a terrible, terrible backseat driver. I wouldn't wish me on anyone. And I feel for my husband, John, who's been blindsided by my anxiety way too many times. There he'll be, driving us along, listening to music and thinking about whatever, when out of nowhere I'll yell, "Be careful!" Or worse. Sometimes I've even ducked below the dashboard as if a sniper was shooting at us.

"What?!?! What is it?" he'll scream back, as he frantically looks every which way to find the source of my alarm.

Unfortunately, the only thing my panic and shrieks of "Be careful!" successfully do is cause him to panic. Which in turn causes him to take his eyes off the road, which, more times than I care to admit, has nearly gotten us into an accident. And it has most certainly gotten us into a number of really "unpleasant exchanges." I've tried to explain that my reaction is beyond my control. It's not that I don't want to trust his judgment, it's that I'm afraid for my life! I *have* to say something. He sees it differently. He's unnerved. Insulted. And pissed. He's been driving for more than thirty years with a virtually spotless record, thank you very much. And, he certainly wants to avoid an accident as much as I do. *Do I really believe my panic is beyond my control? Therapy, anyone? Meditation? Blinders! A little faith! Something!* "You're the one who's going to cause a wreck, not me!" he tells me.

Which is not to say that there's never been a legitimate cause for my concern. We live in Los Angeles—crazy drivers abound. And once in a while, John may not be looking in the right place at the right time. In those situations, however, he'd be best served by some concrete information like "'the red car is running the light" spoken quickly but calmly. Unfortunately, what he usually hears is a panicked "Be careful!" which just raises the question "Of what?" Fortunately, John and I have landed on a solution: I drive. Unless, of course, I've had a drink, and then I'm sufficiently sedated to be a proper passenger—one who leaves the driving to the driver. Trusting others' judgment is hard for me, and yet not trusting it makes life more stressful and more dangerous for everyone around me.

> "Children have never been very good at listening to their elders, but they have never failed to imitate them."
> —James Baldwin

I know I inherited my anxiety from my dear mother. As James Baldwin, the novelist and social critic, once said, "Children have never been very good at listening to their elders, but they have never failed to imitate them." I remember our one and only family river-rafting trip. The boat next to ours was full of rowdy twenty-somethings splashing one another with their paddles and generally having a boisterously good time. Unbeknownst to anyone, it was making my mom increasingly anxious. Perhaps she was afraid they weren't listening to the guide's directions, or maybe their fun said to her that they weren't taking this life-or-death situation seriously. Whatever it was, when she just couldn't take it another moment, seemingly out of the blue, she *stood up* in the boat—which, of course, almost caused it to tip over—and screamed, "This has gone far enough!" Everyone looked at her like *What's up with the crazy lady?* Mortified, I vowed never to be that person. Not surprisingly, I grew up to be just like her. Riddled with fear.

Play Is Inherently Risky

All this is to say that I'm not the type of parent I'd wish on my kids (or any kids) when it comes to their doing the risky things kids are driven to do—climbing jungle gyms, rocks, trees, fences, and ladders; rolling down steep hills; swinging high on ropes; jumping off ledges; sliding down railings; and running around with sharp sticks. Intellectually I know that these are things kids *need* to do. It's how growing humans learn about the world and what their bodies are capable of. It's the way they explore things like gravity and momentum, friction and density, and how they experience exhilaration and satisfaction. It's how they grow strong, build endurance, and become agile, coordinated, and, ironically, careful. This is all done without direction, which is how people learn best—by following their interests while listening to their instincts, guided by their senses, which tell them things like *hold tighter, too cold, reach farther, too high, bend lower, swing out.*

Another name for all of this climbing-jumping-rolling-leaping activity is "play," and it is, as the revolutionary educator Maria

Montessori declared, "the work of children." Play is at once fun and challenging. In fact, it's the challenges that make it fun. As Peter Gray, an evolutionary psychologist and research professor at Boston College, explains, "If it's not dangerous in some way, it's not exciting and therefore not playful. And if they aren't playing, they aren't learning. . . . A playful activity that becomes too easy loses its attraction and ceases to be play. The player then modifies the activity to make it harder or moves on to something different." This reality is not exactly music to my "I'm terrified my precious kids will get hurt" ears.

> As a society, we've gotten increasingly anxious about our kids getting hurt.

I know I'm not alone in my anxiety. It seems that as a society we've gotten increasingly anxious about our kids getting hurt—to their detriment. While no-brainers like seat belts and helmets are one thing, the incessant haranguing I hear at parks and on playgrounds—"Walk! No running!" and "Come on down from there! That's dangerous"—is making our kids second-guess their instincts. Angela Hanscom, a pediatric occupational therapist and author of *Balanced and Barefoot: How Unrestricted Outdoor Play Makes for Strong, Confident, and Capable Children*, reports, "Many children are kept from falling. Plenty of children are told 'no' when they attempt to climb on top of a rock or pick up a stick. Little kids are told not to spin in circles and are kept from rolling down hills. It is my opinion—supported by observing scores of kids, in clinic and out—that by constantly restricting children's movements we impede the development of strong vestibular systems (balance), which most children will achieve naturally through physical trial and error. If we don't allow children to take (safe) risks and test themselves, they can seem clumsy, uncoordinated, and unsafe at an early age."

Case in point: One day at the park, I watched a nanny "help" a three-year-old boy on a bike *with training wheels* by steering for him and running alongside him as he pedaled. When she stepped away to give him a chance to do it on his own, he cried out for her. "Come! Help me!" He'd clearly become so dependent on her support that he'd lost confidence in his ability and thus was unable to ride a bike with training wheels alone for even a second. When his nanny and I later chatted while we pushed the kids on the swings, she explained that her boss told her she had to stay very close to the boy at all times because last week he'd fallen and scraped his knee (God forbid!) and her boss was furious with her for letting it happen. So now she was super paranoid and overly protective, which obviously wasn't infusing the kid with any confidence in his own abilities or judgment. I was dying to give her a copy of *Free-Range Kids: How to Raise Safe, Self-Reliant Children (Without Going Nuts with Worry)* to share with her boss. In it, author Lenore Skenazy advocates for trusting kids to have good instincts and warns that by trying to prevent all danger and accidents, we deprive kids of the chance to become self-reliant, "Over-protectiveness is a danger in and of itself. A child who thinks he can't do anything on his own, eventually can't."

> "Over-protectiveness is a danger in and of itself. A child who thinks he can't do anything on his own, eventually can't."
> —*Lenore Skenazy*

I found a similar protecting-our-kids-actually-hurts-them message in the article "7 Crippling Parenting Behaviors that Keep Children from Growing into Leaders" from the *Forbes* Parenting for Success series:

We live in a world that warns us of danger at every turn. . . so we do everything we can to protect [our children]. It's our job after all, but we have insulated them from healthy risk-taking behavior and it's had an adverse effect. Psychologists in Europe have discovered that if a child doesn't play outside and is never allowed to experience a skinned knee, they frequently have phobias as adults. Kids need to fall a few times to learn it's normal; teens likely need to break up with a boyfriend or girlfriend to appreciate the emotional maturity that lasting relationships require. If parents remove risk from children's lives, we will likely experience high arrogance and low self-esteem in our growing leaders.

Our need to play, an innate human drive that has been honed over millennia, is risky for good reason. It's the way we become attuned to the environment and our bodies. So when we parents try to become the drivers of our kids' bodies—when we think we know better than they do—they can come to doubt their own judgment, and that's truly risky.

Calm in the Face of Risk

Knowing all of this is one thing, trying to live it is another. Especially when the universe gave me a son who was born a traceur. A what? A traceur, I've come to learn, is at once a ninja, Spider-Man, a skateboarder, and a gymnast who sees every ledge, railing, gate, fence, bench, step, and post as something to scale, jump, vault over, flip off from, or to otherwise creatively interface with. To traceurs like Hudson, directions like "Get down off that ledge!" "Don't climb that high!" "Slow down!" and "Be careful!" are insults, nails on a chalkboard that disrupt their flow, challenge their integrity and intelligence, and kill their bliss. Traceurs practice what is now known as the art/sport of parkour or free-running. The best of the best don't go to the Olympics, they become the stuntmen in superhero movies. One look at their show reels on YouTube is enough to make me want to lock Hudson up in a box until he's forty. But Hudson got lucky: His innate talent, spirit, and confidence weren't going to be squelched by his mother's overwhelming anxiety. I largely credit my ability to remain calm in the face of Hudson's ninja-like lifestyle to the parent-and-me classes that John and I started taking with Jules at the RIE (Resources for Infant Educarers) Center when she was a baby. Over the course of two years, without realizing it was happening, I was slowly but surely given the antidote to my anxiety. Not entirely, of course. But man, it's really helped take the edge off.

Slowly Introduce Risk

In retrospect, I can see that RIE helped me relax as my children explored the edges of their abilities, because in RIE classes the play space is totally safe and risks are gradually introduced. RIE classes are deceptively simple. It looks like nothing is happening, when what's really happening is that we're learning how to truly respect our children and their abilities.

Each week's class was essentially the same: As each family arrived, we'd remove our shoes and the babies' shoes and socks, place the babies on the center mat, and then take a seat along the perimeter, where we'd simply watch them do their thing for a half hour. Learning from the children being themselves and doing what they do was the curriculum. Afterward, we'd talk about anything we'd noticed and share challenges or questions we had. That's all. I was amazed how much I learned—largely from just watching the kids play. I started becoming more and more aware of details I never would've noticed, like the way a baby used her toe to balance, or how tenacious a child was in trying to roll over.

At first the babies were so young they couldn't do much more than lie on their backs, wave cloth napkins around, and gnaw on little toys—which was just my speed. They were a joy to watch, and I was at peace. Then, like dominos, one by one each child turned over. And then one day, Tatiana started to crawl! All of us new parents were in awe of her out-and-aboutness as we tried to imagine what it would be like when our babies followed suit. As the kids became more and more agile, coordinated, and strong, our teacher, Francesca, introduced new challenges to the space. For instance, one day she brought out a three-inch-high platform and ramp for the kids to clamber up and descend, and cubes to climb in, on, and out of—all of which each child tackled in his or her own way and time. And if they fell, which they sometimes did, they were just inches from the floor. No harm, no foul. If they were startled or momentarily hurt, we were there for comfort. "You fell! I saw that." Essentially we were learning, through observation, to trust our children's judgment. As RIE's founding director, Magda Gerber, once explained, "A child who has always been allowed to move freely develops not only an agile body but good judgment about what he can and cannot do. Developing good body image, spatial relations, and a sense of balance helps the child learn not only how to move but also how to fall and how to recover. Children raised this way hardly ever have serious accidents." She warned, however, "Whenever you restrict an infant from what he could and would do naturally, in my mind you tell the child, 'I know what's good for you.' But you the adult does not know. . . . [A] child may become confused because his body tells him one thing and the adult another, and then the child may fall." In other words: Trust is key. I found the more I observed the kids at play, the more confident I became in their competence.

I remember the day Francesca brought out an empty five-gallon plastic water container for the kids to play with. It was the same size as they were! *Weird!* I'd thought. But it proved to be an ideal challenge. It was light enough for the year-old kids to carry but cumbersome enough to require concentration and coordination.

Some carried it up the ramp. Some lifted it onto a large wooden cube. Some rolled it, tried to flip it over, and even fought over it. As they struggled to achieve whatever they had in mind, we parents struggled to let them. It seemed that learning to rein in our instinct to "help" was part of what we were learning.

Then, when the kids were about a year and half old, Francesca brought out a large wooden rocking boat that up to four kids could sit in—two on each side. It scared me. *What if it rocked onto one of their feet! What if one fell forward when it got going fast?* Some of the kids climbed on right away, but others held back. In fact, one girl didn't climb into the rocking boat for months. But she watched. Only after she'd closely observed how it worked, and how all the other kids interacted with it, did she feel ready to venture out. She was being careful. She knew what *she* needed to know to feel safe to explore it. Every child, we learned, is truly unique. Each has his own internal barometer that provides information about what feels safe. Problems crop up when parents try to restrict kids' exploration because of their own fears or, conversely, push kids beyond their comfort zones: "Come on, you can do it!" We're not them. We literally can't know how their body is experiencing a situation.

No Socks! No Shoes!

What also helped the children be careful in RIE class was that they were barefoot. As yogis, modern dancers, and practitioners of martial arts will tell you, when feet are unrestricted by shoes (no matter how flexible), toes can more easily spread, grasp, and stretch—all of which helps with balance, coordination, and strength. And skin! Unlike any fabric, skin provides just the right amount of resistance to keep us safe. On the other hand, socks undermine kids' burgeoning abilities by turning them into mini Jerry Lewises slipping all over the place—particularly on wood floors. Bare feet help children be careful, which is ironic, because so many parents want kids in shoes to protect their feet. In the *Guardian* article "Why Barefoot Is Best for Children," podiatrist Tracy Byrne explains, "Toddlers keep their heads up more when they are walking barefoot. The feedback they get from the ground means there is less need to look down, which is what puts them off balance and causes them to fall down." So when Hudson refused to wear shoes for the first six years of his life, we didn't force it, because we'd learned he was actually better off without them. As you may imagine, over the years I got very used to questions like "Aren't you afraid he'll step on glass?" (no) and "Aren't his feet freezing?" (we live in sunny southern California), to say nothing about the comments about his dirty feet. (Smugly, I'm sure) I took comfort in seeing him climb everything in sight—railings, jungle gyms, trees, my car, what have you—with the confidence and skill of a chimp. And yes, he stepped on a bee twice—which wasn't enough to convince him shoes were necessary. The momentary pain was a small price to pay for the gift of feeling safe, coordinated, and free that his bare feet gave him.

How Help Hinders

When Jules was a toddler, I remember that our RIE-inspired hands-off, let-her-figure-it-out-on-her-own approach could really frustrate her. For instance, when she was eighteen months old, she was mesmerized by the rocking chair on our front porch. Almost daily, she'd push it and watch it rock. Back and forth, back and forth. And soon she wanted up, but try as she might, she was too little to make it happen. The chair was too unsteady and her legs too short. So she'd whimper and motion for help. Help that

I kindly and gently didn't give her. I imagine many might think, *Come on! What's the big deal? Just lift her up already!* I see your point, and I almost agree. But what I'd come to realize was that if she couldn't safely climb onto the chair herself (or onto anything else, for that matter), it was a sign that she wasn't ready to safely be up there. If she couldn't get up, she couldn't get down. And she'd be trapped, and reliant on me. So instead of helping her up, I'd empathize with her frustration. "You want to climb up there. It looks fun. It's so frustrating! Soon you'll be able to!" If she really wanted to, she'd stick with it, and by sticking with it, she'd develop just the strength and coordination she needed to safely climb up onto and down from the rocking chair. A couple of months later, she did it. It was her own Mt. Everest. She was delighted and so proud. "Me do it!" And then she did it often! And I didn't have to worry or watch her every move because I knew that she knew what she was doing. By not getting help, Jules became both skilled and careful.

If only I could've explained this "be patient, let her struggle, and empathize" approach to Jules's babysitter, Maria, but I didn't speak Spanish and Maria spoke very little English. I suspect, however, that even if we had been able to communicate clearly, it might not have changed much. God bless babysitters and nannies—the safety of their young charges is a big responsibility. More than anything, they don't want the children they care for to get hurt on their watch. As a result, many are apt to be more overprotective and cautious than even the most obsessive helicopter parent. "Be careful!" is their mantra. "Watch out!" "No!" "That's not safe!" are common refrains called out as if their livelihood depends on it, because it does. But, as I've learned over the course of many car rides with John, fear can wreak the kind of havoc it's meant to keep others from suffering. And, unfortunately, Maria's fear of Jules getting hurt ended with a trip to the emergency room.

Returning home one afternoon, I heard Jules's screams before I even reached the front door. I ran upstairs as fast as I could and found Maria rocking Jules in her arms. Jules was shrieking, and Maria looked desperate and worried. I immediately picked Jules up, and almost instantly she stopped shrieking. At first I thought it was because now she was with me. *Mommy's here!* What I'd later figure out was that she'd stopped screeching because by picking her up, I'd taken the pressure off the exact spot that made her suffer most. Soon she stopped crying altogether and seemed totally fine. I was perplexed. I couldn't understand what had upset her so. And then I noticed Jules wasn't moving one of her arms. In fact, she couldn't. It was just dangling there. Remarkably, if no pressure was applied, it didn't hurt. Panicked again, I immediately put her in the car, and the three of us headed to the emergency room.

"It's a radial head subluxation," the doctor explained. "Essentially it means her elbow is partially dislocated. It's commonly known as 'nursemaid's elbow.'"

Then with one swift move, the doctor popped Jules's elbow back into place. Jules let out a short, loud scream, and she was back to normal. Thank goodness. Then, thanks to the doctor's Spanish, I learned what had happened.

Fear can wreak the kind of havoc it's meant to keep others from suffering.

At the park there's a jungle gym that Jules was too small to climb up onto herself. And since I never helped Jules go where she wasn't able to go herself, she'd never been on it. But oh, how she tried. She'd put her fingers in the holes on the first step and try to swing her leg up. While she was sometimes frustrated, she was undeterred. When she'd tire of trying, she'd go back to digging or climbing smaller rocks in the ravine. But when Maria saw Jules trying so hard, she wanted to help. She wanted Jules to be able to play on the structure and slide down the slide like the rest of the kids who were having so much fun. So Maria lifted Jules up and placed her at the top of the slide. Jules had turned onto her stomach to slide down (because that's what felt safest!), but Maria wanted to teach Jules the "right" way to go down a slide, so she turned Jules around and put her on her butt. And off Jules went. But Maria panicked. Jules looked like she was going too fast! Afraid, Maria grabbed her by the wrist to slow her down, and that's when, without realizing it, Maria pulled Jules's elbow out of its socket. Jules screamed and cried. Maria thought she was just scared, as nothing physically seemed to be wrong. Eventually Jules stopped crying and seemed okay—that is, until Maria cradled her in her arms at home, applying pressure to her dislocated elbow, not realizing that her attempt to soothe her was causing the unbearable pain. That's when I came in.

That night, when Jules was finally asleep, I Googled "nursemaid's elbow," thinking it was such a strange name for a dislocated body part. It turns out the injury got the nickname back when the minders of children were called nursemaids, as the injury often occurred on their watch. If named today, it would be called "nanny's elbow" or "babysitter's elbow." It was exactly as Magda Gerber had warned:

> Studying accident statistics in children, Dr. Pikler [Gerber's mentor] found that the children . . . who had been kept indoors and raised by nannies fell victim to fractures and concussions more often than children who played in the street and were allowed more freedom of movement. The children who played in the street and learned how to fall were apparently more aware of their physical abilities and limits. Thus, she felt it was better to allow a growing child unrestricted movement.

Yes, the reason Jules got hurt was because Maria panicked. But the reason Maria panicked was because she had pushed Jules to do something she wasn't yet able to do on her own. If kids are allowed to explore a challenge in their own time, to struggle and conquer it when they are ready, we don't have to worry. But when we push them, then we can panic. And even if we don't panic, if we push them, we have to hover to ensure they're okay, which they probably won't be if we're not right there.

RIE taught me:

- Not to push my kids to do things they're not ready to do.
- To trust that they will do something in the safest way for their bodies.
- The best way to get to know what they're capable of is through observation.
- To give my kids a lot of outdoor time so they got very adept at exploring the natural environment.
- To try not to overreact. (This was especially hard for me.) I want my kids to know I'm concerned and am there if they need me, but that they can also handle minor snafus on their own.

Two years of trying to practice these principles put me in good shape to be the mom of someone who would take risk-taking to another level. I'm proud to say that Hudson's really confident in his body's abilities—he's super agile, highly skilled, and rarely gets hurt. And when he does have an injury, he's totally cool with it.

> If kids are allowed to explore a challenge in their own time, to struggle and conquer it when they are ready, we don't have to worry.

"We Just Stopped Saying 'No'"

That said, recess at school has been challenging for Hudson because there are so many things he's driven to do—climb onto ledges, jump off railings, and do back flips—that he's simply not allowed to. And the rules increase every year. In just the decade that I've been a parent, I've seen our collective anxiety over kids getting hurt drive schools to become more and more overprotective. Rae Pica, an educational consultant who has specialized in children's physical activity for over thirty-five years, confirms the growing trend: "To say we've become risk-averse where children are concerned is to be laughably understated. And it's not just parents (who, arguably, are the easiest to frighten). Teachers and school and city administrators, perhaps in reaction to parents' concerns and certainly in reaction to the fear of litigation, are showing the same symptoms. They're removing monkey bars and swing sets from playgrounds. They're outlawing tag, cartwheels, and sometimes even running—and, oh yes, recess."

In just the handful of years that Jules and Hudson attended preschool, the top floor of the longstanding tree house was made off limits, the zip line was taken down, and the outer reaches of the yard were cordoned off so the kids couldn't be out of eyesight. Similarly, kids were discouraged from any kind of roughhousing, despite warnings from experts like Dr. Stuart Brown, founder and director of the National Institute for Play, who explains that ". . . rough-and-tumble play is a great learning medium for all of us.

Preschool kids, for example, should be allowed to dive, hit, whistle, scream, be chaotic, and develop through that a lot of emotional regulation and a lot of the other social by-products—cognitive, emotional, and physical—that come as a part of rough-and-tumble play." Alas, they're not. With developmentally inappropriate "academic" preschools on the rise, more and more children's free play—that is to say, their oxygen—is being limited in the name of getting a head start. And at the kids' elementary school there is now almost nothing for them to climb on, which drives Hudson crazy. There's only so much handball a child can play.

> "To say we've become risk-averse where children are concerned is to be laughably understated."
>
> —Rae Pica

So I was nothing short of shocked when I learned that the Swanson School in Auckland, New Zealand, had actually reversed its own safety-first, restrictive recess policy. Three years ago, the primary school decided to welcome—truly welcome—all manner of play because the administration saw that the climate of caution was stifling the kids. "We just stopped saying 'no,'" explained principal Bruce McLaughlin. "So when a child started climbing a tree, we let them. When a child started riding a bike, we let them." Giving the children their freedom back didn't mean McLaughlin was no longer afraid they might get hurt, it just meant that he was able to temper his fear with the knowledge that children innately need risk and unrestricted play to be healthy and careful. "I think to myself, *I don't want kids to get hurt on my watch.* No teacher does. And that's probably why we ended up in the world we're in today—where we wrap kids up in cotton wool," he shared.

Swanson's "radical" policy to let kids play unrestricted led to a profile on the New Zealand TV magazine show *Sunday Night*. The piece opens with the reporter explaining, "In this school, children are allowed to play outside of the teacher's view. They can make fortresses or rumble to their hearts' content," as footage shows a handful of kids climbing higher and higher into a very tall tree, followed by another kid riding a skateboard on his stomach whizzing down a hill, followed by two boys wrestling on the ground. Then a montage plays of two young girls carrying a log double their size; a kid climbing a 2x4 that's leaning against a six-foot fence; another group working together to erect a giant climbing wall; and lots of kids jumping their scooters off boards and ledges. Taking the whole Swanson recess scene in, the reporter remarks, "A lot of parents watching this would be horrified."

A lot, but not all. One mother commented, "They're doing everything I did as a kid . . . everything that we as a society have stopped kids from doing." While she admits that her children sometimes come home with a bruise here or a bump there, she knows those are just signs of a child playing hard, and soon they'll heal. Every scrape is a mini lesson that sometimes fun comes at a slight cost, or next time to be more careful.

A Time and Place for "Be Careful"

Just to be clear, I'm not saying to simply trust your kid's judgment all the time and not teach them safe habits. I'm not crazy. I've absolutely taught the kids to be careful of many things, like not walking and playing in the street. I've taught them how to look both ways before crossing and how to be careful of the stove and when lighting candles. I've taught them to stop walking or riding their bikes when approaching driveways that are obscured by hedges so they can see if a car is backing out. (Hudson hated this process. He cried and cried each time I insisted he stop his bike to look. He just wanted to fly on by. But I insisted—and insisted. He *had* to be careful.)

Things can seem tricky when one child's freedom to play infringes upon another child's right to feel safe. So, particularly if the children are quite young, I'll help out. This means, for example, if a child is waving a stick and someone is afraid it will poke them, I'll ask, "Where can you wave it away from people?" Or if a child throws sand, I wouldn't just ban sand throwing. (Personally I love to watch children delight in scattering sand—tiny granules flying through the air can be magical and satisfying in such a unique way.) That said, I'd never want that sand to land in other kids' eyes. That would be awful. So, in such a case, I'll say something like, "If you want to throw sand, make sure

> I'm not crazy. I've absolutely taught the kids to be careful of many things.

no one else is around." And for those worried that the sand can easily get in the sand thrower's own eyes, well, that usually will only happen once.

To be honest, while I've made a ton of progress, I still panic. Particularly in parking lots, where I find myself saying stuff to my kids like, "This is a danger zone! Everyone here is on their phones, texting. They're not looking out for you!" or "This is *the* most dangerous parking lot in Los Angeles." And they're like, "Oh? More dangerous than the last most dangerous parking lot in Los Angeles?" I'm pretty sure I could take my hysteria down a couple of notches and still manage to get us to and from the car safely. My parking-lot lunacy aside, I rarely tell my kids to be careful when they're playing. I trust their judgment. Or do my best to, anyway.

Remarkably, my mom has made progress, too. I remember one day when Hudson was not yet a year old and she came with us to the park. As usual for him, he bear-crawled right up the steps of the play structure, then crawled along the top and paused right at the opening where there was at least an eight-foot drop with no railing.

"Jennifer!" my mom gasped. "Get him!"

"He's fine!" I reassured her. "He's done this a lot. I trust . . ."

"I get the theory!" she said, "I just can't take it."

Her wise solution? She walked away and took a stroll around the playground.

I Got This

Giving children the space to take risks and follow their bliss is not just about cultivating their physical abilities. When kids trust they can struggle and figure something out on their own, it translates into other areas of life. Psychologist Tina Payne Bryson, coauthor of *The Whole-Brain Child*, explains, "Our kids are precious, but they're not fragile. . . . When we . . . protect them from any injury, any distress, or any potential challenge, we actually make them more fragile. We communicate to them, 'I don't think you can handle this, and you need me to shelter you.' In so doing, we deny them the privilege of the practice of feeling and sitting in discomfort and finding their way out, and of seeing that they are strong and resourceful."

> "Our kids are precious, but they're not fragile."
> —*Tina Payne Bryson*

All of this being said, the truth is accidents will happen, and all the "be carefuls" in the world can't stop that fact. We're human. Fallible. And we learn valuable information from mistakes and missteps—*if* we're allowed to make them.

CHAPTER SIX

"CAN YOU SAY 'THANK YOU'?"

"The hardest job kids face
today is learning good manners
without seeing any."
—Fred Astaire

A bunch of moms and their toddlers were over at our house one afternoon, and the mayhem was going so well that when I glanced at the clock, I couldn't believe it was already dinnertime. Scrambling, I found a frozen pizza, and just as I was putting it in the oven, I overheard Avery in the playroom ask her mom for some water.

"You can ask Jennifer yourself, sweetheart! She's in the kitchen," Tammy explained. "And don't forget to say thank you!"

Sure enough, in came Avery.

"Water?" she asked.

"Here you go," I said, filling a cup and giving it to her.

When she returned to the playroom, I heard her mom ask, "Did you say thank you?"

"Yes," Avery replied matter-of-factly. Even I was nearly convinced, though, alas, she had not.

"Good girl!" her mom said proudly.

What was Avery going to say? "No"? At the tender age of two, she already realized that lying about forgetting was easier than admitting she'd forgotten. Had she been honest, would her mom have made her come back in to thank me? Would she have gently scolded her or reminded her to say it next time? Too much to deal with! And so the fibbing begins.

Twenty minutes later, just as I was taking the pizza out of the oven, another mom, Sara, came into the kitchen to say good-bye with her son Marcus in her arms.

"We're gonna take off . . ." Sara began.

"Peeetza!" Marcus howled excitedly, reaching out for it.

"You're welcome to stay for some," I offered.

"No, no, no, honey," Sara said blocking Marcus's reach toward the pizza. "We're going home to meet Daddy for dinner!" Then to me she added, "Tim's on his way home, so . . ."

"Peeeeetzzaaaaa!" Marcus wailed desperately.

"No pizza. Dinner is at home," Sara patiently reiterated.

Then Marcus started bawling. "Peeeetza! Peetza!" he cried.

"Can you say thank you to Jennifer for having us over?" Sara asked Marcus, as if he wasn't totally apoplectic.

"That's okay!" I said, not wanting to drag out Marcus's suffering any longer. "It was great to have you over."

Unbeknownst to Tammy and Sara, they'd hit on a subject that was slowly but surely becoming something of a pet peeve: the manner by which we teach kids manners. Now that Jules and her friends were expanding their vocabulary every day, I'd begun to notice just how popular this "Can you say . . ." approach was with parents eager to have their kids say "please" and "thank you," "hello" and "bye-bye!" It seems as if the moment kids can start saying "Milk?" folks feel the need to make sure they say "Milk, please," and that every hello and good-bye needs to be responded to, even if it means picking up

> The moment kids can start saying "Milk?" folks feel the need to make sure they say "Milk, please."

the child's hand like a marionette's and waving it for them. What struck me this time in particular, however, was Sara asking Marcus if he could say "thank you" when he was clearly in no condition to thank anybody for anything. (Other than, perhaps, to thank me with a scowl that said *Thanks for torturing me with pizza I can't have, lady!*) And how could a two-year-old possibly understand that he should be thanking someone for "having them over"? It's not like it was Marcus's idea to come play in my yard in the first place. Young kids don't—yet—see themselves as inconvenient impositions who should be thanking everyone for efforts on their behalf. After all, just a few months earlier, as babies, everyone seemed more than happy to cater to their every need. Realizing that they should now start thanking everyone for milk when all they previously had to do to get some was purse their lips takes a shift in perception. A necessary shift, but one that takes time.

Honestly, I don't mention this to criticize Sara. She's an adoring, thoughtful mom who had a lot going on, and reminding a child to say please or thank you is hardly the worst thing a parent can do. I know that! It's just that this one incident got me thinking. To me, asking a wailing two-year-old desperate for pizza to thank a grown-up for "having them over" seemed so absurd that it was a sign of just how knee-jerk this habit of asking kids to thank adults is. To me, something that deeply ingrained in us begged for a closer look.

A Broken Code

For starters, we all know "Can you say . . . ?" isn't a genuine question. Certainly parents know whether their kids are *able* to say what they want them to say. Instead, it's code—a thinly veiled cue to our children to say what we want them to say at the very moment we want them to say it. The problem is that everyone— parents, teachers, children, and the people to be thanked—knows the code. And because codes only work if the outsider isn't in on it, "Can you say . . . ?" can't do its job, which I presume is to save a child the humiliation of being publicly controlled. I mean, I know exactly how I'd feel if my boss "asked" me something like, "Jennifer, can you thank Keith and Lisa for listening to our presentation?" I'd feel mortified. Demeaned. Resentful. And yet, curiously, we seem to think nothing of saying it to children. I can't imagine a child ever thinking, *Oh, thanks Mom for reminding me! You really have my back.* Or that the person being thanked would actually think the show of appreciation had an ounce of authenticity—not that that seems important to anyone. It's more like we adults all have an unspoken pact with one another. For the sake of teaching our kids manners, we've all agreed to go through the rigmarole of:

"Can I have a candy?"

"What's the magic word?"

"Please?"

"Well, sure, when you ask so nicely."

Or:

"Can you thank so-and-so for having you over?"

"Thank you."

"Good job!"

I realize the hope is that after many years of these mini-training sessions, all of our reminding will kick in and our work will be done. And perhaps that's the case. Nonetheless, I remained dubious. This "say what I want you to say when I want you to say it" approach to teaching manners felt too ventriloquist-operating-a-dummy to truly impart such important values as respect, appreciation, and consideration.

Don't get me wrong: I think helping to nurture good manners is an essential part of my responsibility as a parent. After all, appreciating others and knowing what to say and when to say it so that others feel that appreciation will undoubtedly help Jules and Hudson navigate all manner of social and business interactions with greater ease and confidence throughout their lives—no small things. But, man, I had to hope that there was a better way than me perpetually prompting them to say what I wanted them to say. On the lookout for other options, I found many variations on the same theme. For instance, I noticed that the go-to classic "What's the magic word?" is often ditched as kids grow older in favor of "the do-over," which is couched in yet more rhetorical questions, like, "Can you say it in a way that makes me want to get it for you?" or "Is that the way we ask for things?" Other grown-ups, however, just tack on the omitted "Pleeease!" in a way that screams *Didn't you forget a little somethin'?* And then there's the shocked "Ex-cuuuuse me?" that tells a child how rude they are for failing to say the word. And still others issue the ultimatum "You can ask nicely or you can do it yourself!" It's a do-si-do adults and kids seem very used to dancing—adults eager to inspire some show of respect and appreciation, kids saying what they must to get grown-ups off their backs, often while hiding their rolling eyes. Believe me, I get it. We do stuff for our kids day and night! We're worn out, and they seem oblivious to it. A little gratitude would go a long way.

> Don't get me wrong: I think that helping to nurture good manners is an essential part of my responsibility as a parent.

There've been plenty of times when I, Miss Holier Than Thou, couldn't resist the lure of the pregnant pause at the end of a play-date that beckoned me to prompt Jules to thank the host. Thinking myself quite clever, instead of overtly asking Jules if she *could* say thank you, I'd do my best to discreetly ask her if she *wanted* to say it. The problem is while technically I was letting myself off the hook, I'm not convinced Jules saw my question as giving her a genuine choice. She knew the drill, and a "thank you" was quickly forthcoming. Yes, I think asking out of earshot of the person to be thanked is better than a rhetorical question in front of them, but was it really the best route? Hudson certainly doesn't think so. "Don't tell me what to say!" he once responded to me when I'd quietly asked if he wanted to thank someone—outing me in front of them, effectively giving me a taste of exactly the medicine I was trying not to give him. Suffice it to say, it's mortifying.

Double Standards Abound

As infant specialist Magda Gerber would say, "What we teach is ourselves." In other words, if we want thankful, kind, thoughtful children who say the right things at the right time, the solution is to be that person as much as possible. Obviously no one is perfect, but I really had to ask myself, *Am I the kind, considerate, appreciative person I want my kids to be?* I embarked on a period of self-scrutiny, and much to my dismay, I found that too often the way I spoke to others—like to my mother (when I was triggered) or to John (when he forgot something) or to impossibly slow checkout clerks (when I was in a hurry) or to a babysitter (when she cared for my child differently than I would have)—left something to be desired. That is to say, people who live in glass houses shouldn't throw stones (insert frozen grin emoji).

When it comes to politeness, it's difficult to be a consistently good role model, as a reconnaissance trip to the playground revealed. Over the course of fifteen minutes, I observed the following:

A little boy toddled up to a three-year-old girl and pointed at the cars she was playing with. She glanced up at him and went back to playing. The boy continued to watch her play. Hovering behind the boy was his father, who "asked," "Eric, can you say, 'hi?'"

Eric didn't say hi. (Neither did his dad.) The boy continued to watch the girl play for another minute until his Dad "asked," "Eric, why don't you go play with your brother?"

Obediently, Eric ran off. He found his brother riding a bouncy crocodile in the sandbox and wanted to get on. His brother wasn't ready to get off, and they started to argue.

"Ben, get off for your brother!" both the mom and dad yelled from opposite sides of the playground.

Then, behind me, I heard a mom yell, "I said, come here! If you don't put this sunscreen on this minute, we're leaving the park. Do you understand me?" The boy came, and his mom held his face in one hand and slathered on sunscreen with the other as the boy avoided eye contact with his friends who looked on. "Was that so hard?" she asked him when done. "You can go now."

Then, over by the slide, I heard, "Sebastian, take the steps!" I turned to see a kid climbing up the slide—not sliding down it. (No one was waiting to use it.) The boy continued climbing to the top. He sat down and started banging the slide with his feet.

"Come on down now!" his mom shouted. "It's not an instrument."

My conclusion? Fred Astaire had it right when he said, "The hardest job kids face today is learning good manners without seeing any." These parents seemed to think nothing of directing their kids to do this, say that, go there, come here with nary a please or a thank you, but worse, with a demanding tone that to me implied a total disregard for their children's experience. What's wrong with quietly watching another kid play? Why can't a child use a slide as an instrument? Parents seem able to easily separate the idea of manners from everyday kindness and respect, which is curious because the purpose of manners, as etiquette expert Tamar Adler explains in the *New York Times Magazine*, is to express consideration of another person. It's less about saying the "right" thing at the "right" time and more about letting people know you care about them enough to treat them with respect. She writes, "True courtesy will instinctively check faddish manners at the door in the interest of kindness—which is the root from which the entire family tree of courteous behavior . . . has sprung." Indeed, while we so desperately want our children to remember to say this or that to show their appreciation, the speed with which we can we throw our own patience, consideration, and respect out the window is fairly astonishing. It's as if we have one standard for the way we want our children to present themselves to the world and another standard entirely when it comes to the way we talk to them.

> It's as if we have one standard for the way we want our children to present themselves to the world and another standard entirely when it comes to the way we talk to them.

Is Modeling Enough?

While I was working on becoming a better role model (i.e., a better all around person!), I couldn't help but wonder whether modeling manners was going to be enough to "teach" Jules and Hudson how to be kind and considerate. It required faith and patience, and caring a lot less about what others thought of my parenting and of my kids when Jules and Hudson didn't follow my example. (This is perhaps the biggest challenge of all—and maybe near impossible when parents or in-laws are around.) Ironically, I was convinced of modeling's efficacy one day while driving with Hudson, who was then just two years old. As I was getting on the freeway, a car came out of nowhere and cut me off. Swerving out of the way, I screamed, "What an . . ." But I caught myself!

"Asshole," Hudson said matter-of-factly from his car seat, finishing my thought for me.

See? I said to myself, looking at the bright side. *Modeling works!* What was Hudson going to do? Selectively opt not to learn please and thank you from me and John and only adopt our curses?

In fact, sometimes I could be pretty smug about the success of my modeling approach. I remember the day when Jules, then four, asked me for a smoothie (without saying please). After I'd chopped and blended, I gave her a frothing masterpiece, which she took without a thank-you. *Hmmm,* I thought. *A little gratitude would be nice.* However, she did smile broadly. That counts! My "thank you" shouldn't have to come exactly as the world expects it. Then, a couple of minutes later, she put her glass down and said, "That was *so* good! Thank you, Mama!" *See?* I said to no one. *You couldn't ask for more genuine appreciation than that!*

And Hudson, man, he can be so polite that sometimes he takes it to another level.

> My kids could be pretty damn polite. Sometimes. When they were well fed. Not tired. Not focused on something else.

"Ready for dinner?" I said one day.

"No, thank you," said Hudson. "But thank you for asking." I don't know where he got that one, but it's as disarming as it is charming.

So my kids could be pretty damn polite. Sometimes. When they were well fed. Not tired. Not focused on something else too intently. And I have to admit, it felt good. But of course, sometimes they weren't. As the kids got older—more into the sixes, sevens, and eights—I had to admit there were times when they didn't say what I had hoped they would, and it stung. Or I was embarrassed because in front of others they'd sound so demanding or abrasive. Or insensitive and inconsiderate. Self-centered. Sometimes I'd feel incensed. *Don't talk to me like that! I'm your mother! After all that I do for you?* Other times I'd wince and think, *Did you not hear her just say hello to you? How hard can it be to say hi?* Sometimes they'd open a gift and run off to play with it without thanking the gift giver. *Modeling isn't enough!* I had to admit to myself. I wanted to be able to say something to my kids when I felt unappreciated or disrespected, but what? What could I say without spoon-feeding them what I longed to hear? The answer was simple: I'd tell them how I felt.

Share Your Feelings

Instead of assuming a position of superiority—i.e., acting like the all-knowing grown-up whose job it is to remind my kids how to be proper—I decided to be vulnerable and share with the kids how what they said (or didn't say) made me feel. My intention was to be both honest and informative. Back in my couple's therapy days I learned to use "I messages" to tell John how something he did made me feel—it allowed me to tell him the problem I had with what he did without blaming him personally, because blaming only makes people defensive.

Essentially, an I message is: "I feel ____ when you ____ ." The great thing about I messages is that they inherently acknowledge that the problem is based on one's personal experience and not objective fact. The truth is, what offends one person may not even register with another. For example, while I may feel disrespected when a child doesn't ask me for something "nicely," someone else may genuinely not give a rat's ass. Certainly, plenty of families communicate without the pleases and thank-yous that I like to hear and they don't seem to feel disrespected.

When you're forming an I message, it can also be very helpful to request what you'd prefer in the future. For instance:

> "I feel unappreciated when you tell me to get something for you. In the future, I'd appreciate it if you'd ask me in a kind way."

That's all. No need for anything like "Excuse me? How dare you speak to me that way! You expect me to get everything for you like you're a princess?" Here are a couple of other examples of I messages around the issue of manners:

> "When Carolyn says hello and you don't respond, I am concerned she feels you don't care for her all that much. In the future, it would be polite to say hi or wave."

This gives the child the chance to say, "Well, I don't like her that much," which could be the start of an important conversation. Or the child might realize that Carolyn felt slighted and say "hi" next time.

"When you open Aunt Sandy's present and don't say thank you, I worry she feels you don't appreciate the gift or the time and energy she put into getting it for you."

This might present an opportunity to talk about gifts and how it's not always easy to guess what someone likes, but it always feels nice to be thanked for the effort of getting or making the gift.

It's Never Too Late to Say Thank You

've found that often Jules and Hudson respond to these kinds of I statements with a genuine "Oh, sorry, Mom, I didn't realize. . . ." Then, for instance, in the case of opening a gift without saying thank you, we can brainstorm how to let the gift giver know the present was appreciated.

A phone call?

A thank-you note?

A quick video wearing the sweater or playing with the toy?

An email with a photograph?

There are so many options. It's never too late to say thank you. My motto is *better late than coerced*. Remembering that you can always follow up later can take the pressure off you and your kid in the moment. In the meantime, *I* can do the thanking for my kids. I can be the role model. "What a gorgeous sweater. I love the color, and it's so cozy. Where did you find it? I'm sure when she's finished playing with her friends, she'll try it on!" Which brings me to my overall approach when it comes to my kids and manners in public. Modeling, yes. But beyond modeling, I aim to be their wingman.

Be a Wingman

Just because our children are often welcoming, chatty, and polite doesn't mean they will be in every situation. Sometimes kids won't reply to a "hello" or won't answer a question a grown-up has asked because they feel shy or overwhelmed or insecure or just not quite adept at grown-up conversation. There are so many variables to take into consideration. Do they know the person? Are they in familiar surroundings? Is the person genuine or condescending? I find it helpful to try to imagine how I'd feel if, say, I was walking into the Lakers' locker room. All these huge basketball players towering over me; everyone else feeling comfortable in the space, and me feeling at once intrigued and totally overwhelmed.

"Uh, hi."

Or, I know that if I were meeting someone like Beyoncé or Barack Obama, I'd appreciate a wingman—a friend to introduce me and make chatty conversation that gently includes me. And that's what I try to do for my kids. For example, when my friend Stacey, whom I hadn't seen in a couple of years, came over for a visit, Jules wasn't her usual outgoing self.

> Sometimes kids won't reply to a "hello" because they feel shy or overwhelmed or insecure or just not quite adept at grown-up conversation.

"Hi, Jules!" Stacey said in a very friendly way. "How are you!? What are you up to these days?"

Jules looked down at the ground and started to back away. So in jumped her wingman.

"Jules, I bet you don't even remember Stacey. Last time she visited you were only four. Why don't we all go into the living room and color for a bit? I'll get some markers and paper."

Coloring together took the pressure off making conversation, which ironically allowed it to start flowing naturally. Soon Jules and Stacey were deep into talking about everything. My work as a wingman was done. There certainly was no need for something mortifying like "Jules, I heard Stacey just ask you a question. . . ."

Chill

And sometimes, when it's just us and my kids sound abrupt or curt, I just go right ahead and give them the benefit of the doubt. They're in a hurry. They're preoccupied. They're hungry. I know they love me. So it wasn't the nicest way of asking—it also wasn't the worst. I let it go. As I'm sure they—and John—*often* do with me.

CHAPTER SEVEN

"SHARE!"

"Any euphemism ceases to be
euphemistic after a time and the
true meaning begins to show through.
It's a losing game, but we keep on trying."
—Joseph Wood Krutch

I t took me a couple of years into my life as a parent to realize
that making your kid give her toy to another kid who wants it is
the way of the modern playground. It's called "sharing." And boy
can it cause lots of drama. For kids. For their parents. And certainly
for me.

I'd been forewarned.

Back when I was pregnant for the first time, I was hiking with
my friend Marni, mother of one-and-a-half-year-old Timmy, when
she told me about a playdate gone wrong.

"Timmy wouldn't give Oliver his toy! He just kept on playing with it! All the moms were just looking at me. Waiting for me to *do* something . . . Finally, one of them told me I should give him a time-out so he'd learn to share. I was so embarrassed. I didn't know what to do. What do you think?"

"Oh, gosh, how would I know? Is that really what I have to look forward to?"

"Just you wait!"

Two Babies, One Toy

Jules was eight months old when her first mini-battle over a toy broke out. The object of contention was a Wiffle ball. Fortunately, we were at our Saturday morning parent-and-me class at the RIE Center and our teacher, Francesca, could manage "the crisis," because I had no idea what to do.

What happened was, Jules had inserted her finger into a hole in the Wiffle ball and was happily waving it around when, unbeknownst to her, it caught the eye of ten-month-old Carter, who was crawling across the room to get a closer look. In an instant, Carter's finger went into another hole. And so it began. He pulled. She held on. He pulled harder. She pulled back. They grunted. They tugged. When I couldn't take it anymore, I shot a *Do something!* look at Francesca, who, as it turned out, was on it.

"Jules, Carter, I see you both want the ball. I'm coming closer," she informed them as she slowly moved over and sat down near the struggling duo. "It's *frustrating*, isn't it?" she added knowingly, as if they spoke perfect English.

Just then, Jules let go. Carter had won! *Well, of course he had! He's so much bigger!* I thought. *So unfair! She was playing with it first!*

Seconds later, Carter dropped the ball and crawled away. Apparently, it wasn't so interesting after all. Jules didn't seem upset by it; she'd already moved on to playing with something else. *What ball?*

The people who cared were me and the other parents.

"That's all we're supposed to do?" Carter's dad, Ed, asked incredulously. "'You both want it. I'm coming closer'?"

"Not always," Francesca said, laughing softly. "I said that to let them know an adult was aware of their struggle and that I was here to help if need be."

"But they can't understand you!" Ed replied, still skeptical.

"Well, actually, babies understand more than we think. And they sense our attention and support. And as you saw, they didn't need my help! They worked it out on their own, though maybe not in a way we think is fair."

I hadn't thought she'd seen my glare. *I guess if Jules didn't care, why should I?*

"But sometimes they don't just let go and move on!" Carter's mom, Julia, interjected. "I mean, there've been plenty of times when Carter and another baby will both just hold on and scream until they're blue in the face! Then what?"

"It can get overwhelming for children sometimes," Francesca said. "If they seem stuck, depending on the situation, I might say, 'Let's look around and see if there are any other balls to play with.' Or for very young babies, I may offer another ball. But another ball may not satisfy them, because it isn't the ball in question."

"Okay, but what if there isn't another ball?" Julia pressed.

"If both children are just too upset and can't seem to move on, then I'll explain to them, 'This seems too hard right now. I'm going to put it away for another time.' It's not meant to be punitive—more practical, so that they can calm down."

"I don't get it," interjected Melinda, another mom. "How are they supposed to learn how to share?"

"Well, that takes time . . ."

"Like how much time?" Melinda asked.

"Years, really. Babies and toddlers are naturally self-centered. Caring how others feel is a process, and one that starts with us caring how our children feel."

Hmmm. Interesting. Food for thought.

Two Toddlers, One Toy

When Jules was two and a half, she started going to preschool a couple of hours a day. It was there, thanks to the support of her incredibly patient teachers, that slowly but surely all of the grabbing, tugging, pushing, hitting, and calls of "Mine!" "No, mine!" were replaced with "I'm using it now" and "Can I have a turn when you're done?" Not always, of course. Sometimes, kids would give their toys away when someone asked for them. Who knows—maybe they were done with them or weren't particularly interested. Other times, kids would end up playing with the toy together. Certainly their struggles and tears didn't disappear altogether, but that was to be expected—after all, learning how to stick up for yourself, how to ask for a turn, how to wait for yours, and figuring out how to play together takes time and practice with support from us grown-ups.

> Learning how to stick up for yourself, how to ask for a turn, and how to wait for yours takes time and practice with support from us grown-ups.

Much to the surprise of some parents, the teachers never imposed any "You get it for five minutes and then it's Taylor's turn for five minutes" rules, because although such a system may seem fair, it's not, as

Jules's preschool teacher, Kathleen, explained to all of us during a parent education meeting one night. "At the core of our philosophy here," she said, "is children's *self-directed* play and exploration of materials. A child at play is a child learning—in their own way, at their own pace. So, if we were to stop kids every five minutes so someone else could have a turn, not only would we be directing their play but we'd be interrupting their work. Which would be frustrating. Think of yourselves. You wouldn't want someone to stop you in the middle of writing at your computer or reading a book so someone else could have a turn with it for five minutes. I know it would drive me crazy! It would break my train of thought. It's the same principle." Furthermore, she added, "Whereas one kid may be satisfied with a quick burst of playing with something, another may need a half hour to fully explore and enjoy it."

It made sense. Duly noted.

The Moral Correctness of Sharing

As a new mom, I'd forgotten all about my friend Marni's warning about parents expecting their kids to "share" in the "immediately hand over your toy to a kid who wants it" sense of the word, but a few trips to our local park soon set me straight.

At first when Jules and I would go to the playground and the inevitable struggle broke out between her and some kid over a toy, I'd naively do my best to embody Francesca: "I see you both want the truck. . . . It's hard, isn't it?" Or if someone was grabbing something from Jules, I might remind her, "You can let them know you're using your shovel right now." Or I may have said to a grabbing kid, "This is Jules. I see you like her truck. It's pretty cool, isn't it? You can ask her for a turn when . . ." Well, other parents looked at me like *Enough with the new-age parenting psychobabble, lady, just make your kid give my kid the toy already.* When I wouldn't, some parents would speak to me through their kids saying things like, "I know honey, it's *really sad* when a child can't share, isn't it?" or "Obviously she's still learning to share."

I also noticed that when other kids did "share" in the way the parents expected them to (i.e., immediately), they'd be lavishly praised: "Now that's my good girl! See how happy you made your little friend? That's very generous of you!"

Some kids, when they didn't get the toy they sought, were pretty good at trying to convince other kids to let them have it.

"Share to show you care!" one kid repeated over and over like a campaign slogan.

I even overheard a five-year-old say to a girl, "You *have* to share with me. Those are the rules! God likes it when we share!"

"Who's God?" she asked.

Good question, I thought.

> Sharing has somehow come to mean "Immediately fork over your toy to someone who wants it."

Apparently, not only has sharing somehow come to mean "Immediately fork over your toy to someone who wants it" but, as such, it has also managed to acquire a reputation as the morally right, just, and proper thing to do—no matter the circumstances, no shades of gray. Which, when I stopped to think about it, is no small feat for a prosaic little word that can actually mean "use simultaneously," "divide up," or "take turns"—all of which are actions that could just as easily be inspired by genuine generosity as not. Nonetheless, as a result of sharing's exalted playground status, I've seen many parents go to great lengths to get their kids to hand over their toys to those who want them, when they want them, with the hope, I imagine, that in so doing, they're teaching their kids how to be kind, considerate, generous, and neighborly. Here's but one example of such a lesson.

Sharing at All Costs

I was pushing Jules on the swing when two-and-a-half-year-old Theo walked up carrying an enormous orange drum and a single drumstick, wearing a huge smile. Oh, the simple joys of life. Theo proudly set the drum down at the edge of the sandbox and had at it.

Thwack. Bang. Bam. Bam. Bam.

He was in heaven for a good solid twelve seconds until a much taller three-year-old named Sam ran over, wrangled the stick out of Theo's hand, and started banging the drum himself.

Bam. Bam. Bam.

"Mine! Mine!" Theo screamed, reaching and jumping for the drumstick that Sam had lifted high over his head.

Instantaneously, from opposite ends of the playground, their parents descended on the scene.

"Sam!" Sam's mom whisper-screamed. "Give the drumstick back to the little boy. It's not yours."

"Theo," Theo's dad calmly said to his screaming son, "Remember? You *have* to share your toys."

When Sam didn't just say, "Oh, right, Mom! Sure. I just got carried away because his drum is so awesome. But yeah, I'll give him his drumstick back. No problem" and Theo didn't say, "Ahh, sharing! That's right. I'm supposed to be generous! I'm more than happy to let this kid (who I've never seen before, who yanked my stick out of my hand) play my drum all he wants. I don't know what came over me," the parents continued to try to get their sons to do what they believed was right.

"Saaaaaam! Give. It. Back."

"Theeeooooo! Toys are for sharing."

"Mine! Mine!" Theo continued to shriek.

Finally, Theo's dad put his hand up to Sam's mom and said, "Thanks, but Theo needs to learn to share." So she shrugged an *as you wish* shrug and let her son play Theo's drum while Theo continued to scream and thrash about in enraged desperation. When it was clear that Theo wasn't about to sit quietly by while Sam had all the fun, his dad picked him up and carried him away so Sam could play in peace. Ten minutes or so later, when a calmed-down Theo returned to the playground, he naturally beelined for his drum just as Sam's mom managed to get Sam to hand over the drumstick.

Bam. Thwack. Bam. Thwack. Bam. Bam. Bam. Bliss at last.

Then, not more than a couple of moments later—I kid you not—Owen showed up at the park, and, that's right, Owen wanted to play Theo's drum. But this time, Theo was on it: When Owen reached for his drumstick, Theo held onto it with his life as another heated battle broke out.

> It was as if Theo's dad felt a responsibility to every child at the park who took a fancy to Theo's drum.

"Mine! Mine!" Theo wailed.

At this point, all eyes were on Theo's dad, who quickly returned to his son's side.

"Don't you like Owen?" his dad gently asked, this time employing a new strategy: logic! "Isn't he your friend? Don't you want your friend to enjoy your drum? We share with our friends." (*Apparently "we" also share with strangers like Sam*, I thought, wondering if every kid at the park qualified as a "friend.")

Clearly the answer was no. No, Theo didn't want "his friend" to enjoy his drum. He wanted to enjoy it himself—which is why, I imagined, he brought it to the park in the first place. And so he firmly held onto his drumstick. Undeterred, Theo's dad unfurled

Theo's tiny fingers and took the drumstick and handed it to Owen.

"Here you go, Owen," he said. And then to Theo he added, "Toys are for sharing."

It was as if Theo's dad felt a responsibility to every child at the park who took a fancy to Theo's drum. As if no child, God forbid, should have to suffer the pangs of interest for longer than a single second. Which, I imagined, confused Theo. Why should his dad favor them over him, his own son? And so it went, that every child's desire became Theo's burden.

Well, if I thought Theo had lost it before, I was mistaken. I translated his Wailing and Thrashing Mach II to mean *Eff you Dad! Why can't I play my own drum for two minutes? You only care how other kids feel but what about me?! Sharing sucks!* And away Theo was whisked, all eyes on them. I imagined Theo's dad thinking something like *This is the work of parenting—not always pleasant, but I have to stand my ground. It's my job to teach him right from wrong.* I knew in my heart that Theo's dad was trying his best to do right by both his son and the community. Nonetheless, I went home that day pretty rattled by the whole episode. And I couldn't help but wonder how Jules processed the whole thing from her perch on the swing. It was all pretty dramatic.

I kept replaying it over and over again in my head, trying to pinpoint what distressed me so much. It's not like Theo's dad ever raised his voice; on the contrary, he remained exceedingly calm throughout. And based on what he was saying to Theo, it seemed he'd warned him in advance that if he brought the drum to the park it had to be "shared." However, it's uncertain whether Theo, at just two years old, understood what he was agreeing to. After all, toddlers, with their still developing brains, aren't known for their ability to think ahead.

Maybe what most upset me was my hunch that at some point in the not too distant future, Theo would eventually start to "share" in the way his dad wanted him to, because who would want to go through that level of pain and humiliation over and over again? I cringed at the thought of his dad then praising him for being "generous," satisfied he'd accomplished his goal, as if his son was now truly magnanimous instead of just cowed.

Or maybe it was because if the tables were turned and someone came over to Theo's dad in the middle of an important phone call and forced him to give up his iPhone simply because the other person wanted it and then held him back when he protested, it would never be construed as remotely positive. In fact, it could be characterized as *stealing*. So how did we come to think that making a kid "share" a toy that he is clearly still playing with is not only okay to do, but a good way to teach generosity?

Or maybe it was because I'd recently read blogger Vicki Bergman's satirical post about how parents should give their kids "gifts" with warning labels that read:

> This item is on loan to you under certain conditions. It can and will be taken away from you at the will of your parents, for any reason, including but not limited to: your room is too messy, your grades are too low, you were grumpy one day, you made a mistake.

To her list I'd add "If you don't 'share' it with another kid when they want it." For if a kid doesn't have a genuine choice whether or not to give someone their toy, then it shouldn't be called sharing, and the toy shouldn't be called "theirs." Enough with all the euphemisms. Call a spade a spade: "Here's my parent's toy that they're forcing me to give you. Enjoy!" And if you never truly own anything—if you never have control over your toys, your food, your room, or your clothes—then how will you ever know what feelings and relationships would genuinely inspire you to want to let someone use something special to you? Feelings like love, appreciation, and fear of losing a friend. These things can't be rushed or forced.

And speaking of force, I also found it depressing that Theo's dad resorted to using his size and strength to get his son to "share." He didn't physically hurt him in any way, but I consider prying his hand open and removing Theo from the playground using force. What lesson did that teach Theo? That if someone doesn't do what you want when you want him to and you truly believe it's the *right* thing to do, you can use force to make it happen?

All of that upset me, but I finally pinpointed what hit me the hardest: that Theo's protests fell on deaf ears. Here he was doing everything he possibly could to be heard—screaming and crying, yelling "Mine!," jumping up and down and trying to hold onto his drumstick with every ounce of strength he had—and yet his dad's response was essentially *You can cry all you want, but this is the way it is.* To his father, Theo's distress—which I imagine was a caustic mix of feeling betrayed, powerless, angry, and confused—was merely an inconvenience to overcome in the name of teaching him an important lesson rather than actual suffering to be heard, understood, and responded to in a caring way. It's hard enough to feel those painful feelings; it's even worse to feel them and think that no one—particularly your own dad—cares that you are so upset. That's a recipe for feeling alone and helpless. And in this case, not just alone and helpless, but feeling, likely subconsciously, that you must be bad if you don't want to do something Dad thinks is so good. All this anguish over what? A few minutes banging a drum? It strikes me as nothing short of astounding that one highly subjective interpretation of a single verb—"Share!"—can contribute to so much collateral damage.

> Theo's distress was merely an inconvenience to overcome in the name of teaching him an important lesson rather than actual suffering to be responded to.

It's Okay Not to Share

magine my delight when I discovered a new book that hit the parenting market in 2012: *It's OK Not to Share and Other Renegade Rules for Raising Competent and Compassionate Kids.* In the title chapter, author Heather Shumaker similarly, if not more elegantly, argues that "Sharing on demand interrupts play, erodes parent child trust, and teaches false generosity." Indeed. In particular, I appreciated Shumaker's research on how a child's ability to empathize and their desire to be generous evolves over the course of several years and can't be rushed by good intentions:

> You can wish your two-year-old could share, but developmentally, she's not ready. Sharing comes in stages. Young kids can be trained to give up a toy on command to please an adult, but experts on children's moral development, like William Damon, say a notion of true, altruistic sharing doesn't begin until elementary-school age. Children younger than five share sometimes, most often to get something they want.

> "Sharing on demand interrupts play, erodes parent child trust, and teaches false generosity."
> —Heather Shumaker

Elementary school! I wish that could be announced with a megaphone at every playground across the country.

Furthermore, Shumaker shares that studies show "true generosity is slower to develop in children who are forced to share on demand. Kids will often get sneaky, share only to please an adult, and never share if an adult isn't watching." Shumaker recommends what she calls "extended turns"—letting kids play with something until they are good and done with it—which is very similar to the model

Jules's preschool advocated. She writes, "Keeping a toy when another child wants it is not the mark of a selfish child, simply a busy one. Protect your child's right to play and teach her to say, 'I'm not done yet.' Interrupting play—and instantly rewarding the other child—doesn't benefit either child. Waiting for a turn teaches great lessons in delayed gratification. Young children aren't ready to share; they are ready to take turns. Turn-taking empowers kids and helps teach courtesy, awareness, and spontaneous generosity." Touché.

Theo and Sam, Take Two

So how, in a perfect world, could Theo's dad have helped both Theo and Sam? Perhaps something like this:

"Hey, guys! It looks to me like you both want to play Theo's drum, is that right?"

Maybe the kids nod.

"I'm Theo's dad, George. What's your name?"

"Sam."

"Hi, Sam, do you know Theo? Sam, this is Theo. Theo, this is Sam. I can see you both love drums! And this big orange one is pretty cool. Sam, I bet you saw Theo playing and it looked so fun that you wanted to try it yourself, huh?"

Sam nods.

Then, perhaps, "Theo, I saw you trying to tell Sam that you were still playing. Is that right?"

Theo nods.

"Well, Sam, I can't let you just take Theo's drumstick from him, but you can definitely ask him if you can try it when he's done. Or maybe you guys have some other ideas how to work this out in a fair way?"

You never know what kids may come up with—particularly when properly introduced and not treated as adversaries. Maybe Sam would pick up a stick from the ground and they'd play the drum together. Or Sam might play with his hands. Or maybe Theo would say he was still playing and then Theo's dad could ask Sam to respect that while also empathizing with how hard it might be to accept. Theo's refusal to give up his drum may not win him any friends, but right now friendship might not be a priority for him. It isn't for many toddlers, who are known for parallel playing—playing alongside others without engaging very much with them. We can't ask Theo to be someone he's not yet.

Conflict Is Healthy

Conflicts over objects are as inevitable as they are healthy. When we insist kids "share," it robs them of the opportunity to work things out on their own. My goal is to equip my kids with tools so that (eventually) they can advocate for themselves, negotiate, and creatively problem-solve based on what they think is fair and how others feel. Working things out through play is a great way to do this. As Peter Gray, research professor of psychology at Boston College and author of *Free to Learn*, explains, "Play serves many valuable purposes. It is a means by which children develop their physical, intellectual, emotional, social, and moral capacities. It is a means of creating and preserving friendships. It also provides a state of mind that is . . . uniquely suited for high-level reasoning, insightful problem-solving, and all sorts of creative endeavors." And so, it follows, when and how to share is something that will change based on who our kids are playing with, how old they are, what they are playing, and how they feel about it.

CHAPTER EIGHT

"SAY 'SORRY'!"

"I'm sorry that my forced apology
sounded insincere. I'll try to make it
more convincing next time."
—Unknown

I f I step on someone's toe, "Oh, I'm sorry!" rolls off my tongue
before I can even think about it. However, if I do something gos-
sipy like tell a friend something another friend has told me in
confidence and she finds out (!), well then, I'm really sorry. I'm
mortified and ashamed of myself. And I can imagine my friend
feels a mix of betrayed, indignant, and maybe embarrassed. It's a
mess and, of course, I know I need to apologize. And yet, in cases
such as this, I've often found myself doing everything to avoid it.

I'll blame the friend with whom I shared the information (*I told
her not to tell anyone!*) even though she did exactly what I'd done.

I might even blame the person I've hurt. (*For being so damn private in the first place! For caring what others think! For trusting me!*)

Perhaps, I'll minimize the harm I caused. (*It's not such a big deal! She'll get over it.*)

And/or, I'll just hope that time will make it all go away, even though I know that time never seems to erase the memory of precisely the things we really want it to.

Curiously, I can be plagued by such feelings. I can empathize with the person I've hurt, and know what I need to do to try to make things right. Yet, too often, just the very thought of swallowing my pride, admitting what I've done wrong, looking someone in the eyes, telling them how sorry I am, and asking if there's anything I can do just kinda kills me. I'm overcome by shame, riddled with a paralyzing discomfort. Intellectually I know apologizing is a gift. What else can instantly tell a friend that I value and care about them while also relieving some guilt? I should jump at the chance to say "I'm sorry." And yet, too often, I don't. *Tomorrow*, I tell myself. It's a day that rarely comes.

I know I'm not alone. Hell, if apologizing was easy, or even just not too hard, Judaism wouldn't carve out a full ten days each year—the so called "Days of Awe" between Rosh Hashanah and Yom Kippur—to right the wrongs we've left dangling. During this time, Jewish tradition encourages us to *Reach out! Ask for forgiveness. Start the new year unburdened, healed, and connected. Those you've hurt will feel better. You'll feel better!* Most of us know this to be true and yet too often we let our guilt continue to fester.

As a parent, I hoped there was something I could do to make apologizing come more easily to Jules and Hudson than it has to me. I wanted them to be able to face their mistakes and those they've hurt, knowing it's part of being human, and to do their best to right their wrongs. I wanted them to understand that apologizing is about learning, communicating, growing, and strengthening friendships. Was that possible?

I knew for certain what I didn't want to do: Instruct them to "Say 'sorry'"—an approach I'd noticed was quite popular. Countless times I've watched as a parent of a child who has just hit or grabbed something from another kid admonish, "That's not nice!" followed by a push to "Say 'sorry!'" If the child demurs or flat-out refuses, then a time-out or some such threat is put on the table, which is usually enough to get the child to capitulate.

"Sorry," he mutters.

"That's better!" the parent pronounces, seemingly satisfied.

Whenever this happens, I'm always struck by how unimportant it is to the parent whether the child is truly sorry. It's like *Sincerity, shmincerity, remorse, shmorse. Overrated!* Folks also don't seem to care why their kid did whatever he did or even how the hurt party feels about it. It's as if it's assumed that the "victim" should be satisfied by seeing the child forced into apologizing, and that's that.

> **When we force our kids to apologize, we skip over all of the essential stages that often lead to a genuine apology.**

Not only do problems not get looked at, but apologies get framed as a punishment. Which they shouldn't be. When we force our kids to apologize, we skip over all of the essential stages that often lead to a genuine apology. The blaming. The realization of what you've done. The self-reflection and pangs of remorse. Working up the courage to apologize. Finding the humility. And then feeling the unparalleled relief that comes with getting the words out. Each stage has its own time line and serve its own important purpose.

Their Brains Aren't Ready

Meanwhile, when we make our kids say "sorry," we're rushing them to a place where they aren't ready to be. Being egocentric is a hallmark of young children—they're literally not yet able to see a situation from another's point of view. Not being able to adopt another's perspective means they're not yet able to feel genuine empathy, thus there's no genuine apology. Dr. James M. Herzog, a psychiatrist and professor at Harvard Medical School, explains that a "toddler cannot feel empathy for a friend who gets hurt at the playground. She may match the friend's mood and begin to cry, but she won't feel true empathy, which demands a more highly developed cognitive faculty as well as emotional identification." Which is not to say children can't appear to be sorry. They can! Karen Alonge, an interpersonal communication expert, explains:

> **Being egocentric is a hallmark of young children—they're literally not yet able to see a situation from another's point of view.**

What may look to some adults like remorse in a young child may in fact be something else—perhaps simple curiosity, an instinctive mirroring response (such as crying when they hear another child cry), or even a learned response, such as an empty "I'm sorry" with no real regret behind it. Children may also react from shame or fear and try to smooth things over with a quick apology if they have been frequently chastised or punished. But it's not likely to be true chagrin or regret for harm they have caused until after age six or seven.

Mediator Instead of Judge and Jury

So what to do when your kid hurts another child?

Forget playing judge and jury. Instead, go more the route of mediator. This I learned one morning at Jules's preschool during the period when parents hang out for a bit before saying good-bye, while the kids play in the yard. I was sitting on a bench when I saw a conflict erupt.

Neva and Maggie were playing "potion" with some sticks and a puddle of water. It must have looked like fun to Albert, because he picked up another stick, walked over, and start poking at the water, too.

"Go away!" Maggie said to him.

Albert didn't.

"You can't play!" Maggie added.

Albert pushed her. And she cried. And Neva? Well, she had an idea. "I'm going to tell on you!" It seemed to me that Neva figured that if Albert was in trouble for pushing Maggie, then they could get back to playing their game in peace.

Then Diana, one of the teachers, arrived on the scene, and I watched a master in action. "Are you okay, Maggie?" she asked.

"Albert pushed me!" she said through her tears.

"I saw that," she said softly. "I'm sorry that happened." Then she turned to Albert. "Albert, pushing isn't the way to solve a problem," she explained. "I saw you wanted to play potion with the girls."

"Yeah."

"Is that why you pushed Maggie? You were mad she didn't want you to play?"

Albert nodded.

"I can understand that. Do you want to tell Maggie and Neva how it felt not to be included?"

No, he didn't.

"Girls," Diana said, "it seemed like you were having so much fun playing that you were worried Albert joining you might mess up the game."

"Yeah!" Maggie said in a way that said Diana had nailed it.

"I know that feeling," Diana said, empathizing.

"He doesn't know how to play potion. . . ." Neva added.

"Ahh. You were worried it would take too much time to explain?"

More head nods.

"Well, girls, can you think of a way to include Albert in the game?"

This got them thinking.

"He could get the cups!" Neva offered.

"Or be my assistant!" Maggie said, smiling.

"Albert . . ." Diana started to say, but they were all off and running. Albert had gone to get some cups from the sandbox, and the girls were back mixing their potions.

Whoa! I was impressed. Did they "work through it" all the way? I don't know. They all seemed over it.

Albert didn't have to apologize for pushing Maggie.

Maggie didn't have to apologize for excluding him.

Neva didn't have to apologize for trying to get Albert in trouble.

Hitting wasn't condoned.

Tattling wasn't condoned.

Excluding wasn't condoned.

Hopefully they all got some glimmer of insight into what fueled their hurtful behavior and could see there were other ways to work things out. What wouldn't have served anyone was what I see more often:

"Albert, go say 'sorry' to Maggie."

"Sorry."

"Good job. Now leave them alone and let them play."

I realize that it's not always going to work out as well as it did with Maggie, Neva, and Albert. A kid might be more seriously hurt, which means they need to be attended to first. Do they need some ice? A hug? The kids may be screaming and crying. Some may have run off or refuse to be a part of the conversation. The idea is to wait until everyone is calmer before proceeding. And if one party has left the scene, go to the others and figure out what happened from their perspective. Even if it doesn't wrap up so neatly, the goal is to help the kids communicate and figure out a solution as amicably as possible. Every effort toward this is a step in the right direction and sets the groundwork for future problem-solving. Expecting young kids to be sorry for hurting someone because they felt hurt is just unrealistic.

> **The goal is to help the kids communicate and figure out a solution as amicably as possible.**

Neutral and Curious

Let's take a look at a bit bigger mess with slightly older kids and less closure.

I had taken Hudson, then four, to his friend's fifth birthday party. I was in the kitchen talking to some other parents when I heard the screams. And then in ran the boy and his wound. While there was no blood, it was dental-impression clear and dental-impression deep. Not surprisingly, the kid was hysterical.

"Oh, my God, Aiden!" his mother gasped. "What happened? My poor baby!"

Through his huffing and puffing, Aiden, a child I'd never met before, pegged Hudson as the culprit.

Shit! Oh, God, here we go. Hudson wasn't a biter per se. He'd done it before, maybe a handful of times, but it had been a year since the last incident. I'd thought we were through that stage.

As Aiden's mom tended to her bawling son, holding him and consoling him with a nonstop string of "Oh, my poor baby," she'd periodically flashed me looks that I read as saying, *Your son is a monster. How could he do this to my angel?*

I was mortified, of course, and rattled. This was terrible! I apologized profusely both to Aiden and his mom, for indeed I was sorry. Really sorry. I brought Aiden some ice and a glass of water. I found some Band-Aids and Neosporin. Then I went to find *my* baby. I found him in the playroom on the sofa, cowering under his beloved blankie, sucking two of his fingers, looking shell-shocked. He was in no condition to talk about anything, let alone offer the apology that I imagined Aiden's mother was expecting. Hudson needed comfort, too and time to recalibrate his nervous system.

What, I had to wonder, *had caused Hudson to bite Aiden like that?*

Kids just don't bite other kids out of nowhere, for no reason. Wondering what provoked Hudson wasn't excusing his violence, but there's always a reason. My intention, as always, was to approach Hudson as neutrally and curious as possible. I was upset. I was worried. But I wasn't mad. *Neutral and curious*, I reminded myself, *neutral and curious.*

"Aiden's really hurt, honey," I said, not telling him anything he didn't know. My approach only caused him to retreat deeper into his blanket, like a turtle retracting into its shell. *Sigh.* I took a few beats and began again.

"Something must have really upset you," I said.

His eyes peeked out.

Doing my best CSI impression, I looked around and found a Styrofoam sword on the floor.

"You guys were playing with the sword?" I surmised.

Hudson barely nodded.

"Hmm, one of you had the sword? And one didn't?" I continued, trying to put the pieces together.

"Actually," another voice started to say—and there was the birthday boy's big brother Ollie, who was eleven—"I saw what happened." (Really! This isn't just convenient storytelling.) "Hudson and Aiden were playing," he continued. "They were both laughing and having fun. Aiden was waving that sword at Huddy, kinda in his face, and Huddy kept pushing it away. He said 'Stop!' but Aiden didn't. And then Huddy bit him."

Aha!

"That sounds scary, Hudson," I said, "having a sword waved in your face over and over again."

He nodded.

"So you bit him to get him to stop because he wouldn't listen to you?"

He nodded again.

So who owed whom an apology?

The kid who wouldn't stop waving his sword in the other kid's face? Or the one who bit him? Of course, I never wanted Hudson to bite again! But when we feel under attack, whether perceived or real, our primitive brain takes over and we go into freeze, fight, or flight. And in this case, Hudson fought back. I'd much prefer him to flee, but I understood why he reacted the way he did. I wanted Hudson to think of a better way to get out of the situation.

> When we feel under attack, our primitive brain takes over and we go into freeze, fight, or flight.

Meanwhile, we had a hurt kid. *Could I get the two boys talking?* I wondered.

I let a little time pass, and then I asked Hudson if he'd like to come with me to check in on Aiden to see how he was feeling and to talk about what happened. Not surprisingly, he just retreated back into his blanket.

So I went back to the kitchen, where Aiden was still cuddled up in his mom's lap.

"How are you doing Aiden?" I gently asked.

"It still *really* hurts," he said.

"I'm so sorry, Aiden. I hope the pain goes away soon. Maybe when you're feeling a bit better, we can all talk together?"

He didn't say anything. And his mom looked at me like I was crazy. *Talk? About what? Your son the monster attacking my angel?*

Ten minutes later, through the window I saw Aiden going down the slide, having a ball. I was glad to see him feeling better. Meanwhile, Hudson seemed totally worn out by the whole episode and asked to go home.

"I think we need to check on Aiden before we leave," I said. He turtled again.

So I went outside to talk to Aiden myself. "Aiden, I'm really sorry Hudson hurt you, and I'm glad you're feeling better. We're going to be leaving soon. Is there anything you'd like to say to Hudson before we go?"

"No," he said, eager to get back to playing.

Okay then. I wasn't going to push it. Another time.

That night, after reading books in bed with Hudson, I brought up the incident again. Time had passed. He'd eaten. He was relaxed. I thought we might be able to give it some closure.

"I don't want to talk about it," Hudson said.

"I can understand that. You probably feel badly about what happened."

Silence.

"I'm worried that when you get really mad or don't feel safe, you'll bite someone again. Biting really, really, really hurts. And you can't do that to people. Ever."

"I know," he said.

"It can help to have another plan in your mind already so if you feel scared you can do that plan instead," I said.

He just listened.

"If that happened again, and he didn't stop when you said stop, what else could you do?"

"Run away."

"Yes! I like that. You can always go away, and if you need help, get an adult. Do you feel bad that you hurt him?" I asked.

He nodded yes.

"You know what I do when I feel like I've hurt someone?" I asked.

He shrugged.

"I tell them I'm sorry. It usually helps them feel better. And me, too."

I left it at that. My lecture was over. Next time we could inch things farther along. And of course, there would be a next time.

In His Own Way, in His Own Time

Now comes the moment you've all been waiting for. Or at least the moment Hudson's mother had been. The moment when he apologizes—unprompted, in his own way, in his own time, after cycling through all the phases that lead to a genuine apology.

Hudson, now seven, was playing at his friend Lane's house when Lane's slightly younger brother Duke came home from his gymnastics class super excited to show Hudson and Lane that he could now do a cartwheel! As I'd hear later, Duke did his best, and Lane was very enthusiastic about it, telling his brother how happy he was for him. Hudson, however, responded by saying, "You're showing off!" Which he wasn't. And not just that, but Hudson added, "I've been able to do that for years!" Ouch. And then finally: "Your legs weren't even straight." Oooff.

Not surprisingly, Duke's feelings were hurt. Really hurt.

Apparently, Duke told Hudson as much. But instead of apologizing, Hudson said Duke could make fun of his flip on the trampoline as payback. (This may not make sense to us, but it was logical to them in a I-hurt-you-so-now-you-can-hurt-me way.)

Which Duke proceeded to do.

Over and over and over and over and over again. He obviously wanted to hurt Hudson's feelings as much as Hudson had hurt his.

Hudson began to cry, but Duke and Lane didn't seem to care, as now they started to watch a video. This hurt Hudson's feelings even more, because he felt his friends didn't care about him.

This is where I came in.

"You guys, Hudson is upset. Can you pause the video and work it out?" I asked.

> You can make your child say sorry, but you can't make them mean it.

"He's just upset because I made fun of his flips, but he said I could because he was mean about my cartwheels," Duke explained.

Hudson tried to defend his poor behavior, "But his cartwheel wasn't even good!"

Oh, God, I thought. *Where is this coming from?*

Duke ran off upset, and with some convincing Hudson and I sat down with Lane to figure it out—even though Hudson was hysterical and furious at Duke for making fun of him, somehow blocking out his part in it entirely.

It finally emerged that Hudson was jealous that his friend Lane seemed to like his brother better than him. Hudson said, "Lane said Duke's cartwheels were so great! And he was so proud of him. But he never is that proud of me." It seems the reason Hudson had pointed out that Duke's cartwheels weren't so great was because he was hurt. Lane tried to explain that he was being supportive of his brother and how hard he had worked, and how much it hurt Duke's feelings that Hudson said his cartwheels were bad.

Then Hudson let out a howl that came from deep within. He realized what he'd done and how he'd hurt Duke. And instead of saying he was sorry or showing any remorse, he said, "Now you hate me! Now everyone hates me." Which is so natural. He wished he hadn't done something so mean, and now he feared everyone would turn against him because he had.

I did my best to assure Hudson that we all say things we later regret. Lane did too. Eventually Hudson started to relax. He didn't go and apologize to Duke, but things calmed down enough for the boys to all play together, and both Hudson and Duke even felt comfortable with Hudson sleeping over. The next morning the boys' mother told me that she happened to be walking by their room when she saw Hudson wake up and say to Duke, "I'm sorry" and then fist-bump. Hudson didn't *have* to say he was sorry to Duke, because all was already copacetic. He certainly didn't have to say it because any adult was watching. But he felt driven to. He just needed time—time to process what happened and to get up the gumption to apologize. His way. And Duke accepted it in his own way.

Certainly you can make your child say sorry, but you can't make them mean it.

CHAPTER NINE

"TICKLE, TICKLE, TICKLE!"

"Appearances are often deceiving."
—**Aesop**

"**H**ere comes the tickle monster . . ." some of us may say as we gleefully wriggle our fingers in the air. Others, preferring the element of surprise, just jump right in and tickle kids under their chins or arms or along their sides, hoping to get a good giggle going.

This chapter isn't about the hidden dangers of something we say as much as something we *do*. Tickle kids. Some love to be tickled. Some hate it. And some love it until they hate it. Me? I've always hated it—though it probably looked like I loved it. And therein lies the problem.

When I was a kid, my sister used to play tickle torture with me. (Never has a game been so perfectly named.) Older and much stronger, it would take her no time to wrangle me onto my back, sit on my stomach, and pin my arms over my head with one hand while she tickled me with the other. Under my arms. On my sides. And somehow she managed to turn around and go at my feet— which are *beyond* sensitive. I'd writhe around utterly miserable, trapped in uncontrollable laughter, unable to squeak out a cry for help. I was entirely at my sister's mercy and had to just suffer until she was good and done with me. Given my early experiences with tickling, you probably won't be surprised to learn that when I was at a kid's birthday party and I overheard my friend Jordana say to her friend Sara, "Lily doesn't want to go on the trip because she's afraid Sam is going to tickle her," I leaned in closer. (I know both families fairly well: Lily is Jordana's five-year-old daughter and Sam is Sara's husband—a good guy.)

So how did Sara respond to the news that her best friend's daughter was afraid of her husband tickling her? She laughed.

"Actually," Jordana continued quite seriously, "I've already talked to Sam about it, and he's promised not to tickle her."

"Oh, you know that doesn't mean much with Sam!" Sara said. "He's such a kid himself! He just loves to have fun with the kids," she continued, laughing.

For some reason, Sara didn't understand that Jordana was not only serious but seriously worried. I thought it was pretty obvious that Jordana was fishing for an assurance like, "Oh, I'll talk to him! Of course I'd hate for Lily to feel nervous around Sam. Not to worry!" Instead what Jordana got was something closer to "That's ridiculous. It's just tickling! Kids love it!" Was Sara embarrassed that her husband inadvertently made Lily uncomfortable, or did she genuinely not get that for some kids tickling can be anything but fun? Particularly when you're a little girl and you're being tickled by a six-foot-three man who can't tell you're not enjoying yourself. That can be pretty scary—scary enough that you told your mom you don't want to go to Hawaii.

> I'd writhe around utterly miserable, trapped in uncontrollable laughter, unable to squeak out a cry for help.

Their exchange reminded me of a similarly strained phone conversation I'd had with my friend Elizabeth. Instead of laughing when I expressed my concern about tickling, though, Elizabeth hung up on me. (I'm not sure which is worse.) We were chatting away when I heard her nine-month-old daughter Poppy start screeching in the background.

"Ooooh!" I winced. "Is Poppy okay?"

"She's not crying. She's laughing!" Elizabeth explained. "Greg's just playing Tickle Monster with her. It's their favorite."

Oh, no! Not Tickle Monster! I thought, my heart racing. "Are you *sure* she loves it?" I asked gingerly.

"Yes! Why?" she replied in a way that said *This better be good.*

"Well," I started, "just because a baby's laughing when tickled doesn't mean they're necessarily enjoying . . ."

"Are you serious? Can you please lay off the parenting advice for once? Believe me, I'm her mother. She loves it," she said. "Anyway, I gotta get some stuff done while Greg's taking care of her."

Click.

Shit!

I was sorry I'd said something, but at the same time I thought *How could I not have? You can't tickle a helpless baby, for God's sake!* Obviously I knew Greg would never tickle Poppy the way my sister had tickled me—not even remotely. And maybe she *was* enjoying it. But the issue isn't whether or not she liked being tickled, it's whether at nine months old, Poppy could let her dad know if it got to be too much. Maybe if her dad was a particularly sensitive observer, yes; but I imagine that like most parents, he took her giggles at face value and assumed she was enjoying it. *That's* the problem: Tickling causes the same physiological reactions as humor—i.e., laughter, goose bumps, and convulsive muscle contractions—which means we can look like we're having the time of our lives while suffering, sometimes greatly.

While my experience told me this was true, it was affirming to read that Richard Alexander, an evolutionary biologist at the University of Michigan, said as much in *The New York Times*. In the article "Anatomy of a Tickle Is Serious Business at the Research Lab" Alexander explains, "Ticklish laughter is not the happy phenomenon that many have assumed it to be. . . . A child can be transformed from laughter into tears by going the tiniest bit too far. . . . [Tickling] does not create a pleasurable feeling—just the outward appearance of one." Vindicated! (Or "Duh"? Depends on your experience.) While I wanted to share the article with Elizabeth, I knew she was expecting an apology, not an "I told you so."

> **We can look like we're having the time of our lives while suffering, sometimes greatly.**

I find it nothing short of fascinating that the laughter ignited by tickling can, on the one hand, express the way someone feels so accurately and on the other, mask one's true feelings so thoroughly. What evolutionary purpose could this possibly serve when, to me, this phenomenon only seems to lead to unnecessary pain?

Theories abound. Many evolutionary biologists and neuroscientists believe (and have proven, to a point) that tickling evolved as a way to show dominance without the threat of serious injury. Like a "friendly" first warning from the mob, tickling someone sent the message "I'm in charge. Don't mess with me"—which I imagine was what my sister was going for (and succeeded at). Others believe that our ancestors tickled their kids because it was a "fun" way to help them build self-defense skills, similar to how today we might send our children to a kung fu class. *Be prepared! It's a cruel world.* And still others suggest that tickling may have evolved as a life-saving mechanism: For instance, if someone had a knife at your throat, which is a particularly sensitive area, and it actually caused you to laugh (in spite of the terror you felt), it just might send the message to your attacker "I'm nice! Don't kill me!" *Hmmm, interesting.*

The Dark Side of Tickling

The truth is, tickling hasn't always enjoyed the sparkling reputation that it does today. Throughout history, there have been many cultures well aware of tickling's ability to inflict pain, and as a result, it's been used as a form of punishment. For instance, during the period of the Han Dynasty, Chinese tickle torture was the punishment of choice for nobility as it caused sufficient suffering but left no marks. And apparently, the Ancient Romans let goats do their dirty work. Offenders would be tied up and have their feet soaked in salt, and then the animals would have at them with their tongues. More recently, I read a harrowing account of a Nazi literally torturing a Jewish prisoner in a concentration camp by tickling him with a feather. So how is it that today we seem to be so oblivious to tickling's dark side?

> Throughout history, there have been many cultures well aware of tickling's ability to inflict pain.

A couple of years ago I wrote a piece for the online parenting magazine *Babble* that exposed this shadier side of tickling, and many readers responded by sharing their own childhood memories:

"I hated and feared being tickled as a child and still do as an adult. It reminds me of gasping for my breath while being suffocated and unable to communicate."

"My mother always tickled me even if I said stop. It was SO FRUSTRATING because I wanted to show her that I was happy and having fun with her, but I felt powerless and controlled."

"I loved being tickled to a point as a child, but several people would ignore the clear requests to stop. Gasping and pinned, it would often end in a panic attack for me that left me crying and running away to calls of 'I didn't hurt you! Don't be such a baby!'"

"Just the words 'tickled pink' provoke horrible flashbacks to a childhood fraught with anxiety."

"My dad never got that I really wanted him to stop. Finally, I kneed him in the balls and then was torn between feeling guilty for hurting him so badly and relieved he finally stopped tickling me."

"Even though I'd yell 'stop!' my dad just *never* got that I meant it—I guess because I was always laughing so hard. So, finally one day when I was 13, while I was struggling to make him stop, I broke his finger! I didn't mean to! But that's when his tickling finally ended for good."

Gasping for breath while being suffocated? Powerless? Pinned? Anxious? Being called a baby? Kneeing your dad in the balls? Breaking a finger? In these accounts, I hear a lot of clear signs and calls to stop, and yet the pleas of each child were routinely ignored. Given that most parents would never want to hurt their children, particularly while having a good time, I wonder whether parents are genuinely deceived by their kids' laughter or are willfully duped. My best guess is that being able to make our kids appear happy so quickly serves us in some way.

A Magic Button

It's almost as if we've come to use tickling like it's a magic button that will change our kids' moods or the way they're feeling about us, for the better.

For example, Jules was playing at the park with her four-year-old friend Maddie when they heard Maddie's name being called from across the playground.

Looking up, they saw Maddie's Aunt Angela smiling and waving. Excited, Maddie dropped her shovel and ran over to say hello.

"Hi!" Maddie said.

"Hi, honey!" Aunt Angela said. When Maddie didn't give her a big hug or otherwise show that she was over-the-top excited to see her aunt, Angela playfully tackled Maddie onto her back in the sand and began tickling her frantically up and down her body. And then it happened: laughter! Maddie was laughing! Wildly! (And squirming as she tried to scramble to her feet.) While not a hug, her giggles were the next best thing for Angela: *proof* that Maddie indeed loved her and that Angela was a fun aunt.

Is it our insecurity that subconsciously drives us to drum up smiles on our kids' faces?

Seconds later, Maddie managed to stand up and quickly ran back to play with Jules.

Somewhat similarly, another day, Jules and a group of her friends were sitting around a table intently coloring when one of the dads walked into the room. The girls were so focused that no one took notice. Soon, the dad came up behind his daughter and started wiggling his fingers in her armpit. Grimacing, she pulled away from him. *I'm working!* she seemed to be saying. Nonetheless, he did it again.

"Stop it!" she groaned.

"What? Relax!" he said defensively. "I'm just tickling you. Be nice."

My guess is that he was searching for a clear sign that his daughter was happy to see him. To his obvious dismay, his tickle didn't inspire the smile he was hoping for.

Is it our insecurity that subconsciously drives us to drum up smiles on our kids' faces? Or our impatience? Something else?

It seems clear that the desire to control our children's feelings and behavior in a "fun" way is at the heart of a lot of tickling, as Tracy, a dad, realized after reading my *Babble* piece. He shared:

> I used to tickle our 3 year old to stop her from doing something I didn't want her to do. But after reading your post, wham! It hit me. It's a form of control! It seemed like a great alternative to yelling or threatening, but it really just immobilizes her and limits her movement. It was something we used as a last resort because if we used it at the wrong time, she would cry (late at night, for example, when she was tired). But then I actually started to remember feeling quite violated when my older siblings tickled me. So I have stopped tickling her.

It's important to reflect on what drives us to tickle our kids. Are we looking for genuine connection? Are we worried that our child is unhappy? Are we avoiding being direct about behavior that's bothering us? Or are we genuinely just wanting to have a little fun rough-housing?

Tickling as a Gateway

'd be remiss if I failed to mention that tickling, unfortunately, is one of the means used by sexual predators to groom their victims. This reality makes it that much more important that we're sensitive to our children's requests to stop and honor their wishes *immediately*. Psychotherapist Tracy Lamperti explains how sexual predators use tickling as a precursor to more damaging (and illegal) behavior:

> Gateways to the victim, also called "grooming," [are] successive, thought-out strategies used by a perpetrator with the victim and/or the family in order to facilitate their being able to carry out the acts of sexual abuse on the child with the highest probability of being able to do it without getting caught.
>
> While not all adults who tickle children are paving the way to sexually abuse them, tickling is a good example of the grooming process.
>
> When trust can be won over and defenses can be disarmed, the offender is then able to have their way with the child. With the example of tickling, the perpetrator is able to publicly and/or privately tickle just a little bit. The act is carried out cheerfully and playfully. In this "controlled experiment" the offender is able to see if anyone is going to set a limit, "Oh, Uncle John, we have a no tickling rule in our family. Stop tickling Sam."

Of course no one wants to think about this. But every time we respect our child's "No" or "Stop!", whether they've said "No" explicitly or via their body language, we help them learn that it's their body and their right to decide what happens to it. And every time we advocate for our children, we honor them.

Tickle Responsibly

Am I saying never tickle your kids? No, I'm not. Really! As I said, I know some kids love it. My friend Eric tells me some of his best childhood memories are of being tickled by his dad. And the truth is, Jules loves it, too. Most of the time. But sometimes she doesn't. And sometimes she does until she doesn't. That's why it's so important to keep in mind that tickling can turn dark on a dime, and we may not notice due to the deceptive nature of the uncontrollable laughter tickling can cause. The good news is that tickling is an opportunity to give our kids the chance to have their voices heard. "Stop" means stop. So I think we can tickle responsibly. Here are my guidelines:

1. If a child is too young to talk, *don't* tickle them. Better safe than sorry.

2. Before you tickle, ask. Yes, this takes away the element of surprise, but again, better safe than sorry. And certainly you can be playful about it.

3. Before you tickle, come up with a signal that means "stop" if the tickling gets to be too much and they're laughing too hard to speak. A three-year-old boy I know said to his babysitter, "I like it when you tickle me, but not always. If I pinch your arm, will you stop?" The plan worked.

CHAPTER TEN

"YOU'RE OKAY!"

"An emotion does not cause pain.
Resistance or suppression
of emotion causes pain."
—Frederick Dodson

There are certain situations when I'd love to hear someone tell me that I'm okay—for instance, if I'm being given the results of a biopsy. At that moment, "You're okay" would be the two greatest words in the world. *I'm not dying! No chemo! No radiation! Hallelujah.*

But say I'm crying to a friend, "I lost my job! I'm broke!" and she responds, "You're okay." Or I twist my ankle and exclaim, "Oww! Shit!" and someone responds, "You're fine." It wouldn't make any sense in these situations, because I'm obviously not okay. Certainly, a friend may ask, "Are you okay?"—which, even though I'm clearly not, I know is shorthand for "I care." Or a friend may try to assure me that I will be okay in the near future. But if I'm crying, grimacing, or otherwise looking miserable, it would be silly for someone to tell me that I'm okay. Unless, of course, I'm a kid. Then I've noticed it's a response that's more common than the common cold.

Reassuring?

Perhaps one of the most classic "you're okay" scenes I've watched play out time and again is when a child is excitedly running somewhere and then—bam!—he face-plants. His knees are scraped, his hands are stinging, and his plans are thwarted. Naturally, he cries. And then there they are, the words of reassurance: "You're okay, buddy . . . just brush it off." Is it only me, or does anyone else find it not merely ironic but just plain odd that we tell kids they're okay at *precisely* the moment when they are anything but? If our goal is to assure our kids they're not seriously injured, then why not just tell them that? Or if they've had a bad dream and we wish to comfort them, perhaps, "It was a dream. I'm here now." But a kid who is in pain is not okay, at least not in that moment, so it doesn't really make sense to tell them they are. To state the obvious, we literally can never know how okay anyone other than ourselves is because we're not them. Our kids' bodies aren't linked to our brains. Vulcans might be telepaths, but humans aren't.

> We literally can never know how okay anyone other than ourselves is because we're not them.

Do any of the following *Enough with the emoting already!* scenes sound familiar to you?

Scene from a Café

A dad is talking to a friend at a café while his year-old daughter sits next to him, strapped into her stroller. Soon their conversation is interrupted by her sounds of discomfort.

"Shhhh!" he says to her sweetly, holding his pointer finger up to his lips. "You're okay."

Unsoothed, her discomfort escalates. So her dad rummages around the diaper bag, finds a pacifier, and pops it in her mouth, all the while trying to keep his conversation going.

She spits it out.

He cleans it off and puts it back in her mouth.

She pops it back out and cries. Still half-engaged with his friend, he finds a jar of baby food, unscrews the lid, fills a spoon, and offers some to his daughter.

She turns her head and continues to cry. She tries to get up, but the straps won't let her.

"Shhhh!" her dad tells her again, looking around the café to see if people are annoyed by her.

"Is she okay?" his friend asks.

"Yeah. She's totally fine . . ." he says and then adds, "I don't know why she's crying."

Scene from a Park

I was sitting on a bench at the park while the kids were playing when up walked a woman holding her newborn flanked by her toddler son and mother. The woman took a seat on another bench to nurse her baby while the boy climbed into the play structure and I returned to reading my book. Soon I heard, "Come on, Eric! You can do it!" It was his grandma. She was trying to encourage him to come down the slide.

"Don't be scared, honey! Grandma's here waiting for you!"

He didn't budge.

"You've done it before! It's fun! Remember?"

He relented, and down he went. As soon as his feet hit the sand, he burst into tears.

"You're okay!" his grandma assured him.

He cried and cried and cried.

"Come on, honey. You're not hurt. You always like the slide!" she reminded him.

Still more tears.

"Let's go on the swings!" she offered, trying to distract him. But it didn't work. He continued to cry. Then, turning to her daughter, the grandma called across the playground, "He's not hurt! I don't know why he's crying. He just went down the slide. He's okay. Don't worry."

Scene from a Soccer Field

An eight-year-old boy sits on the ground next to a picnic bench sobbing before his soccer game. His mom is unloading the cooler while his dad talks to another soccer dad.

"I hate these socks. My favorite socks are at home!" the boy wails.

"Come on, buddy! They're just socks. Don't be silly," his mom says.

He cries louder.

The friend dad says half-jokingly, "OCD much?"

The boy's father rolls his eyes as if to say, *Yeah, can you believe it? Over socks? My son!* Then he instructs his wife, "Just ignore him! It'll teach him not to make a huge thing out of nothing. Believe me, he's okay."

Any Way You Slice It

I've been so fascinated by this phenomenon of adults telling kids that they're either not feeling the way they're feeling or that they shouldn't be feeling what they're feeling that I've been keeping a running list of the various ways I've overheard folks send a similar message.

"It can't be as bad as all that."
"Why do you have to make such a fuss?"
"Get over it."
"That's enough already."
"There's no reason to get so upset."
"Don't be a negative Nancy."
"Come on, really?"
"You're overreacting!"
"Keep a stiff upper lip."
"Chin up."
"Come on! Give Mama a smile!"
"Take it like a man."
"Walk it off."
"Big girls don't cry."
"Don't be so dramatic!"
"Drama king!"
"Give it up already."
"Crocodile tears."
"Don't be such a crybaby."
"No use crying over spilled milk."
"Grow up!"

"Stop the noise."

"Enough already!"

"Come on, don't feel that way."

"You're fine, stop crying."

"Really?"

"Go to your room until you can act properly."

"You're so sensitive!"

"You look prettier with a smile on your face."

And then there are those who kick it up a couple of notches, like the clearly distraught and overwhelmed mom I saw at the market who simply yelled, "STOP CRYING!" to her four-year-old son, as if his body was outfitted with a spigot. When he didn't, she snapped, "Stop it already!" But the tears continued to flow. "Do you want your treat?" she threatened. He nodded through his huffing and puffing. "Then stop crying!" While I hate to have to add them, here are two even harsher variations I've had the discomfort of hearing: "Shut up already! It's fine" and "Stop it right now or I'll give you something to really cry about."

We grown-ups seem to be really comfortable telling children who aren't okay that they're actually just fine. That might be because we're ill-equipped to handle unhappy feelings and tears. We also may not realize that telling a child (or anyone) to stop feeling their feelings is unhealthy. As Sigmund Freud said, "Unexpressed emotions will never die. They are buried alive and will come forth later in uglier ways."

Be Careful What You Wish For

S o how might it feel to be told "You're okay" when you don't feel okay or to "Stop crying!" when you can't help it or that "You're overreacting" when you're simply reacting? My guess is that a kid getting these responses would likely feel ashamed, as in *If I wasn't so sensitive (or needy or weak), I wouldn't feel as I do. Something must be wrong with me.* I imagine a child could also feel alone. *No one cares how I truly feel. No one will help me because I shouldn't feel this way. My feelings drive people away, make them annoyed, or frustrated, or embarrassed by me. I'm only lovable when I have it together.* And so it goes that we pile more upset onto their upset. It's not surprising, then, that some kids do their level best to take our words to heart, as this story from kindergarten teacher Christine Lonergan so clearly illustrates.

Lucas tripped over a bump in the sidewalk and came crashing down, hitting his chest on the wood of a low garden edging. His face changed from fear to pain. And then it went blank for just a second, and I saw him set his mouth in a grim line and jut his chin upward. He pushed himself up to his feet as he stated quickly, loudly, and repetitively, "I'm okay. I'm okay." He held his hands up toward me as a signal to stop and not help him.

I got down on my knees in front of him, looking fully into his face. "I'm okay!" he repeated.

"You don't have to be okay," I told him softly.

His eyes started to fill silently with tears. His lips began to quiver as another child who was close by agreed and said he thought that must have hurt. Lucas nodded at this, and tears began to trace down his cheeks. He allowed me to touch his shoulders at this point, as I looked for bruises.

"You don't have to be okay," I repeated, adding, "All people deserve to get comfort."

Indeed, our children deserve and need our comfort and our support. They shouldn't have to be brave for us. The truth is there is nothing wrong with tears. Or feeling upset. In fact, feeling our feelings are beyond our control. We can only attempt to hide what we truly feel but we can't alter it.

What Drives Us to Clamp Down on Kids' Feelings?

So, why is it so hard for us to remain calm, accepting, and compassionate in the face of our kids' upset? Is it . . .

- Because we love our kids so much that we can't bear to see them suffer, so we tell them they're okay because we so desperately want them to be?
- Because their cries push our already frazzled selves over the edge? *Come on already! I can't take anymore.*
- Because we worry that if we respond with too much attention, they'll learn to "use" tears to get more (as if there was something wrong with needing attention)? *Gotta nip that in the bud!*
- Because we're embarrassed in front of our friends that our kid is *still* crying?
- Because we're afraid that if we acknowledge their feelings, it will give them license to "wallow" and then the madness will never end?

- Because we want to give them some perspective? *It's not the end of the world. They're just socks! There are people with real problems in this world!*
- Because we're trying to toughen them up to prepare them for a cold and indifferent world? *When you grow up no one's gonna care how you feel, so you'd better get used to it.*
- Because we believe displays of emotion are an unseemly indulgence of the weak and self-obsessed—something one should be embarrassed of? *A little decorum, please!*
- Because our kids' distress triggers anxiety in us, and so if we can get their pain to go away, ours will, too?

I imagine that for each of us, depending on the situation, it's a different combination of the above. What can help predict what will push our buttons? Our parents!

Not surprisingly, often the way we respond to our kid's distress is subconsciously driven by the way our parents responded to us when we were upset as children. As the psychologist and parenting coach Carrie Contey explains, "The way you relate to . . . the feelings of . . . your children has everything to do with how you were cared for in your early development. Specifically, your first seven years . . . In early life, we are wiring into our neurology the 'language' of emotion that people are speaking around us. This wiring includes both how people respond to our emotions and how they handle their own." If we want to change the way we respond to our kids, it can help to reflect on how our parents responded to us when we were upset. Were you sent to your room when you "acted out"? Did they roll their eyes? Try to placate you? Ignore you? Threaten you? Or did they set the example of a stiff upper lip, as one mother who posted on my Facebook page did:

I can be very strong willed and will not show any "weakness" (no sadness, crying, anxiety) in front of others—that was how I was raised so it's ingrained in me . . . in the past I have not tolerated whining or crying . . . I have picked up that my daughter, like me, now suppresses her unhappiness and will not cry, even when sad or hurt (she will rather walk away or shut her eyes real tight so no tears come out or just deny her pain, much like I do). Seeing this and realizing the impact of my parenting style breaks my heart.

We don't have to be locked into past patterns. As we become more conscious, we can make changes that will better serve our kids (and ourselves!). To start, it can really help to identify our default responses to our kid's challenging emotions.

Dismissive and Disapproving

n his book *Raising an Emotionally Intelligent Child: The Heart of Parenting*, psychologist John Gottman divides most of the responses parents have to kids' distress into two categories: *dismissive* and *disapproving. Dismissive* parents disregard, ignore, or trivialize their children's so-called negative emotions by saying things like "You're okay," "It's not such a big deal," and "Brush it off." *Disapproving* parents are critical of their children's displays of emotions and chastise or punish them for what they deem "inappropriate" expressions. They're more apt to say things like "Why do you have to make such a fuss?" "Go to your room until you can act properly," and "If you respond like that, then I'm taking away your toys."

> If we want to change the way we respond to our kids, it can help to reflect on how our parents responded to us.

Gottman found that even the most loving, devoted, and patient parents can be dismissive and/or disapproving without realizing it. Unfortunately, such responses will not nurture their children's emotional health, which is essential to leading a satisfying life.

The truth is, one's emotional intelligence—often called EQ—is a much greater predictor of a person's happiness than one's IQ, achievements, wealth, and test scores. The importance of being able to understand and work with our emotions can't be overstated. As Gottman explains in his paper "Fostering Emotionally Intelligent Children, Families, and Communities":

> Being emotional does not mean being irrational. Emotions have a logic of their own. They make sense. They guide and instruct. They are real. They are the engine of learning and change. The regulation of emotion only comes through the understanding of emotion, not through its suppression.

So how can we help our kids when they're upset?

Let Them Feel Their Feelings

First, if they are crying, let them cry. EQ 101: Holding back tears isn't healthy. And while I know we all know this, too often we act as if we don't. Crying is good for us. Tears carry toxins out of our bodies and shuddering releases tension from our muscles. And usually on the other side of tears is sunshine. Crying isn't something kids or anyone should feel the need to stop or apologize for. Our culture's knee-jerk impulse to apologize for being "too emotional" is backward. We have so much shame around expressions of emotion, as if they are a sign of weakness instead of a sign of our humanity. Expressing our pain is meant to inspire compassion and connect us to one another, not drive us apart.

Empathy. It's the Only Way

At the risk of stating the obvious, our job is to make sure our kids know that we care and they're not alone. Nothing soothes quite like someone genuinely caring enough to try to understand where you're coming from—without judgment. Without rushing you to just get it out already. Without trying to fix it. No cookie, no promise of Disneyland, no video game—nothing but empathy can provide the deep sense of relief that someone is there for you in your time of need. *Phew! I'm not alone. I'm not crazy. Someone gets it.* Nursing scholar Theresa Wiseman has identified the four characteristics of empathy:

- Seeing a situation from another's perspective.
- Being nonjudgmental.
- Trying to understand another's feelings.
- Communicating our understanding of their feelings to them.

Be Curious

The path to empathy is paved by curiosity. Wondering *How are they feeling?* and *How did they come to feel that way?* is essential. However, directly asking our kids these questions will usually backfire. Just as kids won't say "I've had a hard day, can we talk about it?" they often won't be able to answer direct questions because those can feel invasive and overwhelming. Instead they'll brood or otherwise act out. What's more, often kids need our help figuring out what happened and how they feel. So we at once have to be detectives looking for clues, while also creating a space where they feel safe sharing.

When we're genuinely curious, we can't help but listen in a more focused and open way. And it's our calm, reassuring, undivided attention that helps kids open up.

Listen

Being able to truly hear what a child who is crying, lashing out, whining, or screaming is trying to communicate can be as challenging as it is essential. We help calm our children and "open the door" for them to share their difficult feelings with us when we put our phones down and show them we're listening with our entire body. That way they don't have to be additionally frustrated and hurt because they feel that we don't seem to really care. It can also be very calming for a child if we don't hover over them, but instead listen to them from either their eye level or below. This sends the signal that we are receptive, not dominating.

If a child is overwhelmed or just not ready to talk, we can gently invite them to share with us by using what the great communication expert psychologist Thomas Gordon calls "door-openers."

"I can see something is really bothering you."

"Sounds like you've got something to say about this."

"You seem too upset to talk about this right now. I'm here when you're ready."

"This seems really important to you."

"I'm interested in your point of view."

As Gordon explains, "door-openers . . . convey acceptance of the child and respect for him as a person by telling him, in effect: "You have a right to express how you feel."

Once a child has started to share, we can keep the door open, as it were, by showing that we are still listening (without judgment!) by periodically nodding or saying "Mmm, hmmm" or "I see" or "interesting," etc.

Reflect Back (Just Go There)

Then we need to let them know we get it! And mincing words won't help anyone—just go there. (If we're off base, they'll let us know.)

"Sounds like you hate school and think your teacher is mean?"

"It's scary to be yelled at, huh?"

"You felt left out."

"You felt controlled, like you had no choice, huh?"

"You're worried they're going to laugh at you?"

"You think I love your brother more than you."

"You took her candy without asking and now you feel guilty?"

"You're feeling bored? Like there's nothing to do?"

"You're really nervous about reading your poem in class?"

"You're so sad your fish died. You really miss him."

Even if you're dismayed by what your child is expressing, forego comments like "You don't really mean that" or "You don't really feel that way." They do mean it and they do feel it. And our not liking it (or

> When we're genuinely curious, we can't help but listen in a more focused and open way.

being appalled or otherwise upset by their feelings) isn't going to help anything and just signals lack of acceptance. That can cause kids to start feeding us what we want to hear, not what they really feel.

Often once a child feels genuinely understood, they relax. Sometimes it's just connecting, being heard and understood, that makes us feel better. We've felt our feelings, and like the weather, they've moved through us. The storm is over. Other times, however, identifying how we feel is the first step toward solving the problem at hand. That's the good news about feeling tough feelings: They help us make decisions we couldn't make without them.

Tough Feelings Help Us

From an evolutionary viewpoint, we humans wouldn't continue to feel the wide range of emotions that we do if they didn't serve us. As the mission statement of the Yale Center for Emotional Intelligence tells us, "Emotions drive learning, decision-making, creativity, relationships, and health." Indeed, that's their purpose: to guide and motivate us. Feelings shouldn't be banished by reason, but instead work in concert with it. I love how the three authors of *A General Theory of Love*, Thomas Lewis, Fari Amini, and Richard Lannon, professors of psychiatry at UC San Francisco, explain how feelings influence our decision-making process: "The brain's ancient emotional architecture is not a bothersome animal encumbrance. Instead, it is nothing less than the key to our lives. We live immersed in unseen

> Feelings shouldn't be banished by reason, but instead work in concert with it.

forces and silent messages that shape our destinies. As individuals and as a culture, our chance for happiness depends on our ability to decipher a hidden world. . . ." Our feelings are the key to this hidden world, and helping kids figure out how they're feeling is the first step toward solving a problem. Here are a few examples of how identifying feelings can help kids problem-solve.

PARENT: It sounds like you are worried that I love your brother more than you. . . .

KID: Yeah, you always give him more attention.

PARENT: I bet it really hurts when you see me focusing on him. It makes you think I don't care about you as much as I care about him.

KID: Yeah.

PARENT: Oh, sweetheart! I'm so sorry you feel that way, because I love you every bit as much as your brother, and in your own special way. I'm wondering what we can do so we have more alone time together. What if we could set aside some time every day that's just for us? Our own special time? Do you think that will help?

PARENT: Sounds to me like you feel guilty because you took her candy without asking, is that right?

KID: I guess. Maybe.

PARENT: Feeling guilty is like a little voice in us that tells us we need to make things right. Hmmmm . . . Do you have any ideas on how to do that?

KID: Give her new, better candy?

PARENT: That could help. Do you want to use your allowance to pick some out for her? Do you think that will solve the problem?

KID: Well, that means I have to tell her I did it. I guess I should say sorry.

PARENT: Sounds to me like you're nervous about reading your poem in class.

KID: Yeah. I guess.

PARENT: I know that feeling. Sometimes I get nervous when I have to give a speech for work.

KID: I'm afraid I'll mess up and everyone will laugh at me.

PARENT: I wonder what might help give you more confidence.

KID: I don't know.

PARENT: When I practice a lot, I feel more prepared. Would it help if I pretended to be the audience and you practiced some more?

It's reassuring to know our parents care enough not only to help us understand how we feel, but to help us listen to our feelings and to use them to move forward in a productive way.

Once More, This Time with Empathy

Here are the original three scenes from the beginning of the chapter, reimagined with the adults responding with empathy, instead of telling kids who aren't okay that they are.

Scene from a Café Redux

As the dad at the café shushing his one-year-old daughter discovered, "Shhhh!" will pretty much never quiet a baby. I can't imagine a one-year-old thinking *Ahh, I didn't realize my sounds were interrupting your conversation. So sorry! Sure, I'll be quiet.* So perhaps something like this instead . . .

> **BABY GIRL:** [*crying*]
>
> **DAD:** I hear you, honey. You're uncomfortable! Do you want your pacifier?
>
> **BABY GIRL:** [*spits out pacifier*]
>
> **DAD:** No, you don't! Okay. Are you hungry? [*offers food*]
>
> **BABY GIRL:** [*turns head*]
>
> **DAD:** Not hungry. I see you pushing against the straps. You want out! You've sat here a long time while I talked to my friend. You must be antsy and want some attention. [*To friend*] Shall we move this to the park?

Scene from a Park Redux

> **GRANDMA:** I see you looking at the slide, Eric. Does it seem scary?
>
> **ERIC:** [*silent*]
>
> **GRANDMA:** There's no rush. Only go down if you're ready.

However, let's say Eric did go down as he had after being "encouraged" by his grandma who was eager for him to have some fun, and he ends up crying in the sand.

> **GRANDMA:** Are you hurt?

ERIC: [*crying, shakes his head no.*]

GRANDMA: [*educated guess*] That was scary, huh? You went down the slide too fast?

ERIC: [*crying, maybe nodding head in agreement*]

GRANDMA: [*going there*] Are you upset because I rushed you to come down when you weren't ready?

ERIC: [*nodding yes*]

GRANDMA: That's a terrible feeling. I'm sorry I pressured you. Next time I'll follow your lead. I don't want you to do things to please me or anyone.

Scene from a Soccer Field Redux

BOY: [*crying*] I have the wrong socks!

MOM: Oh, I'm sorry to hear that, sweetheart. I can see how upset you are.

BOY: [*crying*] Now the whole game will be ruined!

MOM: [*door-opener*] Can you tell me more about that?

BOY: These socks suck. They hurt my toes.

MOM: [*reflecting back*] You're worried it will be hard to play in uncomfortable socks.

BOY: Yeah! They're the worst socks in the world. This game is gonna suck.

DAD: [*guessing*] You're worried that with these socks you can't play your best?

BOY: Uh, I guess. I *have* to play my best because Eric is sick and now I *have* to play goalie and I'm so bad at it and we're gonna lose and everyone's gonna hate me.

(*It's rarely about the socks.*)

DAD: Ahh, that's right, son! You've never played goalie in a real game before. I can imagine that feels scary. Like everyone's counting on you?

BOY: [*calmer now, listening*]

(*Sometimes being understood is enough. Sometimes moving on to problem-solving can help.*)

DAD: You're worried your teammates are expecting you to be as good as Eric?

BOY: They know I'm not. He's played goalie all year! I've never even played it before!

DAD: But you're still worried [*naming emotion*] they'll expect you to be as good as Eric?

BOY: Probably not.

DAD: You don't think they expect you to be as good, but you still don't want to let them down, huh?

BOY: Yeah.

DAD: I can understand that. Did anyone else volunteer to play goalie?

BOY: No. Only me.

DAD: So without you, there'd be no goalie? Wow, I bet everyone's grateful you're doing it so the game can go on.

BOY: Maybe.

We Mean Well

The good news is that while "You're okay" is as unhelpful as it is untrue, usually when we say it, our hearts are in the right place. So when we actually try to understand how our children genuinely feel instead of telling them how they should feel or we wish they felt, our hearts can align. And we feel closer. Perhaps that's the upside of uncomfortable feelings—they give us opportunities to connect with those we love.

CHAPTER ELEVEN

"BEHAVE YOURSELF!"

"If parents would strike the word
'misbehaving' from their vocabulary, they
would rarely feel judgmental and angry."

—Thomas Gordon

W hen Hudson was a preschooler, he could really drive John and me crazy, and we didn't know what to do about it.

Case in point. We were at a relative's house for some family occasion when Hudson, then three, removed all of the pillows from their fancy sofa and proceeded to use them like giant building blocks, cordoning off an area of the living room by balancing them against the coffee table and other furniture. When our hosts saw what he was up to, they didn't quite gasp in horror, but they clearly weren't too pleased.

"Hudson, there's a playroom with blocks if you want to build," one of them said with as much kindness as she could muster. "Please put the pillows back on the sofa."

But he wouldn't.

With half the party watching, I explained to Hudson that these were very nice pillows and while I knew we made forts at home with our sofa pillows, these belonged on their sofa. "We'll help you put them back, sweetheart," I added. But not only wouldn't he help, he growled at John and me and anyone else who dared come near him and his mini-barricade.

Oh, God. Always in front of family.

Obviously, seeing that it wasn't our home, John and I started to put the pillows back ourselves as Hudson became apoplectic. Finally John really had no choice but to pick him up kicking and screaming and take him outside, where it took an exceptionally long time for him to calm down. And when they did finally return to the party, Hudson clung to John for the rest of the night. From what I could gather from the murmurs among the guests, they were "concerned" we were raising a spoiled child.

"I'd never let my son get away with behaving like that!" was the general sentiment I was picking up on. *He needs rules! Consequences!*

Another day, we had a big party at our house throughout which Hudson essentially never came down from John's shoulders. I remember looking over at John at one point, maybe an hour or so into the party, and I could tell he was annoyed by it.

"Please come down, Hudson!" John implored. "I need a break. It's hard for me to talk to everyone and get their drinks and answer the door with you on my shoulders."

But Hudson wouldn't come down.

So, eventually John took him down.

And Hudson fell apart. Totally. I had to spend the next half hour or so with him as he cycled through his torrent of emotions.

Were we raising a spoiled kid who always had to get his way?

And then there was his best friend's birthday party. He knew there was going to be a big bouncy house with a slide, so he couldn't wait to get there. But once we did, he just sat in a corner of the yard by himself. Not even the lure of bouncing or chocolate cake made him budge. Eventually, he said he wanted to go home. I couldn't understand it.

Needs Drive Behavior

Fortunately for us—and for Hudson—we'd just started taking a new weekly parenting class from Echo Parenting and Education, an organization that advocates for an empathy-led, nonviolent approach to parenting. And by "nonviolent," they mean parenting with the intention of not causing any harm to a child—be it embarrassment, humiliation, shame, physical pain, what have you. It's a philosophy that does not believe in labels like "right" and "wrong," "good" and "bad," nor does it believe in trying to control children's behavior through demands, coercion, bribes, or threats. *Should be interesting!* I thought. We lucked out with a really sharp, passionate teacher named Eric. While I found everything he said compelling, it was a lot to digest.

On the night of our second class, Eric introduced us to the concept of "needs" driving behavior. *Huh?* Eric encouraged us to shift our focus away from trying to figure out how to change our children's behavior—you know, how to get them to brush their teeth, stop hitting their sister, get ready for school on time, and so on—and instead to try to understand what their behavior was telling us. He told us to look for "the *need* behind the 'no.'"

What? The need behind the no? I didn't get it.

I was confused at first, but eventually I came to understand what Eric meant. And once I did, it made total sense to me. It was as if one moment I thought the world was flat and then I got that it was round. Behavior, I came to realize, is a language. A universal language. It's not something that is "good" or "bad." Rather it's something to be understood. My job as a parent wasn't to try to control my children's behavior as much as it was to understand it. I needed to get better at deciphering what my children's behavior was saying.

> Behavior can be at once an expression of our needs and a way to try to meet them.

You see, no matter when we're born or on which patch of the planet we happen to land, we all enter this world speaking behavior. At first, our behavior does just about all of our communicating for us to ensure that we get what we *need*—not just to survive, but to thrive. We cry. We reach. We scrunch up our faces. And our caregivers do their best to interpret our behavior and respond in a helpful way. Do we need food? Sleep? Are we cold? Do we need some love and attention? Then, based on how we respond to their response to our behavior, our caregivers know if they're on the right track or not. *Hmmm, she's still crying after I've changed her. Maybe she's hungry.*

Sure, there's trial and error involved, but the longer our caregivers know us and the more they pay attention to our cues and patterns, the better they understand what our behavior is saying. And so it goes that our behavior can be at once an expression of our needs and a way to try to meet them. As the psychologist Marshall Rosenberg, founder for the Center for Nonviolent Communication, explained it, "Everything we do is in service of our needs. When this one concept is applied to our view of others, we'll see that . . . what others do to us is the best possible thing they know to do to get their needs met." This is the case when we're born and continues to be true throughout the course of our lives. We never stop speaking behavior.

Interestingly, however, at some point—perhaps around the time children start to speak—adults seem to stop trying to interpret their children's behavior (with the intention of responding in a helpful way) and instead start trying to control their children's behavior through language and discipline techniques. If a toddler is hitting, we may say, "Hitting hurts. We don't allow hitting," and then we may threaten or give a time-out. This approach ultimately fails to stop the hitting in the long run because it doesn't address *why* the child hit in the first place. In other words, the time-out didn't address the need that the hitting was trying to meet. For needs, by virtue of their very essence, long to be met. If they can't be satisfied in one way, then they'll try to find another—relentlessly. In that way, needs are like whack a mole. So if our children are not responding to reasonable requests to change their behavior, our job is to wonder what need or needs their behavior is trying to meet so we can respond in a helpful way. How we help a totally dependent newborn will be different from how we'll help a one-year-old or three-year-old or six-year-old, but the goal remains the same: to help them learn to identify their own needs so that ultimately they can find acceptable ways to meet them.

So what exactly are these universal, basic needs that drive all of our behaviors?

What Are Human Needs?

Needs, as I came to understand, aren't wants. They're not *I need that toy*. Or *I need to go to Disneyland*. Those are merely ways of satisfying needs, and there are an infinite number of ways to do that—some healthy, some not so much. Rather, needs are more like I'm hungry and need food, I'm lonely and need companionship, and I'm curious and I need to understand. In fact, there is only a handful or so of innate human needs, and they are the same for all people across all time. That said, over the years, various folks have identified them in different ways. In 1943, the renowned psychologist Abraham Maslow identified five universal human needs (and would later add a sixth) in his seminal paper "A Theory of Human Motivation": physiological (food, water, sleep, etc.); safety (shelter, financial resources); love (friendship, family, a partner); esteem (respect, achievement, self-confidence); self-actualization (values, creativity, problem-solving); and self-transcendence (helping others, feeling at one with the world).

> A baby nursing is at once satisfying her physiological need for sustenance as well as, perhaps, her need for safety and love.

Maslow explained, "Any motivated behavior . . . must be understood to be a channel through which many basic needs may be simultaneously expressed or satisfied. Typically, an act has more than one motivation." For example, a baby nursing is at once satisfying her physiological need for sustenance as well as, perhaps, her need for safety and love. Similarly, by writing this book I am at once satisfying my need for safety (financial resources), esteem (achievement, respect of others), self-actualization (creativity and problem-solving), and self-transcendence (helping others).

In the 1960s, Marshall Rosenberg developed a method of communicating and solving conflicts known as nonviolent communication that relied on identifying the underlying need or needs driving our behavior in order to find more mutually acceptable ways to meet the need. Somewhat similarly to Maslow, Rosenberg identified seven fundamental needs: connection; physical well-being; honesty; play; harmony; autonomy; and meaning. In fact, during our second Echo Parenting class, Eric passed out a sheet outlining these needs, similar to the list on pages 198–199.

At this point I was overwhelmed, so I took the sheet home and put it on my desk on top of all the other things I tend to avoid, like bills and jury duty notices. I'd review it later.

Looking for the Need

But then at the following class, one of the dads, a guy named Patrick, came in almost giddy. He had a breakthrough story to share with us. And his breakthrough fueled mine.

"So for the past few weeks or so," Patrick started, "every morning has been really hard for me. My husband leaves for work really early, so it's just me and the boys. Aiden's two and a half and Ethan is almost eight months. And basically our routine is always the same: We get up, I get the boys dressed, and first I serve Aiden his cereal then I sit next to him to feed Ethan on my lap. Simple! But inevitably, every single morning for the last few weeks, just when Ethan opens his mouth for his first bite, Aiden climbs up on the table and starts batting our chandelier.

"So at first I told him very calmly but firmly, 'Please come down. Tables aren't for climbing. Tables are where we eat.' But he didn't listen. Which actually isn't like him. He just stayed up there hitting the damn thing. 'That's very delicate. Please don't hit it anymore,' I said. But he kept on hitting it. So, totally frustrated, I put Ethan in the Pack 'n Play, picked Aiden off the table, and said, 'I'm not going to let you climb up here anymore,' then I put him down and picked Ethan up and started over. And then Aiden just did it again! I figured he was trying to test my limit, right? I figured there were only so many times he'd do it before he got the message that I won't stand for it. I figured he'd get tired of the whole routine. But it just went on and on.

Universal Needs

PHYSICAL WELL-BEING

- air
- food
- water
- light
- shelter/security/protection/
  protection from pain/safety/
  emotional safety/preservation
- movement/physical exercise
- rest/sleep
- touch
- sexual expression
- health
- comfort
- warmth

CONNECTION

- care
- love
- closeness
- intimacy
- compassion
- empathy
- consideration
- acceptance
- affection
- appreciation
- communication
- cooperation
- trust
- openness
- belonging
- community/companionship/
  partnership/fellowship
- inclusion/participation
- mutuality/reciprocity
- respect
- consistency/continuity
- nurturing
- support
- knowing
- seeing (see/be seen)
- hearing (hear/be heard)
- understanding (understand/
  be understood)
- sharing/exchange
- giving/receiving
- tenderness/softness
- sensitivity/kindness

HONESTY

- authenticity
- integrity
- transparency

PLAY

- fun
- celebration/mourning
- flow
- humor/laugh
- vitality/liveliness
- discovery/adventure
- passion
- spontaneity
- lightness
- variety/diversity

HARMONY

- peace
- calm/relaxation/equanimity
- ease
- beauty
- order
- communion/wholeness
- completion/digestion/integration
- predictability/familiarity
- stability/balance
- equality/justice/fairness

AUTONOMY

- choice
- freedom
- space
- time
- independence

MEANING

- purpose
- contribution/enrich life
- hope
- self-value/self-confidence/ self-esteem/dignity
- inner strength/power/ competence/capacity/ empowerment
- creativity
- learning
- inspiration
- challenge
- stimulation
- growth/evolution/progress
- efficacy/effectiveness
- expression/self-expression
- clarity
- awareness/consciousness
- liberation/transformation
- mattering/taking part in/ having my place in the world
- presence
- centeredness
- spirituality
- simplicity

"Eventually, of course, I lost my patience and yelled at him. But even that didn't make a difference. Then finally our babysitter walked in, which was such a relief. I handed Ethan to her so she could feed him and then took Aiden to preschool, totally spent. And it's been almost the same every day—except on the weekends, when my husband is home. I was really at my wits' end. Then, thanks to last week's class about needs driving behavior, I had a breakthrough."

We were rapt.

"So the following morning, as usual, just as I was about to feed Ethan, Aiden climbed right up on the dining room table again and started hitting the chandelier. But this time instead of getting annoyed or angry, I wondered—just like you said—what his climbing on the table was *saying*. What *need* was he trying to meet by hitting the chandelier? And almost as soon as I asked myself the question, I had an answer. Connection. Belonging! I figured, well, that Aiden was feeling left out. He was probably jealous of the attention I was giving his brother that I used to give him. He'd had a couple years of my undivided attention every morning, and now I was focusing much of it on Ethan! It wasn't brain surgery, but I'd never thought about it before.

"So instead of sounding like a broken record saying, 'We don't climb on tables,' I said, 'Aiden, every time I'm about to feed Ethan, you climb up on the table and hit the chandelier, even though you know I don't want you to. That tells me you have some very strong feelings about me feeding your brother. Are you feeling left out?' He looked down.

"Well, if you are, I can understand that. Before Ethan came along you had all of my attention at breakfast time. I don't want you to feel left out. I love being with you. Hmmm, I wonder what we can do to include you when it's time to feed your brother.

"I could see him thinking, but he didn't say anything. So I threw out an idea: 'Would you like to help feed Ethan?'" I asked.

"Aiden lit up. He climbed right off the table himself! Without me saying a word. He sat right next to me and fed his brother with me. And he was proud! He felt so much *a part of* the family. And he's helped feed Ethan every day since. He just wanted to feel *included*. Problem solved!"

"Wow!" we all marveled.

Eric said, "Thank you so much for sharing that with us. You know what I find so brilliant is that you didn't just jump to solving the problem *for* Aiden. You helped him know that his behavior was telling you something about how he felt and what he needed. That he felt left out. That he needed connection. And that it was a problem you could solve together. Yes, this time he didn't have an idea of what to do. He's only two! But him seeing the relationship between his behavior, his feelings, and a problem that needs solving is so important. And him thinking about possible solutions and knowing you are too. With time, he'll learn he can identify his own needs and find ways to solve them. Of course they need our help at first."

Click. *Needs drive behavior. We humans need what we need. Needs aren't luxuries. If a child isn't responding to a reasonable request, then their behavior must be meeting a more pressing need.*

> **If a child isn't responding to a reasonable request, then their behavior must be meeting a more pressing need.**

Punishing behavior with a time-out or another form of discipline may, in the moment, scare a child into "behaving himself," but it won't help address the underlying feelings and needs driving the behavior. And so the need won't be met, which means the child will only continue to try to meet it in some other way. Punishing a child only creates more problems without truly solving the original one.

What Did Hudson Need?

That night after class, I started to think about the problems we'd been having with Hudson in a whole new way. *What need was driving Hudson's behavior?* I asked myself. As soon as I got home, I grabbed the needs list that was under yet more bills, and there was my answer: physical well-being. Hudson *needed* to feel safe. He wasn't being defiant. He was trying to protect himself! All of a sudden it seemed so obvious. Hudson had always been a particularly sensitive child—sensitive to noise, to food, to transitions, and now that I thought about it, apparently to crowds of people and people invading his personal space. He brought his blanket most places—Linus style—which, when needed, served as a cozy boundary between himself and the chaos of the world.

With the sofa pillows, Hudson had been trying to create a barrier between him and the other guests. There were too many people (many we didn't know) asking him questions, wanting to say hi, wanting to give him a hug. He was literally building a barricade to keep them out so he could feel safe and secure.

> Hudson *needed* to feel safe. He wasn't being defiant. He was trying to protect himself!

And again, by climbing up on John's shoulders during the party, Hudson was placing himself above the fray. No one could jostle him or otherwise get in his face when he was on such a high perch.

And he planted himself in a far-off corner at the birthday party because the bouncy house was so full of kids, it likely felt like a battlefield where he could get hit at any moment. It was chaotic to say the least. Even though he loved bouncing, his need for safety was greater.

Once I realized that all of these behaviors were a way to meet his need for physical well-being, I shared my theory with John. And he totally agreed. For us, understanding what was driving Hudson's behavior made it so much easier to accept it. Instead of being annoyed or angry with him, we felt compassion for him. Poor little guy! He was scared. Trying to keep himself safe. And now that we knew what he needed, if his solutions weren't working for us, we could all try to figure out other ways to meet the need! He didn't have to go it alone. I was as giddy as Patrick had been.

> **Instead of being annoyed or angry with him, we felt compassion for him.**

The next morning, I found a quiet time and said to Hudson, "Honey, I've been thinking about it, and it seems you don't feel comfortable when we have a lot of people over. Is that right?"

The look on his face was one of total relief. His parents understood! Or at least I thought that's what his look was saying. Maybe he was relieved because I'd made a connection for him that hadn't been clear to him in the first place.

"It seems that when there are a lot of people around or when someone gets too close to you—particularly someone you don't know—you feel scared. And then you try to do something to keep them away, so you feel safe. Like when you climb up on Dad's shoulders. Or put pillows around an area and don't let people in. Or hide under your blanket or in a corner. Do you know what I mean?"

He nodded.

"Well, Daddy and I want to make sure you feel safe and comfortable, and there are many ways we can do it." And over time, together we all came up with various ideas, depending on the situation, and we also made some very fundamental changes to our lives that helped him and ultimately us. For instance, we simply stopped having so many people over at once. Honestly, it was a relief, because we didn't have to worry about Hudson so much, which meant we could relax and enjoy ourselves more. Smaller gatherings worked better for our family.

And as for birthday parties . . . Well, we came up with a plan. If the party was at someone's house, we'd ask if there was a quiet place where we could go and read a book and maybe watch for a bit. I found that in this way the transition to a new space was easier for Hudson, and if he could look out a window and get the lay of the land for a while, he'd join the party when he felt he had a handle on things. And for a while, we just avoided altogether the big birthday parties at gyms and the like, as they were too overwhelming for him.

Hudson's preschool teachers also noticed he could be overwhelmed by large groups and shared his strategies for coping. At the beginning of the year, during outdoor play time, he would stay on the porch simply watching everyone play so that he could get to know everyone's playing styles. Which kids were rough. Who was predictable. Once he had the information he needed, he ventured out. They also said he kept his blanket in his cubby and would go get it when he needed it.

> While some may think we coddled Hudson, I think of it as more respecting his sensitive nature.

Hudson wasn't spoiled. He wasn't "misbehaving." He didn't need discipline. He needed help feeling safe in a way that didn't interfere with other people's needs, which was very doable—it just required some thought and experimentation. Yes, it meant making some changes to our family life. For instance, Jules loved action. She loves baseball games, amusement parks, and farmers' markets, which were too overwhelming for Hudson. The truth is, I don't love crowds either. So often, John would take Jules to games or concerts, and Hudson and I would happily stay home. For family time, we'd plan things that worked for everyone. As Hudson has gotten older (and grown bigger), he's become increasingly more comfortable in crowds and recently enjoyed a day at a Renaissance fair. While some may think we coddled Hudson, I think of it as more respecting his sensitive nature.

"Misbehavior" Is Prejudice Against Children

Once I understood that fundamental needs drive behavior, I realized just how inherently biased against children the word "misbehavior" is. I was heartened, though not surprised, to discover that Dr. Thomas Gordon had identified the troubling nature of the word back in the 1980s.

> Most parents and teachers think of children as either "behaving" or "misbehaving" . . . Interestingly enough, the term is almost exclusively applied to children—seldom to adults. We never hear people say:
>
> - "My husband misbehaved yesterday."
> - "One of our guests misbehaved at the party last night."
> - "I got so angry when my friend misbehaved during lunch."
> - "My employees have been misbehaving lately."
>
> Misbehavior is exclusively parent and teacher language, tied up somehow with how adults have traditionally viewed children . . . adults say a child misbehaves whenever some specific action is judged as contrary to how the adult thinks the child should behave. . . . The "badness" of the behavior actually resides in the adult's mind, not the child's; the child in fact is doing what he or she chooses or needs to do to satisfy some need. Put another way, the adult experiences the

badness, not the child. Even more accurately, it is the consequences of the child's behavior for the adult that are felt to be bad (or potentially bad), not the behavior itself.

The tragedy of it is that once an adult has judged a child's behavior as "misbehavior," it gives them license to make a child suffer, doling out consequences and punishment, in other words, suffering. Which is heartbreaking because what children really need is understanding and help finding more acceptable ways to meet their needs. And the truth is, no matter how much we punish kids, the needs will not go away. Which is not to say Dr. Gordon didn't think problems needed to be solved. Of course he did. He just understood that punishing a child for "misbehaving" wasn't the answer.

Behavior Isn't "Mis" Anything

It is ironic that we say children *mis*behave when in fact the opposite is actually true. Children's behavior that we find disruptive or hurtful isn't "mis" anything. We may find it annoying, troubling, or infuriating, but it isn't intrinsically "bad" or "wrong." On the contrary, a child's behavior is exceedingly *accurate*. It is at once a true expression of their need at a particular moment as well as a reflection of their current ability to meet that need. In other words, their so-called "bad" behavior is actually the best they can do, based on their cognition, temperament, and life eperience. To repeat what Marshall Rosenberg said, "Everything we do is in service of our needs. When this one concept is applied to our view of others, we'll see that . . . what others do to us is the best possible thing they know to do to get their needs met." Imagine getting "in trouble" for doing your best. Confusing, for sure.

What If the Tables Were Turned?

I realize this all may seem totally counterintuitive. It might help to imagine the tables being turned so it's adults who are doing the "misbehaving." I thought about this when I came across the article "Time-Outs Are Hurting Your Child" in *Time* by Dr. Dan Siegel and Dr. Tina Bryson (more about time-outs in the next chapter). Reading the piece, I remembered the talk by Dr. Bryson that I'd attended at our preschool several years earlier. Dr. Bryson had admitted that she, too, like many in the audience, she imagined, used to give her children time-outs for their "misbehavior." That was before she learned through her extensive research and experience that not only can time-outs cause children to feel angry, rejected, and ashamed, but they are also ineffective for changing the behavior they aim to address.

Dr. Bryson shared what she learned was a better way to respond to her children when their behavior wasn't acceptable to her, which started with validating the feelings behind the behavior, giving other options, then moving on without belaboring the issue. But back in the days when she did put her kids in time-outs and it caused them to feel angry, hurt, rejected, and ashamed, would it have been fair for someone who already knew better (perhaps someone like Dr. Gordon) to say that Dr. Bryson had "misbehaved" toward her children? Would getting mad at her

> "Everything we do is in service of our needs."
>
> —*Marshall Rosenberg*

or punishing her for her "misbehavior" have helped her learn a better way to handle the situation? Of course not. It's *absurd*. Rather, I imagine most people would give her the benefit of the doubt, claiming she was doing *the best she knew how to do* at the time, that her behavior (giving time-outs) was her best attempt to meet her need for peace and consideration. She simply hadn't yet been introduced to better ways of handling the situation—even though she was a grown-up *and* an expert in the field. In other words, we afford her, as an adult, the benefit of the doubt that she was doing her best, even though her actions weren't helpful and actually were harmful. And the way she learned to be more helpful to her children was through education, not discipline.

And so it is with children—when they do something we don't like, we need to understand what the behavior is telling us so we can help them. Then, we can try to find a different, more acceptable way to meet that need.

Lest you think that by not disciplining kids you will create self-centered brats who believe the world revolves around them, I point to the research of Dr. Peter Haiman. A psychotherapist who has worked with kids and teens for over four decades, Dr. Haiman aims to eradicate the "virulent myth" in our culture that meeting our children's needs will spoil them: "The research literature clearly says that the opposite is true. The well-disciplined child is created when parents appropriately fulfill the needs of childhood and adolescence."

And so I am deeming "misbehavior" the Parentspeak Word that Does the Most Damage because it inspires anger instead of compassion, it's evidence of prejudice against children, and it inevitably leads to their suffering unnecessarily. Congratulations "misbehavior." May I never hear from you again.

CHAPTER TWELVE

"I SAID, 'RIGHT NOW'!"

"The first thing you have to do if you want to raise nice kids, is you have to talk to them like they are people instead of talking to them like they're property."
—**Frank Zappa**

I know we all absolutely adore our children and love them for who they are. That is, until who they are is someone who has locked herself in the bathroom and we're going to be late to a job interview. Or someone who has just poked his helpless infant sister in the eyes and she's shrieking in agony. Or someone who isn't getting into bed an hour after bedtime and we've had it. The day has been long. We've schlepped. We've shopped. We've helped. We've been as patient as one can possibly be. And now we're done. We're not reading another book. We're not going to get another snack. It's *bedtime!* It's at moments like these when our children aren't doing what we've asked them to do in the nicest ways we know how—*for the millionth time*—that it can feel like our kids have extracted our blood, put it in a pan on the stove, and turned on the burner. Our blood isn't boiling yet, but the Incredible Hulks slumbering inside us have opened an eye to see if their brand of influence is needed. Honestly, sometimes it can seem like the only way out of the stressful mess we're in is to show our kids that *we mean business.* I'm talking about using the not-so-secret weapon of parents, grandparents, nannies, teachers, coaches, and principals everywhere: "raising our voices." Otherwise known as YELLING!!

"I said right now!"

"Don't make me ask you again!"

"I've had it!"

Yelling, of course, is a scare tactic, one that "Wolf," a dad who blogs anonymously at Just Add Father, recognized one day just as he was about to let loose: "I realized to my horror that the feeling I had was an impulse to terrify Nick into behaving himself." And it's a tactic that often works. Psychologist Dr. Laura Markham, author of *Peaceful Parent, Happy Kids,* describes how: "Humans, when yelled or screamed at, tend to go into fight, flight, or freeze mode. When kids go into fight, flight, or freeze mode, their learning and ability to absorb information shuts down. Now, picture being a kid and looking up at someone who is four times your size. This person that's glaring down at you is someone, who without them, you would die. You know, on some level, that your survival depends on this person. You will apologize or do whatever you need to do to make this person stop yelling." Sometimes, however, kids will cower and crumble under the torrent of angry sound, because being yelled at can feel so overwhelming and painful.

Unfortunately for everyone, often the more we yell, the more we end up yelling, because we've been training our kids to know they don't really have to listen *until* we start screaming. Soon we're on the path of turning ourselves—our children's source of support, comfort, and guidance—into people to be feared. I imagine for many kids it can begin to feel as it did for the children of Michelle Baxter, a self-professed screamer and mother of two, who shared in an article for *Today's Parent* that her kids "were walking on eggshells around me and they worried about what might set me off." Worse still, if we take our yelling too far, Dr. Markham warns, children "harden their heart to you because their trusted bond to their parent is broken. Once that happens, the child will no longer try to please you. This is the child that will likely grow into a troubled teenager and possibly adult as well."

> The more we yell, the more we end up yelling, because we've been training our kids to know they don't really have to listen *until* we start screaming.

Certainly, no one *wants* to scream at their kids. And yet, we all do it. Well, according to a 2003 study reported in *The New York Times*, at least 98 percent of us do. (I can't imagine things have changed much since then.) I know many parents (like me!) are eager to jump off the yelling go-round but find quitting completely just about impossible. My friend Jill, who's been trying to stop in earnest for a while now, has been both surprised and incredibly frustrated by how impossible going cold turkey has been. "It's given me a sense," she confided, "of how hard it must be to stop drinking or doing drugs. Your body just goes there." Indeed it does. As Wolf said, it's as if we're overcome with an impulse to terrify. But where does this impulse come from?

Our childhoods. In any given moment, there are likely lots of factors, but our underlying responses usually come from the way we were parented. Many in the mental health field describe our extreme reactions to our children's behavior as being "triggered" by experiences from the past. Triggers are unresolved feelings that cause us to overreact. Psychologist Margaret Paul explains, "When we were growing up, we inevitably experienced pain or suffering that we could not acknowledge and/or deal with sufficiently at the time. So as adults, we typically become triggered by experiences that are reminiscent of these old painful feelings." Or as family counselor and parenting coach Sharon Selby explains in her article "How Does Our Own Upbringing (Our Triggers) Influence Our Parenting?": "We have unconscious imprints from our childhood experiences—our schooling, our families, and other childhood influences. . . . Every time we get triggered and our blood begins to boil and our heart beats faster, our *unconscious* has just been activated . . . we get flooded by our emotions, we lose our patience and our rational thinking abilities and act on instinct to protect ourselves."

> Man, yelling can really hit the spot.

That's when many of us start screaming—it's the fight part of the freeze, flight, or fight response. In fact, Dr. Dan Siegel, a clinical professor of psychiatry at the UCLA School of Medicine and Executive Director of the Mindsight Institute, explains that when one is triggered, it can literally feel like "you are experiencing the event for the first time, and it can feel intrusive, confusing, and even terrifying." So we can be going along and then all of a sudden something our kids do or don't do instantaneously reactivates an old wound and suddenly, alarms sound. And we just want it to stop. "Enough already!" we scream. We literally feel as if we can't take it anymore.

And man, yelling can really hit the spot. For a moment there, one glorious moment, we feel better because yelling has drained some of the unbearable stress from our bodies. That is, until, for some of us, the guilt and shame come rushing in like the tide. We may even feel spooked by our own behavior. We may promise ourselves we'll do better next time, hoping our kids will quickly forget about it. *Let's just move on and have a good day! Okay? Just listen to me next time!* Unfortunately, while the flare-up may not be in the forefront of our children's minds—*Kids are resilient!* we assure ourselves—the experience *was* caught and recorded by the synapses of their developing brains, thus giving them valuable information about us as people, about how they deserve to be treated when they make a mistake or don't follow instructions, and about how it's appropriate for adults to react if things don't go their way. And worse still, when we yell at our kids, we're likely implanting triggers in them that their kids may later set off. In other words, when we yell at our kids, it's almost like we're yelling at our unborn grandkids.

Shouldn't Our Children Be Listening to Us?

Hold on for a moment! you may be thinking. *Haven't we asked nicely, over and over again? What are we supposed to do? Let them run the show? We're the adults! We're in charge! Kids should be listening to us.*

Don't get me wrong, I'm in NO WAY saying children shouldn't put down their iPads when it's time to put them down or shouldn't get dressed for school when it's time. What I *am* saying is that we have other options in the way we respond to these frustrations. Indeed, there are actually civilized, respectful, and effective ways we can approach our children when they aren't doing what we've asked. What keeps so many of us from exploring our options is a culture that essentially supports yelling at children. Since virtually forever, a bedrock principle of Western civilization is the belief that children should do as they are told by grown-ups, and if they don't, then they deserve what they have coming. They were warned. And yet another fundamental hallmark of our culture is that we rarely (if ever) think the reverse is true: A parent would never be considered deserving of a child's wrath. If our kids yell at us, we think of them as insolent, sassy back-talkers rather than people trying to stick up for themselves or communicate their needs and feelings without the tools to do so civilly.

This virtually universal double standard is explored in depth by scholar Elisabeth Young-Bruehl in her groundbreaking book *Childism: Confronting Prejudice Against Children* in which she proves how childism functions much like sexism, racism, and homophobia in that a defining characteristic—in this case, youth—is used as evidence of that segment of the population's inferiority and thus legitimizes and justifies all manner of mistreatment. Young-Bruehl explains:

> Children are the one group that, many of us think without thinking, is *naturally* subordinate. Until they reach a stipulated age, they are the responsibility of their parents or guardians—those who have custody. But what does custody permit? What distinguishes it from ownership? One of the essential ingredients of childism is a claim by adults to the effect that children are ours to do with exactly as we see fit, or children exist to serve, honor, and obey adults. These claims make a subordination doctrine out of natural dependency, out of the fact that children are born relatively helpless and need to be taken care of until they can take care of themselves. It seems normal to insist "honor thy father and thy mother" without any reciprocal "honor thy children."

Because we expect children to be deferential to adults, they become easy scapegoats. We get to blame them for "making us" yell, as if they not only deserved it but we literally had no other choice. Without realizing it, we take advantage of their vulnerabilities— the fact that their cognition isn't yet fully developed and that they depend on us to survive. The luxury of being able to blame kids with impunity keeps generation after generation of parents caught in a vicious cycle of stress and anxiety. But, as blame expert and research professor at the University of Houston Graduate College of Social Work Dr. Brené Brown tells us, blame is just a way "to discharge pain and discomfort." And it's a distraction. When we're blaming, we're not thinking about what would be the most helpful way to handle the situation. We're not being curious as to why our kids aren't "listening." We can't empathize with them. And, perhaps most important, blame keeps us from doing the work we need to do to heal the wounds that triggered us in the first place.

> **We can learn to respond to our kids' unwelcome behavior instead of reacting to it.**

But the truth is, we do have a choice.

We can continue to yell at our kids and blame them for making us do it, or we can try to understand our triggers, which, Dr. Siegel explains, ". . . can be an essential starting place in the road to healing." We can learn to respond to our kids' unwelcome behavior instead of reacting to it, and we can be more proactive about preventing situations that work us up in the first place. But it's no easy task: It requires commitment, patience, curiosity, and some fearlessness.

Identifying a Trigger

As a starting point in my quest to stop yelling, I set out to try to identify and understand some of my triggers. It's important work to do because, as Dr. Markham says, "life will keep triggering you until you heal them."

So I asked myself, *When do you lose it the most?*

The answer was easy: Every single morning before school.

Almost daily when I wake up, I pray for a calm beginning to our day. My fantasy goes something like this: First Jules will wake up and call me in. "Good morning, my darling!" I'll say, and then I'll climb into bed with her to cuddle and read a book to ease her into a new day. Then Hudson will wake up, and I'll go into his room to do the same, while Jules luxuriates in bed before getting dressed. (John is busy getting ready for work and walking the dogs before taking the kids to school.) Then I leave Hudson and go downstairs and get breakfast going while they get dressed and then come down. They sit at the table and eat the beautiful, healthy meal I've laid out for them. Then they clear the table, grab their lunches, and head out to the car with John as I give them all a warm send-off. "Have a great day, everyone! I love you!"

If only.

The truth is, no one is getting out of bed. No one is getting dressed. No one knows where their socks and shoes are. Nor does anyone care. No one comes down for breakfast. They want to stay in bed or play, not get ready for school. No one cares about being on time. Except me! "We're gonna be late!!! Let's go!" (Note: No one includes two people: Jules and Hudson.)

At some point, after asking them to come downstairs as nicely as I can for the third time, I lose my shit. We all know the stress of getting our kids out the door in the morning, but I take it to another level. I may not be yelling, but I'm talking in this overly calm, I've-had-it voice that drives my kids insane.

> I may not be yelling, but I'm talking in this overly calm, I've-had-it voice that drives my kids insane.

And in my head, I blame everyone for making me do it.

I blame the kids for being lazy!

For not appreciating the effort I put into their breakfast and their lunches!

For not coming down when I ask them to!

For not caring about being on time!

And then I blame the school for not starting later.

I blame Hudson's teachers for not creating a class environment that he's eager to attend.

I blame the institution of school for existing in the first place.

And I worry about their futures.

If they don't eat a proper breakfast, their day will be ruined for sure!

If they can't do something as simple as getting dressed on time, how will they ever function in the world?

If they can't be on time, how will they ever keep a job?

Before I even know what's happening, all of that blame gets injected into my I've-had-it voice and then it all backfires in a big ugly explosion of upset. Now the kids are crying and screaming and cowering or are otherwise retaliating because being yelled at (even if it doesn't involve a raised voice) feels terrible.

> **If they can't do something as simple as getting dressed on time, how will they ever function in the world?**

"You promised never to sound like that again!"

"You're the one writing the book on not yelling, you should do what you say!"

"Treat others how you want to be treated!"

"Now I'm *really* not going to go to school."

"This is going to be the worst day ever!"

Shit!

And then John emerges from the bathroom and is like, *This again? You've got to be kidding me!*

If I did have any momentum at all getting them out the door, now everything has come to a grinding halt. In fact, the pendulum has swung in the other direction. Because I lost it, they're going to be even later. I feel terrible and they feel terrible. The whole scene is precisely as Dr. Marshall Rosenberg warns: "You can't make your kids do anything. All you can do is make them wish they had. And then, they will make you wish you hadn't made them wish they had."

So in the face of the collateral damage I've wreaked, I sigh a heavy sigh and take a deep breath and remind myself to give myself a break and to remember that this is (yet another) learning experience. As desperate as I am to move past this explosion, I know I can't rush them into feeling better. I need to give them the time they need to recalibrate. I need to give them a chance to tell me how I made them feel—i.e., horrible! I need to give them the time to be calm enough to really hear and digest my apology. And I hate it that once again their not coming down for breakfast has turned me into the bad guy.

Deactivating a Trigger

With that happening day after day, you can probably see why I was eager to understand why I get so triggered in the mornings. If it's not my kids, then what?

What is it, I asked myself, *that really gets you so worked up, Jennifer?*

A little voice answered back, *I don't want them to be late to school.*

Like many people, I think being on time is the "right" thing to do. I believe that being late is rude and sends the message that somehow the rules don't apply to you. But I realized that I was responding to my kids' dragging their feet in the mornings as if being late to school was the end of the world. I think that it's because as a child I learned that it could be. To my grandpa—the family's undeniable patriarch—being on time was beyond a virtue, it was the defining factor of one's character. On time meant you were good; late meant you were bad. No in between. Five minutes late was five minutes way too late. Five minutes of him sitting at a restaurant telling everyone who would listen how inexcusable it was.

And inevitably when I would visit my grandparents—time and again over the course of thirty-plus years—I found myself anxiously caught between my grandmother and grandfather's power play. When it was

> On time meant you were good; late meant you were bad.

time to go, Grandpa and I would wait for Grandma by the elevator in the hall. And we'd wait. And we'd wait, while she did whatever she had to do before leaving at a pace that rivaled molasses dripping from a jar. While she never actually made us late, because Grandpa and I were out in the hall with *plenty* of time to spare, the fear of it was always looming. And I knew what my grandfather's temper could look like. He was six-foot-three, headed up his own company, and had always expected everyone to do as he said, when he said it. I never wanted to be on his bad side—hence it took me no time to be ready (an expectation I obviously had for my children). When my grandmother would finally emerge from the apartment and I'd start to breathe a sigh of relief, inevitably she'd walk back in to get something she'd forgotten. *Oh, God, Grandma, please! Come on! Grandpa is going to lose it!* And often once she did finally start to lock the door, she'd remember yet one more thing and have to GO BACK IN! AGAIN! *Oh, Grandma, no!* Standing with my grandpa, trying to make small talk to take his mind off Grandma not coming, I felt anxious and powerless. And afraid Grandpa would blow at any minute. *So could it be,* I wondered for the first time, *that when my kids are running late for school I feel like I'm a bad mother for having children who don't respect the golden rule of being on time? Or I can't take feeling that the anxiety and powerlessness I felt as a child, so I yell at my kids to keep it at bay?* It made sense.

Becoming aware of what triggered me was a good first step. But being aware wouldn't all of a sudden make my anxiety and anger go away. So what to do?

Feel the Pain

I've learned that the first thing to do when triggered is nothing. Well, not nothing, but the idea is, as psychologist Shefali Tsabary explains in her book *The Conscious Parent: Transforming Ourselves, Empowering Our Children*, to let yourself feel the feelings you so desperately don't want to feel:

> As you learn to be with your emotions, they will no longer overwhelm you. In the full acceptance of surrender, which is of a quite different character from mere resignation, you come to see that pain is simply pain, nothing more and nothing less. Yes, pain is painful—it's meant to be. However, when you don't fuel your pain by either resisting or reacting, but sit with it, it transforms itself into wisdom. Your wisdom will increase in line with your capacity for embracing all of your feelings, whatever their nature. Along with increased wisdom comes a greater capacity for compassion.

For me, understanding that the surge of anger I'm feeling is something to just let myself feel but not necessarily act on helps me keep my cool. Understanding that beneath the anger often lurk more vulnerable feelings like fear also helps. Now, when I feel the rage filling me up like I'm a syringe, I try to force myself to take some slow, deep breaths—which can be remarkably challenging. Sometimes I have to literally walk myself out of the room. I find there's nothing like a change of scenery to help calm the nerves as I struggle to allow myself to just feel my feelings without doing anything about them.

Take Stock

I 've also found it helpful, when I'm not triggered, to take stock of the present situation. As Vannevar Bush, an electrical engineer and inventor, once said, "Fear cannot be banished, but it . . . can be mitigated by reason and evaluation." So what is the *reality* of our family's particular morning situation? What am I afraid might happen if the kids were late? What actually does happen? Here's the reality:

1. While the kids' school officially starts at 8:45, it doesn't really get underway until 9:00. Many kids come at 9:00 and life is just fine.

2. John drives the kids to school so I don't have to deal with the panic of trying to drive fast or getting overwhelmed by the traffic, or need to respond to any flak they may get from teachers.

3. No teacher has ever complained to either of us about the kids being late.

4. John always gets to work on time.

All of this is true, and yet based on the way I lose my shit in the morning, you'd never believe it. You'd think we had a bus to catch or we went to a strict, no-tardiness-tolerated school and our kids had been given their final warning. So now in the morning, I try to remember to remind myself of these realities while also bearing in mind that my kids' moving slower than I want is bound to trigger me. And it helps.

Problem-Solve Together!

Another important step in making our mornings go more smoothly was to talk to my family about what being on time means to me, to their teachers, and to them. I asked:

"Is it important to you to be on time?"

"What are mornings like at school? . . . Is anyone ever late? . . . Is it disruptive?"

As it turns out, it was a lively and informative conversation.

JULES: Our teachers have been working with us all year long to come in quietly and join the morning meeting if we are late. And if we've missed anything, the plan they're going over is written on the board, so we can just look at that. The same kids are late every day, but their parents don't seem stressed about it like you are.

ME: Do you mind being late?

JULES: I'd rather be on time. But it's not really a big deal.

HUDSON: I don't care if I'm late at all.

JOHN: I'd like to be on time, but not at the expense of your mental health. I just feel like the added stress to our lives is worse than being a few minutes late.

Clearly being on time doesn't mean to my family what it means to me. Yes, I want to share with my kids my values of respecting others by arriving promptly, but not at the risk of making them resent it. The truth is, they have the right to their perspective, even if it's one I don't agree with.

However, my perspective also counts, so I shared with them why being on time is important to me. I asked Jules, John, and

Hudson if there was anything they'd be willing to do to help our mornings go more smoothly, so I wouldn't feel alone trying to get everyone out the door. Here's what they came up with:

- Hudson wanted his alarm clock set earlier.
- Both kids said they were happy to eat breakfast in the car, if necessary.
- Jules recommended setting the shoes and socks by the front door at night.
- John said he'd be in charge of prepping the toothbrushes.
- Jules asked if I could ask her to come down in person instead of just yelling up to her.

In fact, Jules's suggestion was life altering. When I could see what she was (or wasn't) doing, I had more information and I could be more empathetic. "Jules, I know you love that book. That's wonderful, but I'm worried that you're so engrossed in it that you'll be late to school. Why don't you get ready first and then read?" I found that when I could say this calmly and with eye contact, she was much more amenable.

This multipronged approach to solving the mornings has been very effective. And perhaps most important, thinking the problem through together has helped all of us realize that we can work as a family to try to solve challenging issues, taking into account multiple perspectives.

Enlist Support

've also explained to the kids that when I speak to them in a way I know is hurtful, it's my problem and not theirs, and I'm working on it. I've asked John, if he's around, to please step in and help—which he'll do *if* my being upset doesn't trigger him too much. That's part of the problem with triggers: They can snowball. When he can say, "Honey, I see this is hard for you, let me help," I feel supported instead of like a bad person. And, I've told the kids they are welcome to simply say to me, "Can you please talk to me in a nicer voice?" And sometimes, if they aren't too hurt themselves, they do. And it's pretty damn disarming.

"Yes, honey. I can. Thank you for the reminder."

Other Strategies

t's no wonder my friend Jill has found trying to stop yelling so hard. It is hard. You just can't simply make a decision to stop and then, boom, no more yelling. I never realized how much can go into it. And while I've touched on many things we can do— i.e., identifying triggers, deactivating them, letting yourself sit with the pain, taking stock of the reality, problem-solving with your family, enlisting their support—there are more options. Certainly, meditation and mindfulness practices, as well as therapy and even anti-anxiety medication in more severe cases, can help. It's also true that if we find ourselves prone to screaming a lot, we may not be taking good care of ourselves. Likely we could use more exercise, more sleep, and/or more time alone, with friends, or our partner. And honestly, the Internet is filled with other tips. One I liked in particular was from a mom named Amanda who blogs at *Dirt and Boogers*. Amanda puts cut-out hearts around her home and in her car, particularly in places she finds herself losing it, to serve as gentle reminders to soften when she feels the surge of anger building inside her. I also like that visible reminders can let our kids know that we're trying to make a change, and I think that counts for a lot.

CHAPTER THIRTEEN

"DO YOU WANT A TIME-OUT?"

"Absence from those we love
is self from self—a deadly banishment."
—**William Shakespeare**

Right around the time spanking was starting to get a bad rap, maybe in the late sixties and early seventies, and increasingly so in the eighties, time-outs came to parents' rescue. Now we could put our foot down, but gently. Phew. If our kids are kicking or grabbing or screaming or melting down—or some fun combination thereof—we can give them a time-out, a break from the chaos. This usually means a parent insists their child stop the unacceptable behavior and go to their room or just off to the side somewhere for a period of time without parental attention. Over the years, time-outs have become so popular in the United States that, according to *Time* magazine, they're now the number-one way parents try to change their children's behavior, as well as the number-one method of discipline recommended by pediatricians.

In fact, I vividly remember Jules's doctor recommending time-outs to me during her eighteen-month wellness visit. He was talking about developmental milestones that were coming up when he added, "And now's the age to start disciplining. When she does something naughty, you can put her in a time-out. I always say a minute for each year—so for Jules, just begin with a minute and half. Even if she won't stay where you put her and even if she cries, just make sure you ignore her for the full time. Be firm. She'll learn soon enough."

Who died and made him a relationship expert? I wondered, taken aback. But I said nothing.

Time and Space: Friends or Foes?

I get the appeal of time-outs. I know that when I'm upset, sometimes a little time and space, perhaps in the form of a walk around the block or even just stepping into the sunshine for a moment, is just what I need to cool down and gain some perspective. If during a heated discussion I can manage to say, "You know, I'm feeling overwhelmed and need a little time to collect myself. Can we can pick this up in twenty minutes or so?" then I can save myself from saying things I'm bound to regret. So I totally understand how folks might think about time-outs as if we're giving our kids the respite they don't realize they need.

But let's be honest: Do any of us truly believe that a child in a time-out is thinking anything like *Ahhh! A little space to reflect. Thanks so much, Mom! Now I know what I did wrong, why I did it, and what I should do differently next time.* It's much more likely that our children are stewing—about how coldhearted and unfair we are. Indeed, as Dr. Daniel Siegel and Dr. Tina Payne Bryson, coauthors of *The Whole-Brain Child* and *No-Drama Discipline*, report in their *Time* article "Time-Outs Are Hurting Your Child," "Time-outs frequently make children angrier and more dysregulated, leaving them even less able to control themselves or think about what they've done, and more focused on how mean their parents are to have punished them." Particularly if they're put in a time-out in front of others. As Dr. Aletha Solter, a developmental psychologist internationally recognized as an expert on attachment, rhetorically asks in her article "The Disadvantages of Time-Out," "Who wants to be isolated from the group and totally ignored?" Obviously, *no one.* Even for a minute and

Alas, there's a significant difference between excusing oneself for a break and being forced to leave your family, friends, and the fun.

a half. No one wants to walk that walk of shame. No one wants people to see them sitting off alone because they've been "bad." Alas, there's a significant difference between excusing oneself for a break and being forced to leave your family, friends, and the fun—particularly with everyone looking on. Personally, I can still remember with remarkable clarity at least half a dozen instances from my childhood when friends got "in trouble" in front of me— they were grounded, sent to their rooms, had TV time or dessert taken away, were screamed at and even spanked. For me, just watching was awful enough. I always felt helpless and mortified for my friends, knowing their experience was made that much worse because I was there. Although we'd never speak about it, we both knew it happened. It's like second-hand smoke—others are adversely affected even though the smoker doesn't mean for them to be. So beware, parents, when you "discipline" your kids in front of others. You're not just hurting them.

Time-Outs Can Trigger Our Primal Fear of Abandonment

The truth is, for many kids, time-outs do indeed cause real pain. Siegel, Bryson, and other experts in the field tell us that time-outs can leave children feeling rejected, unworthy of love, and genuinely scared.

Unfortunately, they're not exaggerating.

As newborn *Homo sapiens*, we are utterly dependent upon our caregivers for the food, warmth, shelter, and nurture we need to survive. And so from birth we are wired in a profound way for connection to our caregivers. In other words, in order to feel safe, we need to feel confident in the strength of our bond with the people in charge of our welfare. We need to know unequivocally that they care for us and will not leave us—no matter what. So, if we sense the connection isn't solid, we might react as if our very survival is at stake. Our parents may know they'd never let anything happen to us, their precious children, but *we* don't know that. Why? Because our parents have sent us away from them when we are struggling. Not only would they let something happen to us, they're causing it to happen. As Dr. Laura Markham warns in her article "What's Wrong with Time-Outs," time-outs can break

> From birth we are wired in a profound way for connection to our caregivers.

a "child's trust in you by triggering his fear of abandonment." She adds, "Banishing an upset child is pushing her away just when she needs you the most. Worst of all, she only calms down and becomes more 'obedient' because you've triggered the universal childhood fear of abandonment." In other words, time-outs can threaten the vital connection that makes children feel safe, and that's genuinely scary. In fact, Dr. Solter tells us that "Nothing is more frightening for a child than the withdrawal of love." She explains that along with a fear of being abandoned comes "insecurity, anxiety, confusion, anger, resentment, and low self-esteem."

When I was growing up in the seventies, my parents didn't use the term "time-out," but I was definitely sent to my room—though they also didn't quite put it that way. What they often told me when I was "throwing a fit"—when my brain was flooded with stress hormones and I was wailing on the floor, kicking and screaming, feeling at once out of control, angry, hurt, and profoundly misunderstood—was that I was welcome to act however I liked, just as long as I did it in my own room. To me, their message was clear. When I could act as if I wasn't feeling the feelings I was feeling, I was welcome to come out and be with them. In the meantime, I was left to try to make sense of the cyclone inside me on my own—a task, of course, for which I was entirely ill-equipped. It was just as marriage and family therapist Susan Stiffelman describes in her article "Why I Don't Recommend Time-Outs":

> Time-outs send a child the message that she is only lovable and acceptable when she is behaving as we wish. The problem with this notion is that to be human is to be complex; we have both our light and shadow side, and to develop healthy self-esteem, we need to embrace all of who we are. When we send a child away because she isn't managing her dark side, we're reinforcing the notion that to be loved and lovable requires splitting off from the part of us that is messy. . . .

Time-outs convey to the child that we cannot handle them unless they're good. Children need confident captains of the ship to help them through life's difficult lessons. When we send a misbehaving child to his room because we can't handle his misbehavior or moodiness, we're effectively "jumping ship," creating anxiety in a child who needs to know that we can handle whatever challenge he may face.

Certainly I *know* beyond a shadow of doubt that my extraordinarily devoted, caring parents were doing their absolute best, which I imagine was better than what their parents did. Maybe they weren't allowed to feel their feelings or act out at all—even in their own rooms. Or maybe as children they just weren't as sensitive as I was. I'm not blaming them, because I know that my parents, like all of us, are flawed, well-meaning people who were raised by flawed, well-meaning people who were raised by flawed, well-meaning people, ad infinitum. My point is, now that I'm a parent, it's up to me to take stock of how my upbringing may have adversely affected me and decide if I want to do things differently. Which I do.

> Even if we try to reassure our kids that we still love them while putting them in a time-out, our actions will speak louder than our words.

What I've learned is that even if we try to reassure our kids that we still love them while putting them in a time-out, our actions will speak louder than our words. Dr. Solter explains, "While parents are often careful to provide reassurances of their love and to distinguish between the child and the unruly behavior ('I love you, but you need to go to your room for five minutes because what you did is not acceptable') . . . concrete experience and perceptions of reality impact more strongly than language." And, according to Dr. David

Simon, a psychotherapist and cofounder of the Chopra Center for Wellbeing, once a child interprets being sent away as being unlovable, it's a belief that can be particularly difficult to shake. "Before we're eight years old," Dr. Simon explains, "we have almost no capacity to filter out information that comes to us. So if parents or teachers, people we count on to nurture us, say something hurtful to us before the age of eight . . . it goes in quite deep and we carry those misbeliefs with us. They profoundly affect our relationship to ourselves, to others . . . [and] our sense of value in the world." This is because, as Dr. Siegel explains, "when an experience is repeated over and over, it deepens and strengthens the connections among our neurons called synapses." When disciplining our children, he asks us to "consider what connections are being formed and how they could play out in your child's future."

In other words, do we know what the long-term impact of time-outs might be?

If we know time-outs can trigger a fear of abandonment in a child, leaving him with a belief that he is unlovable when struggling, and this message is sent over and over again when he is young, wiring the message deep into his brain, how might this affect his future relationships?

According to psychologist and psychotherapist Dr. Susan Lacombe, people who suffer from a fear of abandonment often also suffer from deep-seated feelings of anger and despair and have compulsive behaviors and thought patterns that sabotage their relationships, ultimately driving people to abandon them. This creates a self-fulfilling prophecy, affirming their belief that they aren't truly lovable. Lacombe warns that "unless abandonment issues are resolved [they] will arise in all your close relationships." This is because "What the child learns in the early years gets ingrained in a way that is difficult to access as an adult. Yet, it is often only through our adult relationships that these feelings of abandonment are resolved."

Not My Kid!

Perhaps you're thinking *Not my kid! I've put her in plenty of time-outs and she does just fine. She knows she did something wrong. She pays the price. And we're done. No big deal. Let's not blow things so out of proportion.* I hear you. I've seen plenty of kids put in a time-out at the park—for not sharing, for grabbing a toy, for saying something that wasn't "nice," for hitting their sister, what have you—who sit docilely and then eagerly return to the action when they've been released, like it was no big deal. While this may in part have to do with a child's temperament, it may also depend on how used to the protocol they've become. Perhaps they know there's no point in putting up a fight, or they've realized that protesting only makes things worse. So they stifle their feelings, act like they're totally cool, and ride it out. Maybe they won't give their parents the benefit of knowing how hurt they are.

> Perhaps they know there's no point in putting up a fight, or they've realized that protesting only makes things worse.

Dr. Peter Haiman explains in his article "The Case Against Time-Out" (yes, yet another therapist pleading his case in a similarly titled article) that some children learn to repress their feelings and, as a result, develop various nervous habits to cope, "such as thumb sucking, fingernail biting, hair pulling, skin scratching, tugging at clothes, self-pinching, and many other similar behaviors. The purpose of these behaviors is to ward off uncomfortable feelings and, in identification with their parents' criticism of them, to punish themselves. These defense strategies serve to release anger and ignore uncomfortable feelings."

But my child doesn't have any of these habits. And time-outs are no big deal to them.

I believe you!

But that's not necessarily a good thing. Stiffelman writes, "I am especially concerned when I hear from a parent that time-outs aren't working because a child doesn't care if she's sent to her room. In this case, it's crucial that parents heal the damaged connection and restore trust, while creating a climate for their child to express pain, hurt, or anger. . . ."

Furthermore, it's entirely possible that symptoms of a person suffering from a fear of abandonment may not surface until the child grows up and starts to have relationships with potential partners. Susan Anderson, a therapist who specializes in treating adults who suffer from fear of abandonment, explains, "Much of what they [people who suffer from a fear of abandonment] go through doesn't show on the outside. . . . Outwardly they seem happy and well-adjusted, while inwardly struggling with intrusive anxiety that interferes in their relationships."

Time-Outs Teach That Withdrawing Love Solves Problems

And really, what are we teaching kids about solving problems when we send them away when we don't like how they're acting? That if they don't like what someone is saying or doing, that they should ignore them? That our love and attention are things to be given and taken away to control others' behavior? I know I must have gotten that message, because if John and I are having a hard time, my first instinct is to make him suffer by ignoring him until he realizes how horrible it is to be ignored by me. That's my strategy—one I've learned with therapy not to give in to. I imagine many can relate.

So What to Do?

Okay, *enough already!* I can almost hear you thinking. *Just tell me what we're supposed to do!*

Help.

Help, how?

It depends.

It depends on lots of factors, like what your child did. How he's feeling. What need drove the behavior. The way it adversely affects others. The current circumstances. And the temperament of your child. Alas, appealing as it is, a one-size-fits-all response isn't realistic. Humans are complicated. The reason a child is acting a certain way may be as obvious as someone grabbed her toy and she's trying to stick up for herself, or it may be more complicated. Maybe dad has been out of town for a week and the child misses him, worries about him, and feels left behind, so she takes out her feelings on her brother. Parenting, like all relationships, is not a science, it's an art form, one that requires great sensitivity and a profound respect for the child as an individual with his own valid experience. It also requires parents to take a child's needs as seriously as a grown-up's and to approach the situation with a staggering amount of patience, at least a passing understanding of how the brain works, and with the knowledge that there will be some serious trial and error. As I discuss in Chapter 12, behavior (whether we approve of it or not) is *never* without legitimate cause. Ignoring a legitimate cause will only make things worse. Often when kids are doing something we deem time-out-worthy (a determination that varies from person to person, mind you) it's for one these six reasons:

> Parenting, like all relationships, is not a science, it's an art form.

1. **They're overwhelmed by painful feelings** like hurt, fear, jealousy, anxiety, and/or sadness. In this case, they need our help calming down, and to know that we're attempting to understand their feelings and empathize.

2. **They're trying to meet a fundamental need in the best way they know how** (but their best isn't good enough). In this case, they need our help finding a better way to meet their needs.

3. **They don't have the information they need to make a better choice.** In this case, they simply need more information.

4. **They have yet to develop the cognition to control themselves.** In this case, they need us close by to help them make better decisions.

5. **The environment isn't set up for them to succeed.** In this case, we need to set up our space to support them better.

6. **Our expectations aren't realistic.** In this case, we have to adjust our expectations.

Or some combination thereof.

The good news is that there is a place between punitive and permissive, between strict control and giving in, and that's where problem-solving, growth, and connection live. Some characterize this third approach as "family-centered." Others, including Dr. Thomas Gordon, author of *Parent Effectiveness Training*, think of it as more "democratic." Alfie Kohn, author of *Unconditional Parenting*, believes in "working with" a child to problem-solve (as opposed to "doing to" them). Dr. Ross Greene, author of *Raising Human Beings*, advocates creating a "collaborative partnership" with children. Whatever you call it, the process includes loads of empathy, sending clear messages about what behavior is unacceptable, listening to the child's feelings and needs while also being clear about our own, and problem-solving together.

Safety First

As always, the first order of business is to keep everyone safe. We're the adults; that's our job. If you need to stop your child from hitting someone, try to do it as gently as possible. "I can see you're very angry, but I can't let you hit. That hurts. . . ." If they've already hurt someone, do your best to separate the children and attend to the hurt child, while remaining neutral. You might say something like "I'm sorry you got hurt. Can I get you some ice?" or offer other suggestions to help the hurt child feel better. Then to the child who hurt the other child, "I know you're angry, but hitting isn't the way to solve a problem. I know we can solve this together. . . ."

Acceptance

When our kids are having a hard time, we're like first responders to an accident: We're there to help, not judge. (Imagine a paramedic screaming at a drunk driver who has multiple fractures, "I'm not going to help you. You deserve this! You never should drink and drive!") Perhaps the most difficult thing to do when your child is acting out is to let them know you still love them. Anything like "I can see you're having a rough time, and I want to help" can signal to them that a calm, caring individual is on the scene to provide comfort and support. In the book *Hold on to Your Kids: Why Parents Need to Matter More Than Peers*, developmental psychologist Dr. Gordon Neufeld and coauthor Dr. Gabor Maté, the internationally renowned physician who specializes in treating addiction, write, "Unconditional parental love is the indispensable nutrient for the child's healthy emotional growth. The first task is to create space in the child's heart for the certainty that she is precisely the person the parents want and love. . . . The child can be ornery, unpleasant, whiny, uncooperative, and plain rude, and the parent still lets her feel loved." In fact, they tell us, it is essential for a child to "be able to bring her unrest, her least likable characteristics to the parent and still receive the parent's absolutely satisfying, security-inducing, unconditional love." Or as Mister Rogers more succinctly put it, "To love someone is to strive to accept that person exactly the way he or she is, right here and now." So obviously, and at the risk of sounding like a broken record, time-outs can literally never say: *I love you unconditionally.*

> "To love someone is to strive to accept that person exactly the way he or she is, right here and now."
> —*Mister Rogers*

Soothing

So we're not going to let anyone hurt anyone. We're accepting our children as they are in their struggle, and we're signaling that we're here to help.

Now, before they can actually take in anything we have to say, they need to be calm. And helping them get calm is part of our job. "Young children depend upon, want to be with, love, and need their parents," Dr. Haiman tells us. Similarly, Dr. Siegel and Dr. Bryson explain in no uncertain terms that children "have a profound need for connection" and that "decades of research in attachment demonstrate that particularly in times of distress, we need to be near and be soothed by the people who care for us."

Scientifically speaking (in layman's language, of course), if our child has become dysregulated—that is to say, if her brain is flooded with stress hormones—she literally can't think straight. Dr. Dan Siegel

> **How you will help your child calm down depends on his or her nature.**

calls this "flipping your lid." He explains: "When we 'flip our lids,' our rational brains have a very poor connection with our emotional brains. Our feelings are intense, and we're not able to access the logical, problem-solving part of our brain. To restore our rational brain to its coherent state, we need to calm our anger and ease our fears." How you will help your child calm down depends on his or her nature. Certainly what Jules responds to when very upset is different from what helps Hudson. For instance, for some children just signaling our acceptance can help. For others, being held and otherwise physically comforted relaxes them. Some may want a little space, while knowing we're close by when they're ready to talk. Some need a really good cry to get it all out. Some can start to settle down by sucking their fingers or thumb. Some need a special blanket or toy. Some need a book. Some like to suck their fingers *while* holding a special blanket and reading a book. And sometimes just diving right in and naming what they're feeling and why they may be feeling it hits the spot like nothing else. Perhaps something like, "You're so furious because it just doesn't seem fair. Is that right? You've been waiting for your chance patiently for three weeks, and she just gets to do it the first day?" *Ahh, someone gets it.* Or, "You hate it that I won't let you watch a movie this late at night. You think it's unfair because your sister got to watch a movie late one night, huh?" As Dr. Siegel and Dr. Bryson say, "Name it to tame it."

Realistic Expectations

Just because we're grown-ups, just because we're annoyed, just because we're embarrassed, just because we're mad, that doesn't mean the way we want our kids to behave is the only viable solution. The truth is there are many ways to solve a problem.

Let's say we're in a nice restaurant and the kids are being too loud and fidgety. People are looking at us. They've paid a lot of money for a civilized meal, and our kids are ruining their night out. Yes, we're getting annoyed. Yes, we've asked the kids to settle down nicely several times. Now what? Threaten? "Do you want a time-out? No? Then sit properly." Bribe? "If you're good, we'll go out for ice cream after." Or problem-solve? "How can we make this situation work for everyone?"

> Is it realistic to expect a child to sit at a table quietly and listen to adult conversation? Maybe, for some kids. Not mine.

Is it realistic to expect a child to sit at a table quietly and listen to adult conversation? Maybe, for some kids. Not mine. But I've seen it. And now that Jules is older, she can do it longer. But asking Hudson to sit quietly at a grown-up restaurant is setting him up to fall. My options are this: Bring something to occupy the kids, like action figures and paper and pencils, take them outside to run around until the food comes, or don't take them to the restaurant in the first place.

Information Please!

S ometimes kids just need more information. Instead of getting them "in trouble" for what they have done, we can simply tell them why what they're doing isn't working in the current circumstances. For instance, one day when Jules was three-ish there was a group play date in a friend's backyard. Four kids were playing in and around the sandbox, and all was going well until India started throwing sand. She wasn't throwing it at anyone; rather, she was throwing it on the ground outside the sandbox.

"India, honey! Remember, no throwing sand," her mom calmly reminded her.

India paid no attention and kept at it.

"Indie! No! No sand throwing," her mom reiterated, this time more forcefully.

But India was in a trance. She seemed mesmerized by the white specs hitting the green grass. Delighted, even.

Just as her mom seemed on the verge of taking things up a couple of notches, Linda, whose house it was, stepped in and came up to India, made eye contact, and said, "You know India, I love throwing sand, too. It feels good, and I like to watch it scatter in the wind. But the reason I don't want you throwing it out of the sandbox is that if we all did that, there wouldn't be any more left to play with. Sand is too hard to pick up from grass and put back in the box." India seemed to register what Linda had to say. Apparently it made some sense to her, because she stopped throwing the sand and actually started to try to pick some up off the grass and put it back in the sandbox. She understood what Linda was saying and soon changed her course, moving on to digging.

Help Them Be the People They Need to Be

Our kids may not yet be able to control themselves the way we want them to, as I quickly realized when Jules was two and I was close to nine months pregnant with Hudson. Out of nowhere, my easygoing Jules started scratching kids' faces in the middle of playing. I was mortified and worried. My best guess was that Jules was feeling lots of confusing feelings about the imminent arrival of a new family member, and I guessed that she was taking it out on other kids. Perhaps she was looking for assurance that we'd still love her no matter how she acted. Jules didn't need a time-out; she needed me. Not just more love, time, and assurance, but she physically needed me closer to her while she played, should she act out again. Which she did. Over and over. For a couple of weeks, maybe even longer, every time Jules was playing with other kids I had to remain close and really keep an eye on her, because things could be going just fine and then, in a flash, I could see a look on her face and her claws would come out. I got better at seeing it, and I'd step in and gently stop her arm. "I can't let you hurt your friends. I can see you didn't like that. You can tell her 'Stop.' Or 'Don't grab.' Sure, it was a bummer—as in a total bummer—to have to be so vigilant, but worth it. She eventually got the message that I wasn't going to let her scratch other kids' faces and that I was interested in how she was feeling.

And So . . .

And so I submit, because we now *know* that children are wired for connection in order to feel safe and loved, and because we *know* fear of abandonment is a primal fear, it makes no sense to respond to a child's unacceptable behavior in a way that exploits their base need.

What I find particularly interesting about time-outs is that they were devised ostensibly to be a kinder, gentler alternative to spanking a child, and now I'm not so sure that when we take the long view they're even that. Likely they are, but not by much. When I consider that a time-out can break a child's trust in his parents, that it can trigger feelings of abandonment, that it can

> **A time-out can break a child's trust in his parents.**

leave a child feeling unloved for who he is, and that it can even possibly lead to a life of self-sabotaging relationships because he is plagued by a fear of abandonment, I really have to wonder. My conclusion: Neither isolating nor striking a child serves us well. Far better to help them find better ways to regulate themselves.

CHAPTER FOURTEEN

"DO YOU WANT A SPANKING?"

"Through violence
you may 'solve' one problem,
but you sow the seeds for another."
—the Dalai Lama

"Do you want a spanking?" my friend Stuart "asked" his seven-year-old in front of me and some other friends and family while we were hanging out at their swimming pool. A question doesn't get much more rhetorical than that. What Stuart was obviously saying was, *Stop it or I'll hurt you, and I don't care who knows it.* And it freaked me out. *Is this really* *happening? It's the twenty-first century!* I'd known Stuart for twenty years and he's about as progressive a guy as you can get, and yet he still thought "spanking" his child was okay. I felt like I'd been living under a rock, naively assuming that spanking had gone out of fashion. Boy, was I wrong.

Alas, a little research told me hitting children is alive and well in America.

(Please note that what many people refer to as "spanking" I call "hitting," because I think "spanking" is a dangerous euphemism that makes the act seem as if it's a viable form of discipline instead of a harmful act of violence. The truth is, according to the common-law definition of assault, if it's an intentional act by a person that makes another person fear imminent harm or offensive contact, it meets the criteria of violent—you don't even have to actually hit. The only time I'll use the term "spanking" is when I'm quoting a study or expert.)

So as I said, adults hitting children when they don't like how they have acted is alive and well in America. A 2013 Harris Poll tells us that 81 percent of Americans believe it's acceptable to "spank" a child, and 82 percent of Gen X parents do it, while 72 percent of Millennials do. While I wasn't particularly surprised to learn from a Columbia University study published in *Pediatrics* that the majority of parents are "spanking" children between the ages of three and five, I was shocked to read a new study called "Eavesdropping on the Family: A Pilot Investigation of Corporal Punishment in the Home," based on home audio recordings, that revealed that some parents start "spanking" when their babies are only six months old. That's hitting someone who is cognitively incapable of impulse control. It's like hitting someone for not being able to walk.

> 81 percent of Americans believe it's acceptable to "spank" a child.

Professor of psychology George Holden, the author of the "Eavesdropping" study, reported that not only do parents hit their children more than they admit to, but that spanking was so ineffective that the children continued to engage in the same behavior only ten minutes after being hit. Far from using corporal punishment as a last resort, Dr. Holden disclosed, "We heard parents hitting their children for the most extraordinarily mundane offenses, typically violations of social conventions." On average, parents hit or spanked just half a minute after the conflict began. With that kind of timing, it sounds as if striking children is not so much a discipline technique as a reflex or a habit. Or a quick way to release stress.

> It sounds as if striking children is not so much a discipline technique as a reflex or a habit.

We Are Masters at Rationalizing

I wonder if those who "spank" their kids feel the same way I did when I smoked two packs of Camel Lights a day for a solid decade. Certainly, I understood beyond a shadow of doubt just what the warnings on the packages told me—i.e., "Smoking Causes Lung Cancer, Heart Disease, Emphysema, and May Complicate Pregnancy" and "Quitting Smoking Now Greatly Reduces Serious Risks to Your Health"—but I was somehow easily able to compartmentalize that information and light up as if smoking was just fine, and even beneficial in its ability to help me relax and look "good." Maybe it was because I was so young that I just couldn't imagine myself as an older woman in a hospital bed dying of lung cancer. Or, maybe it was because on some level smoking was working for me—i.e., it rescued my desperately insecure self in social settings and helped alleviate stress. In other words, smoking met an immediate need or two that was more important to me in the moment than the abstract notion of my long-term health. I'd quit . . . someday. So I wonder: Is spanking still so widely practiced because the conclusive research that tells us it's always associated with negative outcomes hasn't reached parents? Or does everybody know just how bad spanking is for kids, but they turn a blind eye because on some level "spanking" their kids is working for them—i.e., releasing stress, or making them feel powerful?

Warning: Spanking Is Bad for Children's Health

To be totally clear: The science regarding "spanking" kids is as conclusive as it is regarding inhaling tobacco. There are no positive outcomes. Outcomes are *always* negative. This has been confirmed over and over again by many of our nation's top experts on the subject, including Dr. Elizabeth Gershoff of the University of Texas at Austin, a developmental psychologist who has studied the effects of spanking for fifteen years and has also conducted two meta analyses summarizing hundreds of studies conducted around the world. Explains Dr. Gershoff, "The more kids are spanked the more aggressive they are. The more likely they are to get into delinquent behaviors. The more likely they are to have mental health problems—as children and as adults. The more likely they are to experience abuse from their parents." Full stop. While initial research suggested that at least in the short term spanking made kids more compliant, Dr. Gershoff's more complete meta-analysis disproved that long-held, long-clung-to belief.

Her findings are similar to those of Dr. Martin Teicher, a developmental neuropsychiatrist and professor at Harvard Medical School who conducted a five-year neuroimaging study of the impact of corporal punishment on the brains of predominantly middle-class, well-educated people. Teicher's study, as Stacey Patton reported in her article "Is Being Pro-Spanking a Sign of Brain Damage?", found that "the brain scans of corporally punished young adults showed nearly 20 percent reduction in the volume of gray matter in certain areas of the prefrontal cortex of their brains, compared with those who were not hit. Gray matter is associated with intelligence and intellect, Dr. Teicher said, and harm to that region is linked to depression, addiction and other mental health disorders." However, the consequences are not abstract or only visible on brain scans. Teicher's work and that of other researchers shows that spanking is associated with aggression, delinquency, low IQ, mental-health problems, and drug and alcohol abuse.

> "The more kids are spanked the more aggressive they are."
> —Dr. Elizabeth Gershoff

If the Surgeon General issued warnings to parents about the dangers of spanking, perhaps by printing labels on the hospital baby blankets used to wrap newborns, here's how they might read:

WARNING: Spanking me can reduce gray matter in my brain and lower my IQ.

WARNING: Physical punishment is associated with higher levels of aggression against parents, siblings, peers, and spouses and makes me more susceptible to depression.

WARNING: Spanking me will slow my cognitive development and increase my risk of criminal behavior.

WARNING: Being spanked by the person who is supposed to protect me is confusing and can cause cognitive dissonance.

WARNING: Spanking me will cause me to connect violence and love.

WARNING: Spanking me increases my chances of having mental-health problems, which can lead to drug and alcohol abuse.

For the record, all of the following esteemed organizations expressly condemn corporal punishment: the American Academy of Pediatrics, the American Psychological Association, the Academy of Child and Adolescent Psychiatry, the American Humane Association, the National Association of Pediatric Nurse Practitioners, the American Public Health Association, the American Psychoanalytical Association, the National Association of School Psychologists, the American Civil Liberties Union, UNICEF, and the United Nations.

And yet, hitting children remains legal and widely practiced in the United States.

Legal Legacy

Perhaps you may remember there was a time not too long ago when husbands spanking their wives was also a normalized, accepted, and legal part of our culture. When the practice became illegal and qualified as battery (and thus subject to a fine and/or imprisonment in a county jail and court-mandated anger-management classes), some men lamented their loss of status and power as these quotes from a 1950s Brooklyn *Daily Mirror* article entitled "If a Woman Needs It, Should She Be Spanked?" attest:

"Yes, when they deserve it. I think there are certain cases when it is advisable." —Barber

"Yes. Most of them have it coming to them anyway." —Toy factory owner

"It teaches them who's boss. A lot of women tend to forget this is a man's world and a lot of men who stepped down as boss of a family wish they hadn't. Spanking might help get back some of the respect they lost." —Parking lot attendant

Not surprisingly, the reasons these men gave in favor of hitting their wives—"teaching them who's boss" and "they deserve it"—are precisely how many adults today justify hitting children. On Facebook a parent posted a video of her child having "a tantrum," and many parents responded with how they'd handle the situation if their child dared behave that way:

"Awww my child did this once, bless his heart I pulled the car over to the side of the road and whooped his ass, asked if he had anymore issues, when he said no ma'am we continued on our way."

"Pull over . . . Beat his ass . . . Put his seat belt on . . . Rinse repeat until results achieved."

"This kid needs a good ol fashioned ass busting with a switch off a tree. I don't condone beating kids by any means. . . . But a switch sure as hell taught the majority of us that are 30 plus years old just what respecting a parent is. . . . Kids now days have little respect and there are far too many 'lazy' and 'too busy to deal with it' parents that would rather give a kid a damn pill than take five minutes to talk to the kid or bust their ass. . . . Damn shame. I have three kids . . . All girls, and while they are all three completely different in their attitudes they all have the same manners because they know dad doesn't take their shit."

"She has never spanked that boy obviously! If that was my momma she would give me something to cry about LOL!"

While I find the cavalierness with which these folks talk about inflicting pain on a child in duress chilling, most of the above would likely be perfectly legal—as long as it stays within the confines of what is defined as "reasonable," the definition of which varies from state to state. Here in my home state of California, our law reads:

A parent has a right to reasonably discipline by punishing a child and may administer reasonable punishment without being liable for a battery. (*Emery v. Emery* (1955) 45 Cal.2d 421 . . .; *People v. Stewart* (1961) 188 Cal. App.2d 88, 91. . . .) This includes the right to inflict reasonable corporal punishment. (*People v. Curtiss* (1931) 116 Cal. App. Supp. 771, 775 . . .

Notice that the last amendment to this law was more than fifty years ago in 1961—that's three years before the landmark civil rights act of 1964 outlawed discrimination based on race, color, religion, sex, or national origin. While we have come so far as a society since then (and obviously have a long way to go), this dated law that discriminates based on age still stands.

This right to hurt children is a legal legacy inherited from America's earliest settlers. Under English Common Law, children were understood to be the property of their parents, and as such, parents had great latitude over the treatment of their children. Combine that latitude with Puritans' strict religious morals and belief in harsh

> Children were understood to be the property of their parents.

punishments, and you get generations of children descended from those raised with a horse whip, dunce caps, pillories, and worse. Parents could literally do almost anything to a child—short of murdering them—and there was nothing a child, a bystander, or the law could do about it from a legal standpoint. That changed in 1874 when the American Society for the Prevention of Cruelty of Animals (ASPCA) filed a case on behalf of nine-year-old Mary Ellen Wilson who had been a prisoner in her tenement home, subjected to unimaginable cruelty by her foster parents, Francis and Mary Connolly. The prosecution argued that if a horse or dog was treated as Mary Ellen had been, it would be illegal. As a result, the precedent of "child abuse" was established along with the first child protection agency: the New York Society for the Prevention of Cruelty to Children. And while things have improved *considerably* since then (which gives me real hope for the future), it still remains legal to inflict pain on children to make them suffer for behaving in a way we don't like.

> It still remains legal to inflict pain on children to make them suffer for behaving in a way we don't like.

The one state in our union that has offered a glimmer of hope to children is Delaware. In 2012, Governor Jack Markell signed into law a bill that effectively outlawed corporal punishment. The bill, sponsored by Senate Majority Leader Patricia M. Blevins (my hero!), created a definition of "physical injury" in the child abuse and neglect laws to include the "infliction of pain" on a child, thus making corporal punishment a crime.

Our nation's failure to protect children from violence diminishes the United States' reputation as an international leader in human rights. Fortunately, to date forty-nine nations and principalities are leading the way in children's rights by outlawing corporal punishment based on the argument that as an act of violence it's a violation of a child's human right to dignity and bodily integrity. The first country to stand up for children in this way was Sweden back in 1966, when it removed a parent's right to corporal punishment. It would be another thirteen years, however, before the Swedes would pass a law expressly banning corporal punishment with language that clearly states children may not be subjected to either physical punishment or injurious or humiliating treatment. Finland and Norway soon followed suit in 1983 and 1987, respectively. And then in 1989 the United Nations ratified the landmark human rights treaty the Convention on the Rights of the Child, which sets out the civil, political, economic, social, health, and cultural rights of children and the conditions necessary for children to develop to their full potential. The Convention expressly states that children are not the property of their parents, and as human beings, they are the subject of their own rights. Article 19 addresses the issue of corporal punishment:

> States Parties shall take all appropriate legislative, administrative, social, and educational measures to protect the child from all forms of physical or mental violence, injury or abuse, neglect or negligent treatment, maltreatment or exploitation, including sexual abuse, while in the care of parent(s), legal guardian(s), or any other person who has the care of the child.

Movingly, the Convention on the Rights of the Child has been the most rapidly and widely ratified international human rights treaty in history. Since being adopted by the United Nations in 1989, *all* 193 UN member nations have ratified the Convention with

Forward Thinkers

'd like to recognize the forty-nine countries and principalities that have followed Sweden's lead by prohibiting any form of violence against children. They are:

1979 Sweden	2008 Liechtenstein
1983 Finland	2008 Luxembourg
1987 Norway	2008 Republic of Moldova
1989 Austria	2010 Albania
1994 Cyprus	2010 Kenya
1997 Denmark	2010 Poland
1998 Latvia	2010 Republic of Congo
1999 Croatia	2010 Tunisia
2000 Bulgaria	2011 South Sudan
2000 Germany	2013 Cabo Verde
2000 Israel	2013 Honduras
2002 Turkmenistan	2013 Macedonia
2003 Iceland	2014 Andorra
2004 Romania	2014 Argentina
2004 Ukraine	2014 Bolivia
2005 Hungary	2014 Brazil
2006 Greece	2014 Estonia
2007 Netherlands	2014 Malta
2007 New Zealand	2014 Nicaragua
2007 Portugal	2014 Peru
2007 Spain	2014 San Marino
2007 Togo	2015 Benin
2007 Uruguay	2015 Ireland
2007 Venezuela	2016 Mongolia
2008 Costa Rica	

the exception of one. Which one? The United States of America. What's holding us up? Well, here we need a two-thirds majority in the Senate to approve the Convention in order for it to go to the President for ratification. Today, more than twenty-five years after the treaty was signed, no President of the United States has submitted the treaty to the United States Senate requesting its advice and consent to ratification. Go figure. Where's the outrage? Nowhere.

I am particularly impressed with the language the Israeli Supreme Court used in 2000 to explain why corporal punishment would no longer be legal:

> In the judicial, social, and educational circumstances in which we live, we must not make compromises that can endanger the welfare and physical well-being of minors. We must also take into account that we live in a society in which violence is spreading like a plague; permission for "light" violence is liable to deteriorate into much more severe violence. We cannot endanger the physical and mental well-being of a minor by any kind of corporal punishment. A truth which is worthy must be clear and unequivocal and the message is that corporal punishment is not allowed.

Indeed.

Perpetuating the Cycle

So if spanking children is so harmful, why do so many defend it? The late Alice Miller, the renowned psychologist and author who dedicated her career to helping adults suffering from the effects of being abused as children, explains why so many perpetuate the cycle of violence:

Almost all small children are smacked during the first three years of life when they begin to walk and to touch objects which may not be touched. This happens at exactly the time when the human brain builds up its structure and should thus learn kindness, truthfulness, and love but never, never cruelty and lies. . . . Children very early on assimilate the violence they endured, which they may glorify and apply later as parents, in believing that they deserved the punishment and were beaten out of love. They don't know that the only reason for the punishments they have (or in retrospect, had) to endure is the fact that their parents themselves endured and learned violence without being able to question it. Later, the adults, once abused children, beat their own children and often feel grateful to their parents who mistreated them when they were small and defenseless. This is why society's ignorance remains so immovable and parents continue to produce severe pain and destructivity—in all "good will," in every generation. . . .

Supporting Miller's statement, in one study Dr. Teicher found that 60 percent of the subjects who were hit as children defended the practice—a finding that didn't surprise him. Dr. Teicher explains a common justification people use to defend their parents' choice: "because if I say it was a bad thing that hurt me, set me back and challenges me as an adult, that will truly be upsetting and will cause me to reframe how I view my parents, my childhood, my religion. It will call into question a number of things I don't want to question." But he reiterates, "The science tells us corporal punishment is a failed experiment for producing a beneficial protective effect against antisocial behaviors or incarceration."

While certainly laws that ban corporal punishment don't all of a sudden stop the practice (and because it usually happens behind closed doors, it's virtually impossible to police), they are a leap in

School Safety Zone—Think Again

est you think *Well, corporal punishment may be permitted in schools, but that doesn't mean it actually happens often in this day and age*, according to estimates from the federal Department of Education (Office of Civil Rights), during the 2012–2013 school year alone, 20,083 children received corporal punishment in Arkansas, 12,282 in Georgia, 31,236 in Mississippi, 10,318 in Tennessee, and 28,569 in Texas. And that's just five of the nineteen states that allow physical punishment. Perhaps it won't surprise you to learn that a disproportionate number of those children were boys and African Americans. And even more tragically, many suffered from disabilities.

Unfortunately, being hit by your teachers for "misbehavior" is precisely the kind of education these kids should not be receiving, because as science has now confirmed again and again, violence breeds more violence (toward peers, siblings,

the right direction and have proven to be most successful when accompanied by an educational campaign.

And speaking of education, for the record, a total of 100 countries throughout the world have banned corporal punishment in schools. The first country to lead the way was Poland back in . . . 1783! And then Finland eighty-nine years later in 1872. Again, the United States is not on the list because here corporal punishment in public schools is an issue voted on by the constituents of individual states. For the record, in nineteen states it is legal for teachers and administrators to hit children in public school for behavior they don't like. It is legal in private schools in all but two states.

and, later, spouses) and more antisocial behavior. As the ACLU puts it, "Corporal punishment causes pain, humiliation, and in some cases deep bruising or other serious injury; it also can have long-lasting psychological consequences. . . . Furthermore, it creates a violent, degrading school environment in which all students—and particularly students with disabilities—may struggle to succeed."

The hypocrisy of corporal punishment is particularly glaring in the legal code of a Florida county that allows a child to be paddled but *only through elementary school* and only for "level two offenses," like hitting a child or exhibiting other aggressive behavior. *You better not hit or you'll get hit.* It's as if the only logical and viable response to aggression is aggression. And as Gandhi so succinctly put it, "An eye for an eye only ends up making the whole world blind."

To move forward, I think it is essential to come to terms with the reality that we do not own our children. I think it's rather telling of our society's view of children that when an American child petitions family court to be released from his or her parents' custody, legally speaking, the child files for what's known as Emancipation of a Minor—emancipation meaning freedom. The child is now free from the control of the parent. This is a tacit admission that children who have not been emancipated are not free. Even as many of us may recoil at terms like "own" and "rule"—perhaps even finding them to be grossly overstated—too often the ways in which we treat our children carry many of the hallmarks of ownership, such as "You must do what I say . . . and if not, I will make you suffer." If you can legally cause harm to another person, in a real sense you have ownership over their bodies. When only one group of citizens can legally be subjected to pain and humiliation that is illegal for everyone else, it is a glaring example of inequality. Of injustice. And oppression. Hitting children needs to be considered the act of domestic violence that it is. It needs to be classified as illegal assault and battery subject to arrest, *not* a form of education.

Hitting children needs to be considered the act of domestic violence that it is.

Murray Straus, codirector of the Family Research Laboratory at the University of New Hampshire, doesn't hold out much hope for sweeping change on this issue in the United States anytime soon, lamenting, "We [Americans] believe that physical force is the way to get things done. So it's going to be awhile." Maybe. Maybe not. Many people said the same thing about same-sex marriage, positing that change was so far off that it wouldn't come to fruition in their lifetime. And yet the dominoes started falling in 2003 when Massachusetts allowed same-sex marriage, and by June 26, 2015, it was the law of the land. Boom. Love won. So I'm confident we can change the tide when it comes to hitting kids. And we must.

Are you in?

ALL THAT SAID . . .

"If I have the belief that I can do it,
I shall surely acquire the
capacity to do it even if I may not
have it at the beginning."
—**Mahatma Gandhi**

"Women Are People, Too!" the headline announced. The year was 1960. The magazine was *Good Housekeeping.* The writer was Betty Friedan. And a nerve was hit.

In the article, Friedan identified a highly prevalent "complex and elusive problem" that had no name. She wrote about women being dissatisfied in their roles as housewives and mothers—frustrated that their thoughts, feelings, needs, and ambitions were not given equal respect and consideration as those of men. The overwhelming response to the piece inspired Friedan to expand her research and write *The Feminine Mystique,* a book largely credited with igniting the second wave of the feminist movement. At the time, the idea of equality for women was so radical to so many that the FBI viewed the women's movement as "part of the enemy, a challenge to American values." Thirty years of hard-won progress later, Friedan wrote, "What used to be the feminist agenda is now an everyday reality. The way women look at themselves, the way other people look at women, is completely different." (And of course the fight continues.)

This book could just as easily be called *Kids Are People, Too!* because, in large part, that's its message. Similarly, it's about a highly prevalent, complex, elusive, and equally harrowing problem with no name: Children are not treated with the respect and consideration they deserve as human beings. And it's taking a toll not just on children and our relationships with them but also on who they become when they grow up and how they relate to others and the world. In other words, that we treat children as inferior people subject to our control has affected and continues to affect all of us in profound ways that are so deeply entrenched that we accept them as the norm.

> It's a catch-22. Children are dependent on us adults to advocate for them, and yet it is our minds they would be fighting to change.

President Barack Obama reminds us, "Our nation was founded on a bedrock principle that we are all created equal. The project of each generation is to bridge the meaning of those founding words with the realities of changing times." And that it is up to us "to ensure that those words ring true, for every single American . . ." I believe children are equal to adults, and I look forward to the day when I can say, "The way children look at themselves and the way adults look at children is completely different." Unfortunately, this book (and others with a similar message) literally can't strike a chord with those people who are being discriminated against and ignite in them a desire to do something about it because, in large part, many in that population can't yet read. The reality is, as Elisabeth

Young-Bruehl, author of *Childism: Confronting Prejudice Against Children*, points out, "unlike most of those who suffer from racism or sexism, children are not yet political thinkers and actors. They depend upon adults for the articulation and protection of their rights." It's a catch-22. Children are dependent on us adults to advocate for them, and yet it is our minds they would be fighting to change. And so it falls on us to examine our own privileged perspective and positions of power in order to shift our own thinking.

But are children really equal to adults?

It's a question many disenfranchised groups have heard before.

Are women really equal to men? Are people with darker skin really equal to those with lighter skin? Are people who are attracted to the same sex really equal to those who are attracted to the opposite sex? Are people who were born with a gender identity that does not correspond to their biological sex assigned at birth really equal to those who were born with the gender that corresponds to their biological sex assigned at birth? Yes.

But it's different with children! many argue, because their brains aren't yet fully developed. The brains of children simply aren't equal to adult brains. (And my brain is also not equal to Stephen Hawking's, for that matter.) Yes, it is true that cognition evolves over time. In fact, neuroscientists now largely agree that our brains aren't fully developed until we are in our mid-twenties, which means we are "legal adults" for roughly seven years without the brains that can make judgments as sound as we will be able to later on. (Ever wonder why the price of car insurance goes down when one turns twenty-six? By then we have better impulse control!) Nonetheless, like all of us, children, regardless of their age, are fully sentient beings with equally valid and equally persistent feelings, thoughts, and needs that drive them. To my mind, because young children are so vulnerable, dependent, and unable to advocate for themselves the way older people can, they are actually deserving of even more careful consideration and respect, because it is so easy to disregard their point of view. The truth is, for a relatively short period of time, we can make our children do anything we damn well please. We have all the power. The love to give or withhold. The strength. The money. The shelter. The food. And the law. We can legally scream at them. Shame them. Isolate them. And hit them. And there is not a single thing they can do about it. What do our kids have? Only the faith that their parents know what they're doing. They are entirely at our mercy. Simply keeping this in mind can make such a difference.

Don't get me wrong. I'm not saying we aren't to act as our children's parents—i.e., their guides, role models, nurturers, and keepers of their safety. We must! Of course. As author and feminist Elizabeth Janeway so beautifully explains, "Children do indeed need to be brought up. . . . They need love, stability, consistent and unequivocal care, and lasting relationships with people who are profoundly enough interested in them to look after them with warmth, gaiety, and patience." I would add that children also need parents who will seriously recognize and honor their point of view, who work with them to solve problems to everyone's mutual satisfaction, and who will advocate for them out in the world until they are entirely able to advocate for themselves. I know it can feel overwhelming, like an unfair burden to have to be the one to break cycles, learn new skills, and heal old wounds so that we can be the parents our kids deserve. It can feel like both a blessing and a curse. But it needn't be so daunting.

> Children need parents who will advocate for them out in the world until they are entirely able to advocate for themselves.

Truly.

We can start small.

Each and every one of us can make little changes every day that cumulatively send the message to our children that we value them highly. That their point of view is important. Change comes in the details. It's telling a baby you are going to pick her up and showing her your outstretched arms before you lift her so she knows what to expect. It's taking the extra time to explain why something is important, instead of just making them do it because "I said so." It's waiting to let your child have their own reaction to something they've done before we rush in with a "Good job!" or a "Keep at it!" It's letting kids play in the way they want to without trying to direct their activity or the outcome. It's honoring your child's "no," whether it's a hug they don't want or tickling they're done with. It's letting your child be angry when you think they are overreacting. It's not making them say hello, or good-bye, or thank you, or sorry in the moment, but being their wingman and trusting they'll get there. It's taking the time to figure out why they don't want to do something, not just figuring out what you can do to get them to do it. It's not screaming at them when you're dying to unleash. It's letting them know you get what they're saying.

> "An adolescent does not rebel against his parents. He rebels against their power."
>
> —Dr. Thomas Gordon

Certainly we'll all mess up. We'll be frazzled and snap or running late and not take the time. We'll fall back into old patterns. We're human! What's important is that we make amends when we mess up so that our children don't think our mistakes are their fault. The good news is that every mistake is a chance to model empathy for ourselves so that our children learn mistakes are normal and don't diminish us.

Dr. Thomas Gordon reminds us, "When kids feel we are genuinely interested in their perspective and want to work with them to solve problems, their resistance melts away. An adolescent does not rebel against his parents. He rebels against their power. If parents would rely less on power and more on non-power methods to influence their children from infancy on, there would be little for children to rebel against when they become adolescents . . . parents inevitably run out of power, and sooner than they think." No matter how much control and power we seem to have over our children when they are young, it is at once an illusion and fleeting, for we can tell them what to do, but we can't control what they think or how they feel.

RESOURCES

While it continues to evolve, my thinking about children and parenting has been shaped by numerous people, perhaps most influentially by Magda Gerber, founding director of RIE (Resources for Infant Educarers); Ruth Beaglehole, founding director of Echo Parenting & Education; A. S. Neill, the founder of the revolutionary "free school" Summerhill; Alfie Kohn, the independent scholar, and outspoken social critic; and the psychologist Thomas Gordon, who created the course and book *Parent Effectiveness Training* (PET) based on his Gordon Model of Communication. Over the past decade, I've read many books, attended many talks, and taken many courses and seminars, finding each mode of communication uniquely helpful.

At the risk of stating the obvious, books let me wrestle with ideas at my own pace, and I can come back to the text again and again as needed. And of course being able to be in a "conversation" of sorts with those no longer with us, like John Holt, A. S. Neill, and Magda Gerber, is a gift.

I love going to talks, because I usually attend with friends, and our post-talk discussions are usually as lively and helpful as the talk itself. Plus, I find the Q and As usually hit on questions I have. Furthermore, in this time of digital everything, hearing someone's passion in person is not just different, it's better. (I'm going to make a plug here for Alfie Kohn, who is as articulate and compelling as he is convincing. If he comes to a town anywhere near you, go!)

Personally, I've found that classes have had the greatest impact in a practical sense, because there is no substitute for learning from a real person with others. Questions are wrestled with, skills are practiced, and there's time for reflection between classes. I also found that classes have naturally led to creating a community of like-minded parents, which is so important, particularly when you're going against the grain.

I hope you find these resources useful.

Books

A s we all know, there are literally thousands of books on parenting. The list here includes those that have either been most helpful to me personally, or align with my belief in a compassionate, respectful, non-punitive approach to raising children. Some are more philosophical and truly paradigm challenging, for example, A. S. Neill's *Summerhill*, John Holt's *Escape from Childhood*, and Elizabeth Young-Breuhl's *Childism*. Others are more practical in nature, including Dr. Thomas Gordon's *Parent Effectiveness Training* and Dr. Laura Markham's *Peaceful Parent, Happy Kids*.

Raising Our Children, Raising Ourselves: Transforming Parent-Child Relationships from Reaction and Struggle to Freedom, Power, and Joy, by Naomi Aldort

Playful Parenting, by Lawrence J. Cohen

Positive Parenting: An Essential Guide Ending the Power Struggles and Reconnecting from the Heart, by Rebecca Eanes

Dear Parent: Caring for Infants with Respect, by Magda Gerber

Parent Effectiveness Training: The Proven Program for Raising Responsible Kids, by Thomas Gordon, PhD

Free to Learn: Why Unleashing the Instinct to Play Will Make Our Children Happier, More Self-Reliant and Better Students for Life, by Peter Gray

Raising Human Beings: *A Collaborative Partnership with Your Child,* by Ross W. Greene, PhD

Parenting for a Peaceful World, by Robin Grille, PhD

Escape from Childhood: *The Needs and Rights of Children,* by John Holt

How Children Learn, by John Holt

The Gentle Parent: *Positive, Practical, Effective Discipline,* by L. R. Knost

Punished by Rewards: *The Trouble with Gold Stars, Incentive Plans, A's, Praise and Other Bribes,* by Alfie Kohn

Unconditional Parenting: *Moving from Rewards and Punishment to Love and Reason,* by Alfie Kohn

Elevating Child Care: *A Guide to Respectful Parenting,* by Janet Lansbury

Peaceful Parent, Happy Kids: *How to Stop Yelling and Start Connecting,* by Laura Markham, PhD

Peaceful Parent, Happy Siblings: *How to Stop the Fighting and Raise Friends for Life,* by Laura Markham, PhD

Summerhill: *A New View of Childhood,* by A. S. Neill and Albert Lamb

Raising Children Compassionately: *Parenting the Nonviolent Communication Way,* by Marshall B. Rosenberg, PhD

It's OK Not to Share . . . *and Other Renegade Rules for Raising Competent and Compassionate Kids,* by Heather Shumaker

It's Ok to Go Up the Slide: *Renegade Rules for Raising Confident and Creative Kids,* by Heather Shumaker

The Whole-Brain Child: 12 Revolutionary Strategies to Nurture Your Child's Developing Mind, by Daniel J. Siegel, MD, and Tina Payne Bryson, PhD

The Conscious Parent: Transforming Ourselves, Empowering Our Children, by Shefali Tsabary, PhD, preface by His Holiness the Dalai Lama

Out of Control: Why Disciplining Your Child Doesn't Work . . . and What Will, by Shefali Tsabary, PhD

Childism: Confronting Prejudice Against Children, by Elisabeth Young-Bruehl

In-Person Courses

'm lucky to live in Los Angeles, a big city that is home to RIE, Echo Parenting & Education, and Meike Lemmens, PET instructor and instructor trainer. While there are certainly teachers of these classes throughout the country, they are scattered here and there. Check the websites to learn if a class is being offered near you.

Parent-Infant Classes
Resources for Infant Educarers
rie.org (see Alliance of RIE Associates)

Parent Effectiveness Training
Meike Lemmens, parentingclassesoc.com
Gordon Training International, gordontraining.com

Nonviolent Parenting Philosophy and Practice
Echo Parenting & Education
echoparenting.org

Online Courses

If you live in a place that doesn't offer many parenting class options, you may want to take some classes online. A benefit of these is you can often take them at your own pace—a plus for busy parents.

Parenting by Connection Starter Class
Hand in Hand Parenting
handinhandparenting.org

Peaceful Parent, Happy Kids Online Course
Dr. Laura Markham
ahaparenting.com

Breaking the Anger Circle
Lori Petro
Teach-through-love.com

Supporting Sensitive Children
Lori Petro
Teach-through-love.com

Transform Your Parenting
Lori Petro
Teach-through-love.com

Online Resources

On the following websites, you can find enormous amounts of helpful information on parenting and education—everything from articles and blog posts on a plethora of topics to additional resources, private coaching, speaking schedules, and more.

Ahaparenting.com

Alfiekohn.org

Echoparenting.org

Gordontraining.com

Handinhandparenting.org

Heathershumaker.com

Janetlansbury.com

Littleheartsbooks.com

Livesinthebalance.org

Naturalchild.org

Positive-parents.org

RIE.org

Teach-through-love.com

ACKNOWLEDGMENTS

O ver the course of the nine-plus years I've worked on this book, the help I've received from a handful of people has felt a bit like they've been running a relay race alongside me—each accompanying me for a critical part of the journey then handing me off to the next fresh brain. Early on, both A.J. Dickerson and Dorothy Braudy read a premature draft, and while it must've been just awful, they encouraged me as if I was really onto something. Dorothy passed it on to our neighbors Jay Martel and Alexandra Susman, who offered invaluable insights. (A special thank-you to Alexandra and her husband, Jordan, for allowing me to reprint the letter that appears on page 58.) Then, Colleen Wainwright appeared seemingly out of nowhere and helped me focus and organize the book in a much clearer way, before passing the baton to Lea Payne, who asked me some tough questions for which I had no answers. Then just at a moment when I was overcome with doubt, Jennifer Jason Leigh championed the project and gave me new momentum.

Thank you, thank you, thank you!

Meanwhile, the ever-changing community of writers and staff at the Casbah Café in Silver Lake—including Tracy McMillan, Carla Blair, and Anil Baral to name a few—helped me feel less alone as I plugged away, always knowing just the right chit-chat-to-work ratio so we could enjoy each other while actually getting something done.

Chet Callahan has been there almost from the start, talking through just about every issue the book addresses, helping me clarify my thoughts along the way.

With the help of my friends and readers

Fortunately, I didn't have to wear out the generosity of too many friends as the readers of my Good Job Facebook page have consistently provided me with incredible feedback and a constant exchange of ideas. Whenever I had a draft or even just a partial of a chapter and was hungry for a response, I'd ask if anyone was available to read it and give me their uncensored thoughts. Usually I'd have a handful of volunteers from all over the country (and globe) within minutes, and by morning I had the feedback I was looking for. More than a hundred people took the time to read my work and weigh in, their encouragement was as helpful as their criticism. Please see page 275 for the complete list of folks who stepped up to the plate.

I hope everyone has as devoted a friend as Meredith Morton has been to me. From the beginning, she's been telling anyone who will listen that I'm working on a *very* important book that they *must* read. She knows when to ask how it's coming along and also how to refrain from asking for months and even years at a time. She read numerous first drafts before I turned to my Facebook folks to relieve her of the burden. And her husband, Scott Cutler, periodically injects me with his own particular brand of I-have-good-instincts confidence. They've given me unrestricted access to an incredibly beautiful pub to write in, which was particularly welcome when the Casbah closed unexpectedly overnight.

The last person to receive the baton and take me to the finish line was the brilliant author Raphael Simon. While I hated to prevail upon him, I forced myself to and he never was anything but gracious about it. No chapter was sent in without an email that said either "good to go" or "you can consider it done." And perhaps most helpfully, Rafi articulated for me what I was trying to do with the book in a way I hadn't quite been able to see myself.

It takes a village to make a book

Over the first couple of years as I stumbled along, it helped to know that if I was able to make something decent of the swarm of ideas swirling in my head, Susan Golomb, my truly world-class literary agent at Writers House, would take a look. When I finally had some chapters I thought were Susan-worthy, I sent them over. Her response was something like, "Do this, that, and the other thing and I'll look at it again." One year and eighty pages of this, that, and the other thing later, the proposal was up to Golomb standards and ready to find a home.

I knew it would take a brave editor to embrace a book that goes against the grain like this one—particularly one written without the stamp of a PhD. That brave editor turned out to be Margot Herrera at Workman Publishing, who championed the book to editorial director Susan Bolotin and then-publisher Peter Workman. While they were intrigued, they weren't quite convinced. They generously shared some thoughts and concerns and then, nine months and three rewrites of a single chapter later, Workman committed. I was thrilled to be at a publishing house whose hallmark—accessible books with a strong point of view—matched my ambitions for the project. Workman has turned out to be a perfect fit because they don't rush a book into publication before its time. Throughout the lengthy publication process, Margot's astute questions, comments, and edits have pushed me to sharpen my arguments and create a more cohesive manuscript. I'm so grateful for her faith in this project as it has evolved so much in the three years we've been working on it together. In fact, everyone at Workman, including Galen Smith in design, Evan Griffith in editorial, Kate Karol in production editorial, Moira Kerrigan and Thea James in marketing, and Noreen Herits in publicity, has been more than a pleasure to work with. Their genuine enthusiasm and commitment to the project has been as palpable as it has been reassuring.

Thanks to my mentors

Meanwhile, there would be nothing to write about if it weren't for the guidance of my many teachers and mentors who have helped shape my thinking over the past decade. At RIE, I'd like to thank Antoinette Samardzic, Ruth Anne Hammond, Elizabeth Memel, and Deborah Solomon, all of whom have shared Magda Gerber's Educaring philosophy with me in their own unique ways. Brian Joseph from Echo Parenting and Education gave me a brilliant, compelling, and compassionate introduction to nonviolent parenting. And having the opportunity to hear the ever-passionate child advocate Ruth Beaglehole, Echo's fearless founder, speak on many occasions is always nothing short of totally inspiring. Then there is the incomparable Meike Lemmens, the PET instructor whose course and master classes I've had the privilege of attending. Meike is as sharp, clear, and thoughtful as she is infinitely calm and patient. I'm absolutely indebted to Meike for her generous support, in-depth comments, quick turnarounds, and unflagging belief in the book.

And of course my family

All of that said, the book would have been entirely impossible without its primary patron: my husband, John Lehr. While he's largely stayed out of the fray, he has always made clear that this book coming to fruition is important and worth the financial sacrifices. And although it's certainly taken a lot longer to come together than either of us could have ever imagined, he never made me feel like the clock was ticking while our bank account was diminishing— though that was clearly the case. Thank you, thank you, thank you, John.

And no acknowledgment would be complete without thanking my parents, Judy and Carl Schlosberg, for their unflagging love and support and for instilling in me persistence.

With gratitude to my Facebook friends

Special thanks to all of the folks who follow me on my Good Job Facebook page—people who are engaged with the same issues. I'm especially grateful to those who read sections of the book and shared their feedback. These generous people are Kristen Aumoithe • Erin Ammer Auses • Renee Bakke Dockmanovich • Katy Bankhead • Mega Benston Key • Daphna Bossik • Sara Brodt • Laura Bruce • Katy Brown • Diana Cabera • Calvin Carson • Isabella Carter • Jordyn Castaneda • Michelle Cescatti • Tip Chow • Jennifer Colella • Virginia Cylke • Louise de Dassel • Rena Drechsler • Rose Dunlap • Thea Eaton • Ashley Farnham • Tricia Farnworth • Lara Fong Baldwin • Haley C. French • Hannelle Fritz • Daniel Fuller • Hannah Green • Arianne Groth • Nikki Hammett • Sarah Hoyle • Traci Hill Lupo • Danielle Honeyands • Diane Hyett • Sarah Jebb • Briana Johnson • Jessica LB • Julie Lawrence • Karen Liska Evans • Mary Loewen Reed • Lindsay Olson MacLeod • Melanie MacFarlane • Camille Meigs Haughey • Jennifer Michel Anderson • Pallida Mors • Debbie Moore • April Murphy • Meaghan O'Gara • Tina Olmstead • Casey Orth • Naomi Payne • Tonia Paulsen • Gabi Pezo • Tamara Pulles • Andrea Raleigh Groom • Lauren Rodriguez • Jasmin Romero • Jennifer Savage Matysczak • Danielle Salinas • Kellie Scarbrough • Heather Scharfenberg • Kay Shroff • Anslie Stokes Milligan • Alissa Turner • Sara Urquhart • Katherine Vince • The-Mars Volya • Nellie Webb-Solari • Brandeis • Karen Williams • Wright Conroy • Emily Wolfe • Samantha Yeaton • Bobby Zapta • Melanie Heidorn • Jennifer Mullin • Heloise Abk • Monica Serratos • Kim Snel • Kelly E. McFadden • Kized Juarrez Utting • Grace Li • Camille Anne • Giovanna Drovandi • Michelle Lewis Barnes • Joyce Sutton Ring • Michelle Ann • Shalene • Wendy Beernink • Claire Battersby • Lauren Barker • Melissa Acker • Ginger Calkings • Mary Kay Patrick • Tracy Friedlander • Alison Cooper • Miriam Bettant • Moira Hughes • Stacie Malkus • Jessica Gardner • Karen Holbrook •

Shirley Humann Shanahan • Sarah Freebern • Suz Crichton-Stuart • Kailey Brown • Simone Furtkamp • Kristy Williams • Setsuko Dairymple • Theresa Phillips • Chrissy Chris Muller • Far Zia • Kaitlin Lucier Servant • Anna Chapa • Stellina Gunn • Brianna Coyte • Amand King • Alyson Stears • Jade Chiu • Helena Sorus • Nicole Ellis Lemoncelli • Stacy Jacobs Wynn • Penny Elizabeth • Deanne Carson • Ashley Tinsley Kagan • Asley Williams Stevenson • Amanda Adams Lightfoot • Carla D'Anna • Stephanie Benson Bresike • Jennifer Lyons • Jonni MacArthur • Sarah Buckingham • Jennifer Brown • Eliza Parker • Charlie Woods • Julia Underwood • Toni Trinidad • Rebecca Hawkins • Stephanie Freund • Cassandra Wagner • Jessica Markwell • Nicole Hamelin Luff • Bekah Parker • Lori Erickson • Natalie Davis • Katie Soli • Lindsay Hennings • Julie King • and Lisa Heuneman Townsend.

In short, I'm one fortunate person.